SPRING, SUMMER & FALL

THE RISE AND FALL OF THE LABOUR PARTY 1986–99

Ray Kavanagh

BLACKWATER PRESS

Editor
Margaret Burns

Design/Layout
Paula Byrne

Cover Design
Liz Murphy

ISBN
1 84131 528 1

© – Ray Kavanagh 2001

Produced in Ireland by
Blackwater Press
c/o Folens Publishers
Hibernian Industrial Estate,
Greenhills Road,
Tallaght, Dublin 24.

CONTENTS

Dedicated to the memory of
Alderman Jim Kemmy TD

CHAPTER 1

ENTERTAINMENT FOR THE MEDIA

IN THE *Magill* 'Guide to Election '82', its editor, Vincent Browne, wrote: 'There are indications of terminal decline in the Labour Party vote and in its hold on almost all of its 15 seats.' Nor did he hold out many prospects for the future: 'Hopes of any radical change in Labour's fortune are minimal. The best that can be hoped for is that the decline be halted.' His analysis was based not only on the declining Labour vote since the 1969 general election, but also on a constituency-by-constituency breakdown which indicated that the main challenge the party faced was its own survival. Vincent Browne wasn't alone in this conclusion. Inside the party, signs of impending fragmentation and collapse continued to accumulate.

In 1983 the Director of Elections for the November 1982 general election, Tony Kinsella, wrote in a report on the elections: 'It is my opinion that if the party does not manage to record gains in the forthcoming elections, it is highly likely that it will be by-passed, both from left and right, by political developments.' No such gains were in store for the party however. In the following year, the party lost all its four seats in the European Parliament elections. Among those failing to be elected were: Frank Cluskey, former party leader and government minister; Justin Keating, former Minister for Industry and Commerce; Eileen Desmond TD, former Minister for Health and Social Welfare; and Michael D Higgins, the Chairman of the party. The local elections took place in 1985 with near disastrous results for Labour. The party lost 19 out of its 77 County and County Borough Council seats (almost a quarter of its total seats). This result was ominous on two fronts; it meant that Labour would lose at least one Senate seat at the next Senate elections (councillors vote at Senate elections), but much more seriously, the losses portended general election defeats in many constituencies.

In Dublin City the situation had reached crisis point. Only two councillors were returned to Dublin Corporation; they were Sean Kenny and Lord Mayor Michael O'Halloran. This was below the critical mass, and Labour as a political party in local election terms had been wiped out in the capital city. At a subsequent meeting of Dublin Directors of Elections held in Labour's head office, the following question was asked by Padraig Turley, the Dublin South-Central constituency Director of Elections: 'How do you wind up a political party?' Though the others present pooh-poohed the idea, the fact that it was discussed at such senior level indicated a *malaise* that looked insuperable at that time. Nor could a party leader escape reprobation. 'Are the results of this election a reflection on the leadership of Dick Spring?', an RTE reporter asked Michael O'Halloran during live television on the night of the count. O'Halloran stared straight into the camera and said, 'Yes'. To compound the problem, the decline in Labour support occurred side by side with the rise of the Workers' Party. This party, which originated in a Sinn Féin split, now posed as a replacement for Labour as Ireland's left-wing alternative. Many of the losses sustained by Labour in the 1985 local elections, particularly in the Dublin area, were to the Workers' Party. It was a major obsession with many in the party. 'How do we fend off the threat of the Workers' Party?' Colm O'Briain asked Kathleen O'Meara at her successful interview for the position of Labour Press Officer in 1985. Kathleen inhaled deeply on her cigarette and went, 'Well...'.

Colm O'Briain exits

In July of that year, Colm O'Briain resigned as General Secretary. He had done so at least twice before but on this occasion the party leader and his entourage were determined to let him go. Colm had been Labour's most colourful General Secretary – with his terracotta-coloured trousers, curly mop of hair and shoulder bag. A Wexford delegate had asked Anne Byrne, the constituency organiser at the 1985 National Conference in Cork: 'Who is that fine looking woman on the platform, the one with the curly hair?' Colm took it all in very good humour. His organisational ideas matched his colourful garb. These included insisting that members live in the areas where they were registered, and that constituency organisations that had not paid their National Collection Targets up front should be corralled off at National Conferences until such time as they had. His 'Dublin 4' credentials were impeccable; he had served as Chief Executive of the Arts Council and worked as a producer in RTE. The rural party, who equated Dublin with hostility to coalition and an inability to organise or to win seats, treated him with great suspicion.

The internal opposition

At this time, the Labour Party was in a coalition government with Fine Gael. On Colm's resignation, the appointing body, the Administrative Council (AC) split between those who wanted either a pro-coalition or an anti-coalition replacement. In those days 'anti-coalition' was interchangeable with 'anti-Spring' or 'anti-ministerial'. The opposition to Dick Spring in the party at this stage was wide-ranging. It included 'Labour Left' a group of mainly Dublin activists who wanted Labour out of Government with Fine Gael. It was a well-funded and well-organised group.

The militant faction was also a major feature in the Labour Party, having successfully infiltrated and taken over Labour Youth. Another hostile group was headed and organised by the Kildare councillor Emmet Stagg, who correctly felt that his only way of replacing the sitting Labour TD for the constituency, Joe Birmingham, was to set himself up as a more radical alternative. Whether he was more left wing or not has never been gauged, but he was the internal opposition, and to oppose Joe Birmingham (Junior Minister at the Board of Works) was to oppose Dick Spring and Labour's participation in government.

The contestants

Three people were shortlisted for the position of General Secretary of the Labour Party: Bernard Browne, an official with Ireland's second biggest union, the FWUI; Fergus Finlay, Deputy Government Press Secretary and Dick Spring's media manager; and myself, a 31-year-old national-school teacher who had been active in the Labour Party for the previous 11 years. Bernard Browne had very strong support from Labour Left. He was an anti-coalitionist and a sponsor of 'Trade Unionists for a United and Independent Ireland', the group which had attacked the Hillsborough Agreement. He also had the strong support of his many union colleagues in the party. His boss, Billy Attley, the General Secretary of the union, was on the interview board.

Fergus Finlay was Personnel Manager with Ridge Tool Co. in Cork when Senator Pat Magner suggested his appointment to the new Tánaiste, Dick Spring, in 1983. Dick had found himself propelled into the position after a mere month as leader of the Labour Party. Finlay was therefore appointed Deputy Government Press Secretary (a position usually taken by the Labour Party when in Government). He and Dick did not enjoy as close a relationship as they did later on – especially during the 1992–97

3

Government – but nevertheless they had been working closely together for almost three years. Much of the poor or hostile publicity that the party got in those years was blamed, in most cases unfairly, on Fergus. There were some major whoppers though, from the abolition of food subsidies, to the introduction of service charges.

Friends and allies: Toddy O'Sullivan TD and Frank Cluskey TD outside Leinster House.

Frank Cluskey, who had resigned as Minister in 1983 and now sat uncomfortably on the backbenches, was particularly hostile. He considered Fergus to be a right-wing influence on Dick Spring, inimical to the social welfare and trade union constituency. When Frank Cluskey spoke, many in the party took heed; he still had a considerable following in the membership, in the parliamentary party and in the trade unions. I enjoyed a warm, almost 'father and son' relationship with him, and his secretary/ adviser, Mary Turley, was a personal friend of mine. Frank was a senior FWUI member and its political adviser and as such I did not expect any overt support from him. Nevertheless, my friendship with him ensured that he was not active in support of the candidacy of Bernard Browne. Other than from Frank, I didn't have the high-level support enjoyed by my two rivals for the job. In my favour, I knew the party and the membership as neither of them did and (at that time) I didn't have any particularly entrenched enemies in the party. I felt that out of the three I was the best qualified to rebuild the organisation and instill a sense of pride and purpose in a demoralised membership.

I was delighted with my interview and my good feeling was confirmed some days later when the Leinster House gossip machine confirmed my confidence in my performance. All that was needed now was the call. Of course, things did not work that way and I was very disappointed to hear from Dick Spring a few days later that the interview board was to recommend Bernard Browne for the job. Seemingly this result was leaked and Dick was courteously informing me before I read it in the papers. So embarrassment was added to disappointment as I had not informed my work colleagues that I was applying for another job.

It was at this stage that the appointment of the new General Secretary became hot news. The party had split in a bitter fashion over the appointment and a media circus ensued. Both sides briefed the media on why their candidate should get the job. Instead of being a contest for a person who would work to rebuild the party, it became a power struggle between pro and anti-coalitionists. The winner would then be expected to throw the weight of the position in behind his respective camp.

The *Sunday Tribune* lends a hand

On the weekend of 1 December 1985 I was at home in Ferbane, Co. Offaly. I had purchased the *Sunday Tribune* and was sitting in the kitchen reading it when I burst out laughing. An article written by Máirín de Burca entitled 'The Labour Party in Coalition has Lost Support' outlined an interview given to her by Bernard Browne presenting his views and background. It was a very sympathetic interview from a former comrade, but was bound to cause him terminal damage as it outlined his opposition to Labour's democratically approved coalition arrangement. The ministers and the supporters of the coalition would rightly be up in arms. No one could seriously propose the appointment of a General Secretary whose publicly stated opinions were contrary to the clear decisions of the party. To hold these opinions was bad enough, but to express them publicly even before the appointment was ratified smacked of either innocence or arrogance. Of course, it was neither of these: Máirín de Burca had been the unwitting cause of landing Bernard in the soup. He had been foolish in giving such an interview before he had been formally ratified in the position. He was later to claim that the comments he made were for background information only. He wrote to the Party Chairman, Michael D Higgins, seeking to clarify matters with the party officers. As all hell now broke out in the party, I knew that Bernard's candidature was fatally and irretrievably damaged.

It was now up to Dick Spring to appoint his own adviser, Fergus Finlay, if he wanted. Faced with major hostility to this within the party, he opted for the middle course and I was comfortably ensconced. On 20 January 1986 Fergus put in writing his withdrawal from the contest and the stage was set for a vote by the AC between Bernard and myself. I was to win by 19 votes to 13.

Dick's secretary, Sally Clarke, telephoned me with the news and soon afterwards friends started to drop in. Kathleen Gill arrived with a bottle of champagne and branch members Ann Connolly and Pat McGlynn joined others to celebrate my elevation. These three were to be particularly supportive and loyal to me in the years to come. No phone call came from Dick Spring or from any other Labour Party dignitary. Even then I found this strange. It appeared that I had become General Secretary as part of the ongoing struggle for dominance inside the party, and not, as one might expect, because the candidate who fills this important post would be the one to help rebuild the party. Each of the participants in the drama of the preceding few months was so caught up in their own personal role that they did not see the overall importance of the new situation or indeed the possibilities. I knew then that I would be very much on my own in my new position. This was a prospect that I entirely relished.

CHAPTER 2

PLUGGING THE DYKE

THE MAJOR political story of early 1986 was the founding of The Progressive Democrats (PDs) by Dessie O'Malley. The new party took enormously from Fianna Fáil, encompassing almost the entire anti-Haughey wing. Fine Gael suffered too, but not to the same extent as Fianna Fáil. They lost Michael Keating, their Dublin Central TD, as well as Michael McDowell.

Labour was the political party which was the most distant from their policies, but it would also be threatened, though perhaps in a less significant way. If the 1980s were Thatcherite, Reaganite, and deeply conservative, then 1986, with the rise of the PDs and their monetarist solutions to our economic slump, epitomised the decade. Their success has to be seen in context though; the split in Fianna Fáil, the deeply charismatic leadership of Dessie O'Malley, and the novelty factor, all played a role. From my position in Labour head office at 16 Gardiner Place, the view was not rosy: I could see an impecunious party, a demoralised party membership, and a divided Parliamentary Party. The Labour ministers seemed more under siege than any set of ministers since the end of the second Inter-Party Government (1954–57), which fell apart almost by mutual agreement and exhaustion.

The PLP bear pit

By virtue of my position, I was also Secretary of the Parliamentary Labour Party, usually referred to as the PLP. This was an enormously important position, giving me access to the ministers, TDs, and senators. It gave me an opportunity to build up a relationship with them, which would be crucial when it came to implementing change and development in the party.

My first PLP meeting sticks in my memory. The atmosphere was hostile. Trestle-tables covered with green felt cloth pockmarked with cigarette burns provided the meeting table. The members sat around the tables on brown plastic chairs, many of which were also cigarette burned. The room soon filled with cigarette smoke. My presence was not acknowledged. Dick sat at the top right-hand side of the table alongside Joe Birmingham TD, the PLP Chairman. Dick wore a pink shirt with his initials 'DS' embroidered on the cuffs. During most of the meeting he read from correspondence he had placed in front of him, and even worse, from a magazine which emerged from his post. Occasionally, he looked up from his work and contributed to the meeting. Frank Cluskey TD and Senator Flor O'Mahony puffed cigarettes incessantly while they fumed with indignation. Michael Bell from Louth and Frank Prendergast from Limerick-East were also present. Frank McLoughlin, our outspoken Meath TD, sat there, his mournful eyes cautiously assessing the situation and me. Senator Michael D Higgins was effervescent, frantic and witty. Barry Desmond, the deputy party leader, sat beside Dick Spring, his hand cupped around his ear straining to hear his colleague's contributions. The meeting centred on the proposals to grant licences to independent radio stations. Michael Bell had worked out a deal with Jim Mitchell, the Fine Gael Minister for Communications, which they both hoped would mollify the objections of Cluskey and O'Mahony. They feared a state sell-out would terminally damage RTE. The meeting became so acrimonious that Dick tore himself away from his reading material, held his hands facing out and said, 'Girls, girls', to quieten the din.

The chaos and lack of unity of purpose was even worse than members and observers on the outside considered it to be. It was no wonder that many years later, before he rejoined the party, Jim Kemmy asked Dick Spring: 'Is the PLP still a bear pit?' This was in 1990, by which stage the situation had improved to such an extent that it would have been unrecognisable if set against that spring morning in 1986. I did, however, resolve to do something about the physical conditions of the meeting room. I wrote to the Superintendent of Leinster House, who kindly supplied new tables and chairs, and I decided to start a collection of portraits of former Labour leaders to grace the bare walls. These meetings took place every week when the Dáil was in session and each would contain at least one agenda item that would be critical of the ministers' performance. It must have been sheer torture for the office-holders. However, the meetings did have their lighter moments too.

Solving the fodder crises

It was during these months that Joe Birmingham became a friend of mine. He had a genuine concern for the underdog and an excellent sense of humour. It was in the middle of one of those cyclical fodder crises when a bad winter pushes up the price of animal foodstuffs and farmers apply pressure on the Government for compensation. Before a February PLP meeting, Barry Desmond TD, Minister for Health, and Ruairi Quinn TD, Minister for Labour and the Public Service, discussed the matter. Their concern and sympathy towards the farmers was matched only by their absolute ignorance of rural matters; neither could tell one end of a beast from the other. Joe Birmingham interrupted: 'I've got the solution to the Fodder Crisis.' Joe, who was a rural deputy representing Kildare, was knowledgeable on agricultural matters and his views were listened to with respect. 'The way to solve the Fodder Crisis is to take out ten farmers after Mass every Sunday and shoot them.' For some reason, the ministerial conversation came to an end!

It was impossible not to feel sympathetic towards Dick Spring. He was trying so hard to make the Government work, to keep Labour together and to look after his young family and a constituency that placed tyrannical demands on him. He did all this with little or no support from the media. This was the time when the bar-room experts predicted Labour's wipe-out at the next general election, which could not be long delayed as the Government had entered office in late 1982. Criticism from inside the party hurt him most and I suppose that was understandable given his Kerry North background, where internal criticism was not a feature of the constituency party. It was still very much under the iron grip of his father, Dan, and the organisational and financial control of his mother, Anne. Coming from a Dublin political culture, I had witnessed the bitter Labour infighting since first joining the party and so I was fairly immune to it. Being so sensitive to criticism left Dick very vulnerable, I don't think that there was an Irish political leader before or since who had such an Achilles' heel.

It didn't take me long in those early days of 1986 to sketch the immediate requirements of the party; we had to be put into some shape to fight the general election, after which we would be in opposition or oblivion, depending on the commentators. I was painfully aware that there were many inside the party who were looking forward to the official coalition party receiving a drubbing so that they could ride in and pick up the remaining pieces in a new left-wing way. This was the analysis of Labour Left, a grouping inside the party which had many supporters, especially in the Dublin region, and which had been founded by Brendan Halligan in 1983. Michael Taft, an American who was a member in Dublin South-East, Michael O'Reilly, a senior official in the ATGWU, and Cllr Frank Buckley, a teacher who was a member of Dublin County Council were among its leading lights. My aim was to save as much as possible in terms of votes as well as seats. After the election, the real re-building could begin. All long-term plans would have to wait until after the general election. But first there was a divorce referendum to fight.

The first divorce referendum

In the liberalisation of Irish society, the introduction of divorce and contraception were essential starting points. In 1985, the plucky Barry Desmond TD, deputy leader of the party and Minister for Health, had, in the face of fierce opposition, made a start on liberalising the laws on contraception. The next step was the introduction of divorce laws, which first required an amendment to the constitution. The prohibition to divorce, which had been included in the 1937 constitution, had to be removed. The battleground was already set as the socially conservative forces also saw this issue as central to the Liberal versus Conservative struggle. We were setting up a state based on the personal rights of its citizens. To do this we had to change much of the painstakingly constructed paternalistic and confessional state that had been built up since 1922. As regards his own struggle to introduce the Family Planning Act of 1985, Barry Desmond had succinctly explained it to me: 'It was simply a matter of who runs the country, the Government or the bishops?' On other issues, such as abortion or gay rights, little or no progress was possible until the more universal rights of family planning and remarriage were established. It was to be a gradual process.

The Coalition Government had committed itself to a divorce referendum and proceeded to honour its commitment in spite of the fact that it had made little or no preparation. This was the rock on which this referendum would perish. Divorce has huge property and social welfare aspects which needed to be explained to the electorate. In the case of the granting of a divorce, how would the property of the couple be divided? Horror scenarios of family homes, businesses or farms being split down the middle terrified many. The rather unlikely spectre of middle-aged married men deserting their loyal and hardworking wives in droves was held out as an inevitable consequence. The vulnerability and dependent status of many women in 1986 was shamelessly exploited by the anti-divorce lobby. It was in this campaign that Alice Glenn, the Fine Gael TD in Dublin Central, made her famous statement: 'Women voting for divorce would be like turkeys voting for Christmas.'

10

Spanish ale

The Campaign had to be financed. The Labour Party was just pulling itself out of the large debts it had incurred during the three general elections of 1981 and 1982 and had no money to expend. But help was at hand. Through the good offices of Ruairi Quinn, £40,000 was received from the Spanish Socialist Workers Party (PSOE). Spain was a recent recruit to the European Union and had a friend in Ireland. The closeness was helped by the fact that both Labour and the PSOE were in Government. This was a very substantial contribution at the time and the irony of Spanish aid again reaching Ireland did not escape us, but this time it was hardly for a crusade against Elizabethan England, more of a practical expression of Socialist solidarity! I was Labour's Director of Elections and I immediately set about building a campaign that would reassure the moderate majority in Irish society. Our slogan was to be, 'Put compassion into the Constitution', and we hired the first billboard campaign for Labour. The posters featured an open hand with a rose. It was the first use of the rose as a Labour logo. The idea could have won us a design competition but it didn't win us the referendum. Nevertheless, I think that the moderate tone of our campaign helped immeasurably for the future of the Liberal agenda.

The proposal was rejected with 63.1 per cent voting against and only 36.3 per cent in favour. As the eternal optimist, I considered this to indicate an improved climate when set against the abortion referendum of 1983, which recorded 3 per cent less on the progressive side. The defeat of this divorce referendum had much to do with the unpopularity of the Government. Fergus Finlay very generously hosted a party in his house in Glenageary on the night of the count (Friday 27 June 1986), and the mood was far from sombre. In fact, I recall Niamh Bhreathnach giving a memorable rendition of 'There was an old woman that lived in the woods'. Only Ruairi Quinn showed signs of despair. At a dinner in The Royal Hospital in Kilmainham in honour of the King and Queen of Spain on the following Monday night, he tearfully discussed the matter with me. He was separated from his wife Nicola and had been going out with his partner, Liz, for five years. He now wanted to marry Liz. It was a story repeated in many thousands of relationships around the country. Barry Desmond, in typically hilarious hyperbole, told me that on the morning after the results came in, he had to physically restrain his wife Stella from going to the American Embassy to apply for a Green Card, such was her disgust at the result. The divorce referendum campaign was one that we put down to experience in the certain hope that when the chance would arise again we would not be so unprepared.

Three PLP defections

I now had to build a team of candidates for the fast approaching general election. The succession crisis in the Kildare Constituency had boiled over. Joe Birmingham's decision not to contest in the upcoming general election left the nomination to his favoured candidate, Senator Timmy Conway. Joe Birmingham, who expected Dick Spring to support him, was shattered when the AC decided to add Emmet Stagg as a candidate. He promptly left the party in great bitterness at what he considered his betrayal. With him left Senator Timmy Conway and much of the membership in the south of the constituency. As Emmet was universally expected to win a seat, the defections were not major blows organisationally, but they had a much deeper resonance. It appeared that the party leader could not, or would not, look after his supporters and the Labour Left inspired candidates were in the ascendant. Joe Birmingham's departure was a blow; not only did he epitomise the best of rural radicalism – 'a small man's man' as he described himself – but his extensive organisation in Kildare would not now be available at National Conferences to support the party leader and his line. It was a double blow since the voting strength of Kildare was not only taken from the party leader, but also added to the voting numbers of his opponents.

More was to follow. Helena McAuliffe-Ennis has been elected to the Senate in 1983. Her father Timmy had been a Labour Senator from 1961–69 and from 1973–81. Her sister Ita was the supervisor of the Labour Secretariat in the Dáil and a very influential figure in the Party. Helena was Labour's bright hope on the Longford-Westmeath Constituency, where she was a hardworking and highly respected politician. She had been very friendly on a personal basis with Mary Harney (then a backbench Fianna Fáil TD). She also had a friendly relationship with Dessie O'Malley. Nevertheless, it came as a shock to me when our Press Officer, Kathleen O'Meara, phoned me with prior news of her defection to the newly-formed PDs. Helena was a great loss, not only as a strong candidate, but also as the only female candidate who had any serious prospects of winning a Dáil seat.

Re-organisation begins

It was now time for me to get moving around the country coaxing, cajoling and dragging a candidate list from the Labour organisation. Many thought it couldn't be done. In his very well-meaning way, and on the pretext of discussing his purchase of a new car, Frank Cluskey telephoned me to advise me to keep my distance from the current leadership. 'There has never

12

been so many losses to the parliamentary party in our history. Keep your distance from that lot, son', he warned me. Though I admired him most out of all the parliamentary party, I knew he believed that Spring could not survive. He had lost the leadership himself in 1981 when he was defeated in the general election.

Many people felt that the Labour organisation was neglected. I was greeted in many places with wonder. Contesting a Dáil election is at the best of times a difficult job, but contesting when there is no prospect of victory needs a particular type of mettle. That our candidates were prepared to do this earned my admiration and gratitude. It was not likely to be an election at which Labour candidates would receive a friendly welcome on the doorsteps.

When I visited, I brought a cheque for £1,000 to hand over to the Director of Elections on the successful conclusion of business. In this way, some sort of quality campaign could be conducted without putting the candidates or organisation into too much debt. It was an innocent amount of money in comparison to what Fianna Fáil, Fine Gael or the PDs could produce, but it was a major innovation for Labour. Labour's campaigns were much more dependent on voluntary work than the two other major parties, so £1,000 could go a long way. The members were quite shocked at my tactics. Head office had previously been a place to send money and not from which to receive it.

In constituencies with existing Labour representation, I found it a learning experience. It was a fascinating voyage into Irish political life at its most basic and vital level – the so-called grass roots. In Limerick East, the Convention was held on Sunday 4 May in Hayes Ballroom in Dromkeen, one of the old 'ballrooms of romance'. It was one of the biggest in Ireland during the showband years of the sixties. The sitting TD was Frank Prendergast, a trade union official with deeply held socially conservative views. He had opposed the introduction of divorce and the legalisation of contraceptive facilities. The Labour Party in Limerick was very much a party that considered itself to be a protector of Catholic faith and morals of the old pre-Vatican Council school. Public support had drifted away to Jim Kemmy's small Democratic Socialist Party (DSP), which had won three seats to Labour's one in the local elections.

Frank Prendergast's election to Dáil Éireann in 1982 was to be the last victory for 'old' Labour in the city. Hostility between Labour and the DSP was intense, bitter and hand-to-hand. I arrived early for the Convention, got out of my car on a lovely warm day, and went over to another parked car where a man sat waiting. 'Are you here for the Convention?' I asked hoping to initiate a conversation. 'What Convention? I know nothing about a Convention', replied the man. Later on at the Convention, I was to see him sitting among the crowd.

About 50 people attended and the mood seemed positive and supportive to the party and of the candidate. Then a hand went up for permission to speak. It was Frank Leddin, a former councillor and Mayor of Limerick. He was a nephew of the Labour TD Michael Keyes, who had been a minister in both Inter-Party Governments. 'Is Frank Prendergast entitled to run on account of his opposing party policy in the matter of divorce?' I was flabbergasted. This was from a senior member of a constituency party who I had been led to believe was a mere extension of the arch-confraternity. I sought to explore the topic. The youngest person at the Convention sat near the front. He was a young man no older than 17 years. Being so young, I thought he would come up with a liberal response. I was wrong again. He informed the meeting that the ills of modern Ireland were directly related to the abandonment of Catholic morals in politics. Quite an interesting point of view, but not the one for which I was looking. Frank Prendergast was duly selected as our Dáil Candidate. He was a gentle and cultured man with a commitment to and knowledge of the Irish language, which was uncommon in Labour at that time.

On 27 April 1986 I attended Dick Spring's Selection Convention in Tralee. I drove down in my first new car, a red Mazda 323, accompanied by Dick's Secretary, Sally Clarke, and Ruairi Quinn's Secretary, Denise Rogers. John Rogers, the Attorney General, spoke at the Convention: 'There is one man and one man only that made me Attorney General and that man is Dick Spring.' I cringed with embarrassment. I asked myself where this habit of treating our rural members as mental defectives came from. After the meeting I spoke with Anne Spring: 'We hope to take a seat from Fianna Fáil here,' she said, 'Fine Gael might win a seat here with our help.' I was to remember these words on the night of the count nine months later. What she predicted did in fact happen, but it was a very close thing and we were the ones who almost lost out.

John Rogers was Dick Spring's closest confidante. Dick had really gone out on a limb for him in 1984 when he insisted that he be appointed Attorney General and stood Fine Gael down on the matter. Fine Gael felt that they had a God-given right to this position, but as always when Dick adopted a difficult position, he stuck stubbornly to it. There were other consequences of this appointment however. Mary Robinson, who was a

Labour Senator at the time, was bitterly disappointed at being passed over. She was far senior to John Rogers both in the party and at the Bar. When she resigned from the party in 1985, one wondered if this incident had played more than a little part. John lived in an extensive house in Grosvenor Road in Dublin and at an afternoon party he held in June, I sat in the garden looking at a strange concrete structure. My stares provoked Diarmuid McGuinness, John's fellow barrister, to come to my aid. 'That,' he said, 'is a nuclear bunker.' 'You're joking', I said. 'No,' he replied emphatically, 'it's a nuclear bunker.' I thought it weird, but said nothing. I wondered which great power was expected to drop a H-bomb on Rathgar.

The Dublin constituencies

The Dublin conventions were quite different. For a start, we only held four seats in the capital but had an extensive – if demoralised and defeatist – organisation there. Dublin was always seen as the centre of rebellion in the party. Its anti-leadership and anti-coalition majorities always provided a lively internal opposition within the party and entertainment at our National Conferences. In 1986, all that could be done was to shore up our defences as well as we could against the oncoming election, while pulling the membership together and instilling a bit of self-confidence and self-respect into the party. I asked Mary Freehill to move to Dublin Central, where Joe Costello was rebuilding the party after the disasters that had befallen it in the previous five years. One such disaster was the desertion to Fine Gael of our TD and party leader, Michael O'Leary. Joe Costello and his organisation reacted with vigour to my imposition. My most memorable response from the constituency was in a letter from the constituency Secretary, Mairead Hayes. 'Mary Freehill,' Mairead wrote in a classic putdown, 'had travelled to a meeting in Dublin Central from her home in Dublin 4.' In the following year, Mary left Dublin Central and I soon mended fences with Joe Costello and Mairead Hayes.

Dublin North-West was another political wasteland for Labour and another Dublin South-East conquistador arrived there with even more disastrous results. Billy Tormey was a consultant pathologist and had been in my own Merrion Branch (later the Ballsbridge Branch). Billy thought things should be viewed 'scientifically' and he brought to the Labour Party in Dublin North-East all the usefulness of an ashtray on a motorbike. He has been defeated in every election he has stood for since 1985 – and he stands for them all (local government elections, Dáil elections and Senate elections). He still pursues his quest. My favourite memory of him is after the 1981 general election in the Four Seasons Public House in Dorset

Street. We had just heard that the party leader, Frank Cluskey, had lost his seat and many of us were on the verge of tears. 'Maybe it's all for the best', said Billy with impeccable timing. Dr Caroline Hussey, our Director of Elections spoke for us all when she pulled herself up to full height and in her Holy Faith Convent accent said, 'Billy, would you ever fuck off!'

The 1986 anti-water charges march. Note Dick Spring's photo on the 'wanted' poster!

Party management

While all this was going on, the dissidents in the party did not sit still. Labour Left smelt blood. Holding a National Conference before the general election would have provided a public arena in which maximum hurt and damage could be inflicted on the ministers. So it clearly had to be avoided. This was a difficult task because the AC had already decided to hold the 1986 conference in Cork and the City Hall had been booked. Fortunately, a strike by corporation workmen took place in the autumn and I travelled to Cork and reported back to the AC that because of the possibility of pickets on City Hall we would have to postpone our Conference. This proposal snookered the proponents of a pre-election conference, as they could not oppose my proposal due to its industrial relations aspects. Besides, I had taken care to have a discussion on the matter with Joe O'Callaghan, the ITGWU official and Labour Left firebrand in Cork. It was a close call. The documentation for the conference had already been printed.

The AC met monthly under the chairmanship of Michael D Higgins. It was a forum where the many factions of the party could meet and insult each other in relative comfort. Towards the end of the meeting, the motions placed on the agenda by the AC members were taken. These were invariably hostile to the Government and the bane of Dick Spring's life. That these were taken just at a stage where the members were getting tired and stressed in a smoke-filled atmosphere, added an edge to the sharp exchanges.

The challenge was to get these meetings over as soon as possible, to have as few of them as we could get away with and to make sure that the members who supported Dick Spring were in attendance at every meeting. A week before the meetings, I went through my list and contacted the 'loyalists' who were almost always the country members. It was a great way to get to know the members and to build up a relationship with them. More importantly, it was a vital part of party management. The party leader could not be seen to lose a vote at the Executive of his own party. To do so would have signalled a slide back to the bad old Michael O'Leary days when the party pulled one way and the leader pulled another. There is nothing so demoralising to a party or so unedifying to the general public as to see a party cannibalise its leader. I'm proud to relate that during my thirteen-and-a-half years as General Secretary the decision went against the 'top-table' only once.

The credit for these votes in support of the party leader lies more with the members of the ruling bodies of the party, who gave up a day's leave or holidays every month to come to Dublin to protect the party from internal dissidents. They usually received no reward except my thanks, which was often delivered along with an importunate request for them to attend the next meeting.

Social aspects

Besides the busy organisational schedule that I imposed on myself, and the unavoidable time and work constraints placed on the office by its relationship with and servicing of the parliamentary party and the party leader's demands, other more pleasant duties interloped. The General Secretary is in demand by embassy officials working in Dublin as a source of information and 'feeling' about how the political land lies. The main courtiers are always the British and American Embassies. At this time, with right-wing Governments in power in both countries, the attitude of their respective officials in Dublin was very interesting indeed. The Americans showered me with propaganda about South and Central America, in which the Reagan Administration played a reactionary role. Their policy provoked the deep hostility, not only of the Irish left led by Michael D Higgins, but also of progressive members of the Catholic Church led by Bishop Eamonn Casey of Galway. The great apologia of the year was 'The Challenge to Democracy in Central America', published jointly by the Department of State and the Department of Defence. It depicted American policy as an attempt to prevent the Soviet Union from taking control of the area. Many in Ireland were deeply hostile to the methods used if not so much to the aim.

Officials in the American embassy spent much of their time trying to justify this policy, whereas their British counterparts concentrated on Northern Ireland. The British seemed to know much more about Ireland and the Irish political system. I was constantly amazed at their up-to-date information on the intricate day-to-day goings on.

My social highlight of the year was the state dinner given in The Royal Hospital, Kilmainham, for the King and Queen of Spain on 30 June 1986. It was a glittering occasion and the elegance of the Spanish royals was quite romantic. King Juan Carlos was tall and handsome and Queen Sofia was beautiful. The hosts were President Hillery and his wife Maeve and they performed their role with grace. It was my first time in a receiving line and it was quite a daunting task. I sat at a table with Denis Brosnan, the Managing Director of Kerry Co-op and the entrepreneurial genius behind such brands as *Kerrygold*. I found him to be a friendly and unassuming country fellow and quite an acceptable face of Irish capitalism. Much more interesting to me though was Jennifer Johnston, the world-renowned author. I had been a fan of hers for years and found her much as I had expected and hoped. She was colourful, outgoing and friendly. Her son Paddy Smyth was in the Labour Party, and as the number cruncher for the militant faction he was part of the internal opposition. 'Paddy has such a warm heart,' his doting mother said, 'he means so well.' I gritted my teeth and agreed. Justin Keating, the former Labour cabinet minister was also present. His conversation was a disappointment as the full extent of it came from his anxiety to ascertain whether or not there was a late bar. Of course there was.

Another occasion of social note, but not as glittering, was the lunch held for the New Zealand Prime Minister in Iveagh House on 6 June 1986. The Taoiseach, Garret FitzGerald, was the host in the absence of the Minister for Foreign Affairs, Peter Barry. Among the other guests was former and future Taoiseach Charles Haughey. I quite looked forward to meeting him. When I entered the anteroom of the room in which we were to dine, he was standing at the opposite wall with a small group. He did not circulate, but stood where he was. It was a technique I read about later. Seemingly, it is terribly important to make people move to meet you, rather than you having to move to meet them. I think it's just bad manners really, but anyway I moved over to see what was going on in his group. He held an empty Ballygowan bottle in his hand and declaimed, 'You see the design, it is one of the reasons for their success.' Incredibly, the small crowd murmured assent at the wisdom of this pronouncement. In a flash, I could visualise the fawning of a Fianna Fáil Cabinet in front of this man; even in front of an unsympathetic bunch of dinner guests he had them oohing at his banalities. At dinner, Mr Haughey and Dr FitzGerald squabbled rather rudely over Northern Ireland. In my opinion this was inappropriate in front of the Prime Minister of New Zealand. I forget who started it, but it was surely Mr Haughey's place to support the Taoiseach at a state lunch. It has to be remembered though that Dr FitzGerald was one of the first and bravest exposers of Mr Haughey as far back as 1979. Madeline Taylor-Quinn, then a Fine Gael TD for Clare, was also at the luncheon and I was delighted to have such pleasant company while the big boys made a show of us.

The Commission on Electoral Strategy

In an attempt to shore up the party on the vexed question of coalition, the National Conference of 1985 had decided on the establishment of a wide-ranging body to report on the issue. This was the Commission on Electoral Strategy, which worked right through 1985 and 1986. It was chaired by Niall Greene, one of Labour's few successful entrepreneurs – he was an executive with Guinness Peat Aviation, the aeroplane leasing firm. It was a mammoth and, most thought, an impossible task to bridge the gap between those who wanted Labour to participate in government whenever possible and those who felt that Labour must stay in opposition until it had enough support to dominate, or at least make a very sizeable part of a government. The gap between the two groups and the consequent bitterness is hard to fathom at this remove, but it was the reality of Labour then. The fact that the Commission arrived at a formula owed a lot to the skill of Niall Greene and the respect which he had from the opposing sides, but it also reflected the reality that the party was beginning to accept that the possibility of a government victory in the general election was receding daily. This was an extraordinary situation.

The formula arrived at was that 'Labour would remain outside of government unless urgent national interest required it'. I asked Dick Spring straight out if he agreed that 'urgent national interest' would include a situation where Labour was in a position to form a coalition government with Fine Gael and no other government was available. He seemed surprised at the innocence of my question and replied, 'Of course'. Due to the intensity of the Commission meetings and the fact that the busy ministers would never be able to give full concentration unless some distance was put between them and their offices, it was decided to hold at least one of the meetings outside of Dublin. For some strange reason it was decided to hold a meeting at a centre run by nuns in Co. Meath. The centre was at Ballinter and featured a nun-barmaid in the evening, which added a surreal flavour to our imbibing. The nuns were of the Order of Our Lady of Sion, an order established by a convert from Judaism with the express intention of converting the Jews to Catholicism. Mervyn Taylor was Vice-Chairman of the Labour Party at the time and as Ireland's leading Jewish politician he was hardly likely to appreciate our hosts. I never got round to asking who had booked our venue, but Mervyn, as the soul of diplomacy, just didn't show up to the weekend Commission meeting and made no fuss afterwards.

The Commission held its final meeting in September and its report contained many fine ideas other than the formula on coalition. This formula was a Mexican standoff. Labour Left believed that the general election would be the final rout for the pro-coalitionists. On the other hand, I believed that with the general election out of the way, many things could be sorted out, including the re-establishment of discipline in the party.

The worn-out ministers

The Labour ministers were in a state of physical and mental exhaustion. The Government seemed to be in perpetual cabinet meeting mode. The ministers constantly berated these interminable cabinet meetings, but never seemed to be able to come up with an alternative. Barry Desmond seemed to develop a hearing problem. Liam Kavanagh seemed on the point of collapse from tiredness. Dick Spring, in the backwater of the Department of Energy was involved in the impossible compendium of tasks that included servicing his far-away constituency, fighting Fine Gael pressure for heavy cutbacks to rectify the state finances and holding off a permanent rebellion in his own party. To add to his misery, his health had never fully recovered from the near-fatal car accident he had in 1982, which left him with steel pins in his spine and the victim of recurrent back pain. If all things had been equal, he would not have been the most jolly and amiable of workmates anyway, but his accumulated complaints made him a prickly customer. Ruairi Quinn seemed to be the only minister who actually enjoyed his job. He was a relative newcomer to the Cabinet, arriving in late 1983 on the resignation of

Frank Cluskey over the failure of the Government to nationalise Dublin Gas. He was Minister for Labour and the Public Service and he generally kept himself out of trouble.

Against this background, the Government stumbled on, never quite getting it right but always with the best of intentions. Labour's longstanding policy of forming a National Development Corporation to encourage, stimulate and foster industry finally saw the light. It was very disheartening for the Tánaiste, however, that he'd had the utmost difficulty in finding anyone of substance to take on the position of Chairman of the new body. It just wasn't the time for ideological projects of the left. Finally Richard Burroughs, the public-spirited Chairman of Irish Distillers took on the job. It was not in place long enough to have a great effect; Fianna Fáil's return to power put an end to it and its prospects for success. Now, in much more prosperous times, I can see the wisdom and hope in such a project. It was launched at a time when native Irish industry had proven inadequate to the challenges of wealth creation and many of its main players were sending their money abroad to tax-free havens rather than investing in their own country, the country that had made them rich. The accolades Dick should have received from the party for the delivery of this key piece of Labour policy did not arrive, thereby adding to his bad humour.

The Government crumbles

The National Lottery was devised by that Government, but its launch was left to the next administration. The same happened with the opening up of local radio; having done the groundwork the Government left the granting of franchises to a Fianna Fáil-appointed Commission with Ray Burke as Minister for Communications. In November, I asked Niamh Bhreathnach to approach the Minister for Education, Gemma Hussey, about a small grant to fund half the salary of a Women's Officer in each party (the other half to be funded by the party itself). It was International Women's Year and a small gesture in this direction would have made a real difference to women seeking to rise in the political system. I was genuinely shocked when this proposal was turned down. It seemed that there was a lack of generosity in that Government.

The greatest example of this was when it ignored the EEC directive on equality in social welfare payments, which almost led to the resignation of Michael Bell TD from the parliamentary party. He would have done so except that he had only just arrived back from a previous spell on the independent benches having been turfed out for voting against the 1983

21

budget! This situation was not rectified until 1995, when the payments plus all back money had to be paid on the back of a deal with Democratic Left to enter Government.

The Government was in desperate straits as it faced a contracting economy. In late October of that year, Dick Spring decided that he'd had enough, and would resist pressure for further cuts to the point of bringing down the Government. I was summoned to a meeting in the Mont Clare Hotel. Dick asked quite bluntly: 'Is the party ready for an election?' I told him that organisational matters must always be subsidiary to political decisions, a judgement I still consider to be valid. William Scally, the Tánaiste's Economic Adviser said: 'The Blues have pushed us too far this time', but the Government did not fall and the following day saw a retrieval of relations. But they were never good during that year, at least with Dick Spring and his people. This breakdown was to leave a bitter legacy until the formation of the 1994 Government. A remark made at Cabinet by Alan Dukes, then Minister for Justice, was never forgotten. During a debate on the budget estimates, when Dick Spring indicated that a particular provision could not be bought by the Labour Party, Dukes retorted that Labour, once bought, should stay bought. The first to find this amusing was John Bruton, the Minister for Finance who guffawed loudly. This incident caused such deep offence that it is still quoted today inside the party.

The fragile nature of Labour's continued commitment to participation in Government was underlined by the 'October Crisis'. Dick Spring brought his dilemma to the PLP, much to their surprise. The responses of the members outlined the scenario for Labour's precipitation of the general election. Many, of course, dreaded the prospects. This was only to be expected as they were, after all, deciding on their livelihoods and futures. They had to be careful that they weren't planning their own hanging. Dick Spring demanded the views of the members on the Government's budgetary strategy and, in particular, the limits and nature of cuts in expenditure that Labour could allow. The matter was urgent as the expenditure estimates were being prepared. Michael Bell was quite sure Labour should break on the matter of a budget, which could not contain anything but bad news for our supporters and constituency. He was backed up by Mervyn Taylor, whose contention was that whatever good had been done in social welfare in the last four years, it was the final budget that would be remembered. Frank Cluskey's analysis was that what we were talking about now was the survival of the Labour Party. Fine Gael backbenchers were terrified, he said, and they were ruthless when in this frame of mind. For the first time ever, Garret FitzGerald's leadership was being called into question. 'At this time of great peril for the party,' Cluskey said, 'we must stick together – nothing must be allowed to split the party.' He felt that it would be difficult to find one great issue that would unite us and he had no instant solution.

Ruairi Quinn ruminated on our successor government being headed by Charlie Haughey and the danger of leaving any unfinished business for him. This might mean a wait of 17 years before our return to power, as had happened before. Liam Kavanagh, in what turned out to be a keynote contribution, said that the real difficulty was that the ministers could not come back to the members with specific budgetary proposals and that if this discussion became public knowledge then the entire exercise was doomed. What the leader and ministers needed were directions on budgetary proposals that would be acceptable and this course could be successful if we worked in unison. This meant displaying a confidence in the party leader and in the ministers. After contributions from the other members, all of whom seemed to get the point, Dick Spring summed up: 'We are in control now, demeanour is everything, we must keep our grip.' I reckon that this date, Wednesday 15 October 1986, was when the Coalition Government of 1982–87 effectively ended.

Election countdown

On 20 January 1987, the Labour ministers withdrew from Government. There had been surprisingly little opposition from within. I had been expecting more as there was a widely held belief that the trappings of ministerial power – the extensive clinic office in the Department; the state car; the top level access to other Departments; and the prestige of the office holders themselves – could be crucial to the outcome of an election. Several strategies had been discussed, but that of resigning from office on the basis of the unacceptability of proposed cuts was considered the best for the party in the short term and the country in the long term. Labour had, for over four years now, held back the tide of swinging cuts deemed necessary by the economists, who were accepted by the politicians of Fianna Fáil and Fine Gael as the oracle. Only the far left shouted that there was a massive tax rip-off being perpetrated by the business class, an assertion that has much credibility now with the revelations of the tribunals set up in the late nineties. At this stage, Labour had exhausted itself in defence of a health and social welfare service and had decided to retreat to fight another day. I suggested to Dick Spring that our ministers take the process a stage further and refuse to accept the cuts without resigning, thus precipitating a national debate on the strategy of cutting public services. He replied tersely: 'I will not be fired by Garret FitzGerald.' It was an understandable position after all the hours he had put in in the previous four years.

Labour is written off

We launched into the campaign at breakneck speed. I was the National Director of Elections for the party and had been operating formally in that capacity since October when the party's election readiness programme was started. All parties were ready for this election, but the favourite of the media was the year-old PDs, led by the charismatic Dessie O'Malley. Labour expected no favour and received none. The *Irish Independent* and the *Irish Press* newspapers reverted to type and supported Fine Gael and Fianna Fáil respectively, though John Foley and Chris Glennon of the *Irish Independent* could be relied on to treat us with fairness. *The Irish Times,* while it was never hostile, had little penetration into our electorate and went with the trend of lionising the PDs. RTE was felt by Labour to be permanently hostile to the party. We believed that a group of Workers' Party supporters had taken control of the current affairs department in the early eighties and since then the station had been consistently anti-Labour and anti-National, and indeed had cut down on its investigative side. We had some control over their activities inside the RTE unions, particularly the FWUI, but their dominance of the current affairs department was something we could only rail against. We were always treated fairly by people like Brian Farrell and John Bowman; it was the editorial manipulation that was our greatest bane. All major campaigns in the eighties had been followed by major complaints to RTE by us. We got nowhere. It was particularly galling to a political party committed to a public broadcasting service but we just had to swallow it and wait for better days. Now, however, it added to our troubles as RTE joined certain elements of the print media in announcing the imminent collapse of the Labour Party.

Fergus Finlay took over the media campaign. Kathleen O'Meara, the party's Press Officer, worked on scripts that were mainly for the non-office holders. Fionnula Richardson, who was the Deputy General Secretary of the Socialist Group in Brussels came over for the duration and helped with scripts. William Scally continued his sterling work as a one-man research bureau and proved invaluable as the issues of the election were centred on economic policy. The Government had broken on the budget, how could Labour retain credibility if it could neither agree nor propose a budget? This is where William came in. Almost single-handedly, he produced a budget acceptable to Labour and this was launched one week into the election campaign. The importance of these proposals was that they served, to a certain extent, to silence some of the criticism levelled at us. There were no votes in economic issues for Labour in this election. Ireland, and some would say the Western World, was in the grip of a pernicious right-wing ideology, based on cutting government expenditure and exemplified in Britain by Margaret Thatcher and in the US by Ronald Reagan.

In Ireland, their ideological counterparts were the PDs though, to be fair, both Fianna Fáil and Fine Gael now seemed to discover the enormous benefits of cuts in spending. I told Peter White, Fine Gael's sympathetic Press Officer, that all Fianna Fáil in Government had to do was take out the Fine Gael Budget, dust it a bit and present it to the Dáil! As the differences between them on a policy level evaporated, the question of style came to the fore. Fine Gael orchestrated this by vigorously promoting their own budget proposals, i.e. those already rejected by Labour, but more importantly, by promoting their leader, the Taoiseach Garret FitzGerald, as trustworthy and reliable. Charlie Haughey, the Fianna Fáil leader, was widely perceived as a strong and able leader, but not, however, as a trustworthy person – rather he was felt to be that sort of person described so aptly in Ireland as a 'chancer'. It took many years for people to see real evidence that these suspicions were only too true!

PD–Fine Gael arrangement

The Fine Gael tactic of cosying up to the PDs gave me considerable concern. Fine Gael had been our main source of transfers since the fifties, and for this source to dry up now in our hour of need would be very dangerous indeed. There was another side to the story of course, many Fine Gael supporters and activists, particularly those in the left wing of the party, deplored a move towards the PDs and away from a coalition with Labour. The coalitions had given the country good government on four separate occasions. It was a foolish strategy; it was obvious to me at least that the PDs would eat into the Fine Gael vote very rapidly indeed if all ideological differences were declared to be at an end. To an extent, Fine Gael was in much more danger from the PDs than we were from the Workers' Party. It was, after all, the party of fiscal rectitude. With this in mind, I organised a meeting with Finbarr Fitzpatrick, who was then the Fine Gael General Secretary. We met in the Gresham Hotel in Dublin. It was to no avail, however, and I could tell early into the meeting that he had no interest in proposals. Some crazy scheme had been manufactured somewhere indicating that Fine Gael and the PDs were going to get enough seats to form a Government independent of all other parties. No opinion poll during the campaign had indicated the possibility of such an outcome. Ironically, it was Fine Gael that was the loser in all this. Their famous *rapprochement* with the PDs was a factor in their drop in seats from 70 (in 1982) to 51 (including Ceann Comhairle Tom Fitzpatrick's). Of the PDs' 14 seats, 9 could be said to be gains from Fine Gael. On the transfer front, the solid Fine Gael transfer to Labour was ended where PD candidates remained in the race, but where there weren't any, Fine Gael continued to transfer to us making the crucial difference in many cases.

The election campaign was long by Irish standards (four weeks) and fought in bitter winter weather. For Labour, it was a struggle for survival. We were all too aware that we were not only under threat from the PDs, Fianna Fáil and Fine Gael, but that also, on our left, the Workers' Party were on the move. This was their big chance. Their vote had increased at all elections since their first in 1977 when they appeared as Sinn Féin the Workers' Party. Now they sought to replace Labour as the party of the left and it was the opportune moment.

Whatever about its break-up, the existence of the coalition in the previous four years had necessitated many policy compromises, from the partial abolition of food subsidies, to the imposition of service charges to local authorities. These policy compromises could now be exploited. The Workers' Party fought a sharp campaign and there were bitter exchanges between us in many constituencies, particularly in Mervyn Taylor's Constituency of Dublin South-West, where Pat Rabbitte was his adversary. In Dublin South-Central, the struggle was equally bitter as Frank Cluskey fought Eric Byrne for the left seat. It was during the campaign that Frank learned of the cancer that was to take his life two years later. He battled bravely on, refusing to censor his election literature to suit populist prejudices. When his well-meaning campaign team suggested that he leave out his achievement in introducing unmarried mother's allowance and prisoners wives' allowance on his campaign leaflets, Frank made it quite clear that he would sanction no leaflets without mention of these schemes of which he was so proud. The tragedy of Frank's illness was compounded when, during the same campaign, his adviser, secretary and friend, Mary Turley, contracted multiple sclerosis. I visited the Dublin South-Central workers in the Robert Emmett pub in Thomas Street. Mary was there, presiding over the campaign with her husband Padraig, the Dublin solicitor. She was already sick at that stage but we did not know. Mary was a tall, dark and elegant woman originally from Lorrha in North Tipperary. Though a qualified solicitor, she did not practise, preferring instead to live on a Secretary's salary and work for Frank Cluskey, whose compassionate politics she shared.

In Dublin, the prophets of doom continued their predictions. Michael O'Reilly of the ATGWU, in response to my prediction in the front office of head office that we would win at least a dozen seats said: 'We'd be lucky to get seven or eight.' This I believed to be the Labour Left preference.

The staff at head office at the time comprised Marion Boushell, the Deputy General Secretary; Pat Montague, the Youth Officer; Angie Mulroy, the Membership Secretary; Marie McHale, my Personal Secretary; and Jackie Byrne, who did general secretarial and reception work. They were now supplemented by Fergus Finlay, Sally Clarke, Kathleen O'Meara and William Scally, and it was a united team during the campaign. If each opinion poll showed bad news, then we did not let that get us down, we knew of the quality of our candidates and of their commitment. We would conquer adversity by sheer willpower. A number of innovations I introduced in this election have now become standard practice for Labour. For the first time ever, free candidate posters were issued by head office, thus standardising our design nationally as well as lifting a significant financial burden from the local organisations. Scripts were produced centrally, thus helping the cohesion of the party's response to issues during the campaign. Again for the first time, we hired a hoarding campaign enabling us to further co-ordinate our messages nationally.

Sticking to our core values

On 11 February, we held a press conference in the Clarence Hotel in Dublin on our supportive attitude to the public sector. The press conference was fronted by Senator Flor O'Mahony, our candidate in Dublin North-Central and a close ally and confidante of Frank Cluskey. What was amazing about this press conference was that it took place at all. All indicators showed us that the public service was an unpopular issue, but for us it was a core principle. How can Government deliver to the weakest sectors except through public service? The market economy has no interest in the poor. We held our press conference and stuck to our guns during the campaign. The result was that we dominated the left ground. There may not have been much of it in 1987, but what was there was Labour's.

It was the last chance of the Workers' Party to catch up with us and we out-manoeuvred them simply by sticking to our principles. It seems quite an obvious tactic now, but it is ignored again and again by Labour parties all over the world in the attempt to conquer 'the middle ground'. A Labour Party that abandons its core vote risks losing it. 'Middle ground' squatters can only be shifted when their parties are in disarray. The two major parties,

Fianna Fáil and Fine Gael, would only oblige with this scenario once in a generation. In 1987, these parties joined by the PDs, slogged it out and redistributed the 85 per cent that they received in the elections of the eighties and in most elections since the foundation of the state. Labour, by holding its nerve and running a creditable national campaign, dominated the 15 per cent left-wing vote and lived to reorganise and revitalise just as planned.

In spite of our difficult circumstances, the party fielded candidates in 32 of the 41 constituencies, mainly due to organisational work done in the previous year. In many cases, the candidates ran merely to keep the party in existence. I have always maintained that failure to contest in a constituency can set the party back many years, while running even a weak but respectable candidate can keep the party there as a force that can be restored when a stronger one arrives. If Labour voters are left without a candidate, then their votes will be notoriously hard to recover. In this regard, having Seamus McNamee to run for us in Longford-Westmeath; Tom Phelan to run for us in Laois-Offaly; or Tony Hobbs to run for us in Cork East was a necessary precursor to our winning seats in these constituencies just five years later.

Nor did we fight a totally defensive campaign. Senator Michael D Higgins, the party Chairman, was expected to win back his seat in Galway West; Senator Brendan Howlin was expected to win back the traditional Labour seat in Wexford; but most of all, Cllr Emmet Stagg was to replace Joe Birmingham in the Kildare Constituency after his eventful nomination for the candidacy. Other target constituencies included Senator Michael Ferris' Tipperary South, where he would take on Sean Treacy, who had been elected a Labour TD at the previous election, but who now sat in high pomposity on the independent benches. He had resigned in 1983 over the Family Planning Bill, much to the delight of the liberal section of the party. In Waterford, a young national school teacher, Brian O'Shea was determined to wrest the Labour seat back from the Workers' Party, who had made it their first Dáil gain in 1981. Sean Ryan and Bernie Malone in Dublin North, Senator Flor O'Mahony in Dublin North-Central, Sean Kenny in Dublin North-East and Eithne Fitzgerald, were all expected to do well. Furthermore, we knew that we had more than a fighting chance in Cork South-Central as Toddy O'Sullivan had moved there from Cork North-Central where he had been elected in the first three elections of the eighties.

Polling day 1987

Polling Day was on Tuesday 17 February and the votes were counted on the following day. It was a matter of keeping our nerve all day. I went to the RTE studios for 3.30 p.m. with the message that the Labour seats would be held, but would come in only at the very end when all the transfers came into play. The attitude among the TV journalists was that Labour would suffer a terminal blow. I kept repeating my message almost as a mantra: 'Labour seats would be secured in spite of a first preference vote drop. This would happen due to an accumulation of anti-Fianna Fáil transfers, which would only become apparent at the count for the final seats in most constituencies.' The insults and jibes were flying. Even Proinsias Mac Aonghusa was wheeled on and he duly attacked the Labour Party as being right wing, not mentioning of course that he had been its Vice-Chair in the sixties and had been expelled. For a moment, I thought I might say this, but I held my cool and hoped that the party was doing the same. I only faltered once. Later on in the evening in the reception area outside the studios, I was handed the latest printout of the updated count for Kerry North. It was the result of the fourth count and it showed Dick Spring to be 868 votes away from the quota. The 3370 votes of the last placed candidate, Fianna Fáil's Dan Kiely, were now being distributed between Tom McEllistrim, his running mate who was 2242 votes from the quota and Denis Foley, also Fianna Fáil and 575 votes from the quota. Jimmy Deenihan of Fine Gael had already filled one seat in this three-seater constituency. I couldn't believe what was happening. Barry Desmond, the deputy party leader, who was going into the studio at the time, passed by without comment. But Liam Kavanagh, who was Minister for Tourism, Forestry and Fisheries took the printout, examined it and predicted quite rightly that the transfers from Kiely and Foley's surplus would be enough to keep Dick Spring ahead. This is precisely what happened. Dick went on to win the seat with the small margin of four votes. At the count itself, Dick's sister Kay fainted in the crowd in front of the table where spoiled ballots were being checked. So great was the surge, however, that she didn't fall but remained upright, carried and supported by the crowd. How those four brave voters in Kerry North changed Irish history!

But the story was similarly close elsewhere, and usually to our advantage. We won our new seats in Galway West with Michael D Higgins; in Wexford with Brendan Howlin; and in Kildare with Emmet Stagg. It wasn't until the next day that we also happily learned that Toddy O'Sullivan had been returned in his new constituency of Cork South-Central. He was given a round of applause at the parliamentary party meeting of the following week.

The prophets of doom had been proven wrong. The RTE report of earlier that day, which held out the possibility of Labour returning four or five deputies, was confounded, but, typically, it was not withdrawn. Instead, to cover it up, the results were now interpreted as 'a move to the left inside the Parliamentary Labour Party'. We had returned 12 deputies; a sufficient critical mass to rebuild the party and way in excess of the Workers' Party's four seats. It was also way above what any analyst had predicted for us. Granted, the transfers had come our way, but this was hardly accidental, our strategy of a principled left-wing party made us an acceptable receptacle of transfers for many voters, even (and perhaps crucially) from those who would not dream of giving us a first or indeed a high preference. I went home that night and thanked God for such a magnificent evening. Labour had come through its greatest test. Now we faced the challenge of reforming and reorganising. Exciting times lay ahead.

CHAPTER 3

RESTORING THE PARTY TO ITS MEMBERS

THE IMMEDIATE aftermath of the 1987 general election was a time of contrasting feelings in the Labour Party. I was elated, believing that we had weathered a storm and had great things ahead of us. I was naïve enough to think that my analysis would be universally held in the party. To discuss the situation and make some preliminary plans, a group of us met in Fergus Finlay's house in the Dublin suburb of Glenageary. Besides Fergus and myself, the meeting was attended by the leader Dick, Barry Desmond TD, Ruairi Quinn TD, Senator Pat Magner, and Sally Clarke.

It was a new Dick Spring that emerged. Dick now announced that things would have to change. We looked at him mystified and a bit embarrassed by the tone of his voice. I think I was more embarrassed for Fergus than for myself, as his position was more vulnerable and we were in his house. Dick was expressing his anger at the result in Kerry North, and his demeanour darkened. It seemed as if all the frustration of a hard-working TD who had come so close to losing his seat was coming out. My idea that we were a party renewed and refreshed in Opposition was obviously not one shared by my party leader. I had to tread with care after that: the sensitivities associated with the 1987 general election results had to be factored into every proposal. My enthusiasm for our new position and the wonderful opportunities it offered had to be somewhat masked. The rebuilding of the party would probably require more patience, more time and more work than I had previously anticipated.

The next day, the new Parliamentary Party met. Its first duty was to elect a new Chairman, after which the leader and deputy leader would be elected. I chaired the first part of the meeting and with carefully measured words alluded to the genuine hurt felt by many members over the last few years. I was particularly referring to Frank Cluskey and his people. I appealed to them to let the past alone and to move to the new challenges facing the party. While I spoke, I saw Frank look at me inscrutably from the corner of one eye. Michael Bell was re-elected as PLP Chairman and he then took over. Dick and Barry were re-elected as leader and deputy leader without a contest. Mervyn Taylor was elected Party Whip. A short and vague discussion on the future of the party then followed. There was one memorable intervention however. It came from Liam Kavanagh: 'Our number one priority now,' he said 'must be the defeat of the Workers' Party.'

On Tuesday 3 March, I went over to Leinster House to meet the party leader. I had many things to discuss, including the forthcoming Senate elections and the problems in the Dáil Secretariat, where our loss of seats was likely to lead to job losses. In the lobby, I met Frank McLoughlin, who had lost his seat. He was very weepy; he had always been an emotional and soft-hearted man. He was with John F Conlon, the former Fine Gael TD for Cavan-Monaghan who had also lost his seat. It was heart rending. Dick had been allowed to keep his ministerial offices in Government Buildings in spite of Labour's resignation from office. When I crossed over there from Leinster House, he asked me to go back and fetch Frank McLoughlin, which I did, being very impressed with the gesture. In Dick's office the floodgates opened and poor Frank bewailed his loss. It is a side of politicians rarely seen by the public; now, after his four years in the Dáil he could not pay his phone bill and Telecom had cut him off. 'How much was it?' asked Dick as he reached for his cheque book and wrote out a cheque for the full amount. I was amazed at the whole episode and thought a lot about it – it certainly did not fit into the category of parliamentary politics at the end of the twentieth century. No, this was something entirely different, this was a chieftain receiving his loyal but defeated vassal. I don't think that this scene could take place in any other European democracy.

The results of the Senate elections confirmed the gloomy predictions based on our poor local election results of 1985. Out of 49 elected seats, Labour succeeded in winning only three; these went to Jack Harte from Dublin, Brian O'Shea from Waterford, and Michael Ferris from Tipperary South. The latter two, however, stood a good chance of converting their Senate seats into Dáil seats (which in fact they both did in 1989). On the morale front, we now had 15 Parliamentarians, one more than the PDs. A small point perhaps, but one which is of some importance to the fragile egos in Leinster House.

Fergus Finlay became Special Assistant to the party leader, a new position that gave him a wide brief as spokesperson, speechwriter and political adviser to Dick Spring. There was also a full-time Research Officer who was based in Leinster House. Kathleen O'Meara remained on as Press Officer and soon moved over to the Dáil from Labour head office in Gardiner Place. It was a better resourced party than at any time in our history, in spite of the heavy burden of debt in head office after the general election.

Haughey returns as Taoiseach

On 10 March 1987 Charlie Haughey became Taoiseach for the third time, but now he was leading a Fianna Fáil minority Government. On the following day, Garret FitzGerald resigned as Fine Gael leader. This gave Dick seniority as an opposition leader that he could never enjoy with Garret at the helm of the main Opposition party. Alan Dukes, the new Fine Gael leader, co-operated with the Government in its economic strategy of curtailing expenditure. This departure was known as 'the Tallaght Strategy', due to the location of its first public airing. It was to leave Fine Gael dangerously exposed as a weak Opposition party and, as is always the case in Ireland, any weakness in either of the main parties gives an opening to Labour. The PDs were also experiencing grave difficulties in Opposition. Their *forte* was Government and the hard slog of Opposition was proving an unsuitable role for them and they began to slip in the polls. By March 1987, the shape of the political landscape of the twenty-fifth Dáil had already emerged.

For me it was full steam ahead. This was the scenario I had desired: a reasonably strong PLP in Opposition and a national party outside of the Dáil, rebuilding, reorganising, repositioning and re-emerging. We would construct a party that would enter Government with a mandate. We had not done that before and that would be only the start. I constructed my aims, which had been placed on hold during the previous 12 months when the only aims were survival and salvage. My three aims, which would take the party into a new era and into Government, were as follows:

1. The establishment of party discipline: this included the expulsion of the militant faction from the party.

2. A merger with the Democratic Socialist Party (DSP), the small party founded by Jim Kemmy in 1982. He was its only representative in Dáil Éireann and the party had three councillors elected in 1985. I also hoped

that Declan Bree and his small organisation in Sligo would come on board.

3. The ending of the bitter and futile rift in the party over coalition. This would be achieved by the defeat of the Labour Left group inside and the refocusing of members' energies on electoral success and the election of candidates.

These aims were mainly organisational and extra-parliamentary. A vibrant party would complement a strong Opposition in Leinster House. It was a formula that stood a great chance of success. My main difficulty was, and continued to be, that relations between head office and the leader's office in Leinster House were rarely in harmony. In early 1987, Labour in the Dáil seemed to have shut up shop. Regardless of this, I decided that it was time to hit the road; there was a party awaiting an awakening.

There were monumental problems all around the country. We had lost seats in Meath, Tipperary North, Limerick East, Kerry South and Cork North-Central. Of these, only Kerry South showed any signs of being prepared for recovery. I visited all the other constituencies, assessed the situation and moved towards the appropriate remedial action. In Meath, Frank McLoughlin decided to throw in the towel. This for me meant moving the candidature over to Cllr Brian Fitzgerald, a critic of Frank McLoughlin's, though he had been his running mate in the general election of November 1982.

In Limerick East, a constituency which encompassed most of the city, my strategy was to incorporate Jim Kemmy and his party, the DSP. I visited our organisation there and gauged the depths of bitterness in their feelings. There was an enormous chasm to be bridged. The fact that Jim was now a TD only made matters more challenging. Nevertheless, I knew that I was dealing with pragmatists who would accept a respectful compromise if it were presented properly – but it would take time. The gulf was painfully demonstrated to me on 5 June when I travelled to Limerick. I stayed for the first time of many in the Glentworth Hotel and met the members. Frank Prendergast, the outgoing TD, described graphically the loss of his seat: 'It was like the loss of an arm.' At the meeting, he advocated the compulsory testing of travellers at Shannon Airport for AIDS, a policy that would be detestable to me and to the wider party. I broached the subject of a union with the DSP and the project was denounced in emphatic and free-flowing rhetoric. Not one person out of the 40 attending supported my suggestion. Definitely a job that would take time, I thought.

One by one I clocked up the constituencies, I even managed to fit in Mayo West and the southern part of Cork North-West. It seemed to me that wherever I went, the welcome that I received indicated a positive response to my invitation to enter or return to politics. Some of it was pretty basic, I suppose, as I recalled the great Labour tradition handed down by former generations. Perhaps there was an element of ancestor worship here but the welcome I was accorded was always genuine and the work was to bear fruit later on.

Dick was absent from Dublin, and the party generally, during this period. Soon after the election he came down with a skin condition, caused by stress. The treatment he received necessitated his wearing dark glasses for a period, which did not add to his image. His reticence, of course, precluded him from explaining the reason to his colleagues in the PLP, and yet again he was put down as distant and aloof. He holidayed in America with Kirsti and his family and he took his parents on holiday to the Canaries. This holiday proved to be an unhappy experience as his father, Dan, took ill there. I didn't see him for great periods at a time but Fergus kept in touch. He needed this time to recover and restore himself after the rigours of the previous five years and his close escape at the polls.

CHAPTER 4

THE RITUAL POST-GOVERNMENT DRUBBING

ONE GROUP that was not taking a sabbatical was Labour Left. Reinvigorated by the election of Emmet Stagg and the re-election of Michael D Higgins to the Dáil, they now concentrated on the forthcoming National Conference. This was the one that had been postponed from the previous year (1986). National Conferences that occur in the aftermath of a spell in Government, when the leader remains in position, are always bloody affairs for Labour. In fact, the last time this had happened was in 1982 when the incumbent leader, Michael O'Leary, had received such a lashing from the Conference that he had left the leadership and the party in less than a week!

I hoped this time might be different and that the Conference would be somewhat forward looking and positive. Now, however, in a brilliant strategic move, Labour Left sought to undermine the leadership of Dick Spring, remove the PLP from its central position in the party and move in their own supporters to positions of influence. The method was a motion to Conference to change the way in which the party leader was chosen. At that time, the leader was elected by the TDs in the PLP. To take that power away from it would obviously be a vote of no confidence in the leader so recently chosen by that process. It would also deprive the TDs, who were directly elected by the people, of their key role in selecting the party's leader. However, it was the former strategy that was the premier one. The departure of Dick Spring from the leadership would have fatally damaged the social democratic wing of the party. Coalition with Fine Gael would be ruled out and the new rump party would be free to pursue a full range of far-left policies that would render the party incapable of entering Government.

The National Conference of 1987 was held in the lofty but dreary and run-down surroundings of City Hall in Cork on Friday 25 to Sunday 27 September. The stage set was created by the effervescent Pat Murray, the Cork designer who designed all National Conference sets during my time as General Secretary.

I urged Dick Spring to take the challenge head-on. Other counsels more conciliatory than mine prevailed and the stage was set for the dramatic compromise, 'the Rock Street Amendment', which was carried on the Saturday night of Conference. This was after 9.00 p.m. and only after a direct appeal by the party leader. The compromise set up a Commission on Leadership Strategy, which would report to the next Conference. Niall Greene constructed the compromise motion.

There was a strong list of anti-coalition candidates for the AC. Seventeen of the AC's members were elected at Conference and of these the anti-coalition supporters managed to elect nine, while Spring's supporters elected eight. This was easily rectified as the PLP elected six members onto the AC, all of whom were supporters of the party leader. More serious, however, was the election of certain party officers. Here there was a clean sweep by Emmet Stagg and his people. Mervyn Taylor beat Ruairi Quinn by 631 votes to 517. I had encouraged Ruairi to contest but was somewhat discouraged when his Secretary told me that he would not attend branch meetings to put his case; he would attend constituencies meetings but not the smaller branch meetings. This was at a time when I was travelling the length and breadth of the country to meet groups of 12, ten or maybe even fewer people. It takes a long time to recover from ministerial self-importance.

Mervyn Taylor was hardly likely to be a pushy Chairman though he was quite clearly in the camp of the anti-coalitionists. At Conference, he raised more than a few eyebrows when he referred to 'working people like us'. I suppose it was technically true, as few worked harder than Mervyn, but as the richest man in the Labour Party it did jar, particularly with the top table where they would be a little jealous of him. The election of the second party officer by Labour Left was much more serious. It was Emmet Stagg himself who became Vice-Chairman of the Labour Party. He beat Niamh Bhreathnach to the position by 626 votes to 524 on the elimination of Joe Higgins, the militant candidate. Emmet would use his position to the utmost over the next two years, never taking time out for a second. He came to head office on the Thursday after the Conference. 'You,' he said to me in my office, pointing his finger in a characteristic gesture, 'will in future be the

Secretary of the Labour Party and not Dick Spring's Secretary.' Mervyn arrived on the same afternoon, in part of the same theatrical set-piece, but of course Mervyn just wanted to get the visit over and get back to his office. I told him about Emmet's pronouncement. I think I could detect a look of anguish in Mervyn's face as the constant hassle of the next two years started to show itself.

It was my first Conference as General Secretary and I had to learn everything from scratch. It was only afterwards that I found out about the Conference Arrangements Committee. This body could rule out motions and I could nominate its membership to the AC. This allowed me to remove the crazy motions from the agenda – but I did not know this in 1987. I had to use different strategies. When youth member Gerry Curran of Dublin North-East sent in a motion calling for the resignation of Dick Spring from the leadership of the party, I simply had to avoid Gerry until after the last date for the receipt of motions and then tell him that I had received no such motion. Gerry was livid, especially when I told him that I hoped he wasn't casting aspersions on the workers in a semi-state body like An Post by accusing them of non-delivery of letters. Thank God he didn't think of registering the letter!

Michael D Higgins was the outgoing Party Chairman. He was the darling of the left and enjoyed unparalleled prestige inside the party – and outside of it too – as an unselfish left-wing voice that was nevertheless successful electorally. He had been particularly hostile to the outgoing Coalition and would have been looking for some justification. On the other hand, I was trying to get the party through what was sure to be a bruising Conference, without too much damage being inflicted. Michael D was never afraid to take a risk, but the one he took on the Saturday afternoon of the Conference took the biscuit. As General Secretary, I sat on the left side of the Chairman, assisting him in the calling of delegates and the list of speakers. The session was due to close at 5.00 p.m. to give the delegates a break and to prepare for the leader's speech, which went out on live television at 7.00 p.m. We were running a bit over time but intended finishing the list of speakers before adjourning. There was always tremendous pressure to do this. Delegates had travelled the length and breadth of the country, often at considerable expense to themselves, and to deprive them of their chance of addressing Conference would not be forgiven lightly. At this point, a steward handed Michael D a note. He read it to himself and passed it to me. It read: 'The Gardaí have received a warning that there is a bomb on the hall. Please evacuate the building immediately.' Just then, Michael D called the next speaker, taking the opportunity to remind delegates to be brief, as we were somewhat over our time. The delegates never realised just how brief our time really could have been!

Right from the start it was an anachronism. The debates were dominated by the merits/demerits of the Fine Gael–Labour Coalition that had collapsed in the previous January. It seemed as if the party had to have its therapy session to cleanse itself – at least that was how half the party felt. The other half, who had supported the Coalition, wanted to justify it. Of course, most of the Coalition sections of the party had not whipped in their maximum numbers to attend, as they knew that this would be a bashing session.

Emmet Stagg passionately addressed the delegates. He said he had information that the leadership intended to lead the party back into Government in the election after next. If this happened, he warned Conference, the leadership would be slaughtered by the members. Strong stuff indeed. His 'information' seemed suspiciously like a document I had prepared for Dick Spring on 1 June of that year awkwardly entitled, 'Medium-term strategy for the Labour Party for a period of 6–8 years covering two general elections or three short, unstable governments'. He contemptuously dismissed the reformist section of the party as 'the Vincent de Paul wing'. This was a serious mistake as it deeply offended many of the delegates involved in charity work with that and other organisations. It was great rhetoric though, and very rousing stuff for his own people.

Dick's speech too was sadly very much rooted in the past and in justification of the outgoing Government. Certainly, this had to be done, but now at a six-month remove from power it was, I thought, time to put more emphasis on the future and on plans to rebuild the party. Fergus Finlay told me that up until a fortnight before Conference, Dick had insisted on writing his speech himself, but when at that stage he had only completed two foolscap pages, Fergus felt it was time to take over. The speech received the customary standing ovation, no less enthusiastic than at previous Conferences. It ended in time for the *Nine O'Clock News*, and then the motions on electing the party leader were put to the floor.

The heat of the thousand bodies in the Hall, the tiredness of the delegates, the ranting demagogy, the height of the passions evoked, and the old scores to settle all conspired to turn this into an hour of high drama. Charlie Douglas, the Irish Regional Secretary of the Amalgamated Transport and General Workers' Union (ATGWU) proposed the motion to change the way in which the party leader was chosen. He was no match for a jacketless Dick Spring who humbly identified himself as 'Spring, Rock Street Branch and

ITGWU' to a rousing cheer. The compromise motion he proposed, to set up a Leadership Commission to report to the next Conference was convincingly carried and the Conference adjourned. There was a dreadful social function afterwards in Connolly Hall across the river in Lapps Quay, where the ITGWU had its headquarters. It was a real 'queue up for twenty minutes for your pint affair' and I soon retired to the Imperial Hotel.

There was also a funny side, as always, to this intense and hard fought Conference. It was a brilliantly hot weekend and Anne Kinsella, who was on the check-in desk for Wicklow delegates, announced that the temperature had forced her to remove her knickers! The staid Wicklow delegates were not amused. Another amusing incident was the manner in which Pat Upton received his last vote for election to the AC. The voting for the party officers and the AC members took place on Sunday morning and was based on the delegates surrendering a fully-stamped delegates card for a voting authorisation card. James Wrynn, Pat's colleague from Dublin South-Central went to the toilet and there, on the urinal in front of him, stood a Voting Authorisation Card which some delegate had left behind. The only person they could find who was not a voting delegate and could therefore use the spare ballot was Nicola Quinn, Ruairi's estranged wife. While they reckoned that the chances of her voting for Ruairi for Chair of the party were pretty much nil, it was an adequate sacrifice to make for another Upton vote.

When Conference closed on Sunday afternoon, I dragged myself back to the Imperial Hotel. There in the lobby I met Anne Spring, Dick's mother, whom I hadn't seen for some time. She was very worried and upset. Dick was not enjoying the leadership at all, she confided, and if anyone knew how he really felt, it must be his mother. She was going to advise him to run for the European Parliament when the elections next took place in two years' time. I told her that I thought it would be a horrible life for him and that anyway, there was no one fit to lead the party if he left. I told her that things would get better; the party was always cranky and bitter after leaving Government. She acceded to this but was obviously quite unhappy. 'We'll see', she said. I was deeply shocked: if Dick were to resign now it would be a signal that the party was ungovernable. There was nothing I could do except soldier on and hope that this mood would lift.

Media coverage of the Conference was hostile, as was expected – another Labour internal bust-up. But the party had come through. In spite of my conversation with Anne Spring, I did not expect Dick to do a runner and be gone by Friday morning, as Michael O'Leary had done just five years previously. The party had come through the Conference relatively unscathed: no resignations, no impossible motions carried, and an AC that would be manageable when the six representatives of the PLP were appointed. With the general election out of the way, and now the Conference, it was time for some serious rebuilding.

The Conference, far from depressing him, seemed to give Dick a new perspective on what was required for the party, and to focus his mind on it in a way that had been absent in the previous few months. Much of his low spirits, it must be said, had been caused by simple exhaustion. His performance at the PLP meetings showed a new determination.

Emmet Stagg's group was outnumbered on the AC and even more heavily so on the PLP, with only the support of Michael D Higgins and Mervyn Taylor. His support on the AC would be further eroded when co-options took place. These were to be Flan Honan (a retired ITGWU official) from Clare and Michael Kilcoyne (an ITGWU official) from Castlebar, both strong Spring supporters that I had met on my constituency travels. Logically, it was now time for him to call it a day, but that was not Emmet's way. The battle between himself and Spring was now intensifying and all agreed that 1988 would be the year that would see who was to come out on top.

CHAPTER 5

THE SALLY EMPIRE STRIKES BACK

AT THE back of Leinster House and to the left stands the '1932 Annexe'. It is here in the thirties-style surroundings of an extension to Leinster House that the Labour Party has housed its TDs and staff almost continuously since the beginning of the state. Only one interloper has been recorded. That was between 1948 and 1952 when the leader of the Opposition, Eamon de Valera, occupied the first office on the left on the first floor. At all other times, the leader of the Labour Party has set up office on this floor. Dick Spring re-located here after he left Government in 1987, but opted for the smaller office at the end of the corridor. Directly opposite, across the hall, was the fairly cramped, smoke-filled office occupied by his secretary Sally Clarke, and by Fergus Finlay, Special Assistant to the party leader. The old-world feel of the rooms, and the overheated atmosphere of the offices only served to emphasise their overcrowded nature and their impracticality as offices for politicians.

Dick Spring's office was fitted out with regulation Board of Works furniture; reproduction Victorian style desk, chairs, coffee table and bookcase. On the desk, sat a pink, shaded lamp chosen for him by Sally and adding a feminine and incongruously Barbara Cartland touch to the room. Here he presided from Wednesday morning till Friday, when he returned to his constituency. These offices comprised the 'Forbidden City' or 'The Sally Empire', as Michael D Higgins christened them, for here Sally reigned supreme and no one, not even Dick Spring, could question her mandate. She controlled his diary, his visitors, and his phone calls. It was two years before Fergus was to get his own offices. But Sally Clarke was much more than a strong Wicklow woman. She was a committed socialist who mixed her secretarial expertise with very strongly held views; for example, she never took out voluntary health insurance because she

42

opposed private medicine. She took part in all Dick Spring's inner-circle groups until his retirement. Those who did not take cognisance of the special position of Sally Clarke did so at their own peril, be they minister or humblest branch secretary.

Downstairs in the same building sat Emmet Stagg in his alternative empire. He shared an office with his secretary, Monica Doolan, and his voluntary Assistant and Adviser, that great *bête noire* of the leadership faction and Secretary of Labour Left, Michael Taft. Michael D Higgins TD also shared this office. The nine other Labour TDs and their Dublin-based secretaries occupied the rest of the building. It was a situation of extraordinary claustrophobia and tension, especially after some enormous bust-up at a PLP or AC meeting. These meetings took place at 88 Merrion Square, which had been requisitioned by the Oireachtas to relieve the overcrowding problem.

It was make or break time for Dick's Spring's leadership. Labour Left now had the services of Emmet as a full-time organiser and his energy levels seemed limitless. In Kildare, Emmet had a well-developed and financed organisation, which was bequeathed to him as the sitting Labour TD. Michael D Higgins TD and Mervyn Taylor TD generally supported him, as did most of the Dublin membership, which was traditionally anti-coalition. What had previously been an unequal balance in favour of the leadership now tilted towards equality and unpredictability. The winning of Kildare for Emmet had been the key. What had been an establishment voting and delegate stronghold now became the opposite. The loss of 100 or so delegate votes in Kildare to the other side, making a difference of about 200, accounted for approximately 20 per cent of a National Conference of about 1000 delegates; a very dangerous situation indeed.

I believed that the way to go was to tackle the militant faction. This was a small but influential group of Trotskyites whose dead hand had inflicted mortal damage on the British Labour Party. In Ireland, they were strong enough at this stage to have two members elected out of 17 on the AC. They also dominated Labour Youth, which had been left under their control by a combination of indifference and poor leadership decisions. As they only existed outside Dublin in small pockets, they had never been a priority to Dick Spring. His predecessors, Michael O'Leary and Frank Cluskey, had moved to expel them but balked at the last minute, much to my fury at the time. Labour Left had little time for their far-out fanatical ways and, like me, saw them as a major threat to building up the party. However, when push came to shove, the militant vote always lined up behind the Labour

Left position whether this was on the AC or at a party Conference. It was, after all, the solid transfer of votes from militant Joe Higgins that had elected Mervyn Taylor to the chairmanship of the party. So the rout of the militants would kill two birds with one stone; their expulsion would create space for a more moderate membership and would also seriously weaken the voting strength of the Labour Left grouping.

Joe Higgins was the undisputed leader of the militant faction. A native of Dingle in south Kerry, he had taught for a short time in the Vocational School in Dublin's North Strand, but it was his spell in the seminary that gave him that unshakeable belief in 'the great certainty'. For him, this was the inevitable revolution, just as it would have been the conversion of the heathen for the equivalent believer of 30 years previously. I was always convinced of the similarities between the Church militant and the faction militant. This faction had almost ruined the Labour Party in the urban areas. Young people joining up full of enthusiasm and idealism, intent on changing the world, or even the little Irish part of it, were sucked into the militant faction by its simple certainties. Within three years, these unfortunates were drained of their energies, their good intentions and often their careers. The few who remained, became desiccated repeaters of slogans coined for them in their British headquarters. The great slogan of the militants was: 'Nationalise the commanding heights of the economy.' I was intent on getting rid of them from the Irish Labour Party.

Joe Higgins moves west

Joe Higgins had been a member in the Ranelagh Branch in Dublin South-East, where I got to know him well. Outside of his politics, he was a very personable and kind individual. Dublin South-East was a well-organised constituency with no opening for someone like Joe, so he moved west. Dublin West already had a strong militant presence. They had strongly influenced the selection of Brendan O'Sullivan (instead of Noel Browne) as our candidate in the 1982 by-election when Labour won its minuscule 1.6 per cent. Now Joe moved in, certain of a nomination. The Selection Convention took place on 27 November 1987 in The West County Hotel and Joe secured a nomination along with Eamon Tuffy, the outgoing candidate. Eamon Tuffy and I had already spoken about his contesting again. At the Christmas Party in Dáil Éireann on 17 December 1987, he had given me a long-term undertaking about contesting a number of elections, which was what I required from all Dublin candidates. Eamon had good support in the constituency, so immediately I saw a great chance of fighting the militants. With the expert help of the party's legal adviser, Niall

Connolly, and such constituency stalwarts as Paul Doyle, Colum McCaffrey, and Mick Nagle, we set about ensuring that the candidacy of Joe Higgins would not be ratified by the AC. Eamon Tuffy had contested alone in 1987 and to add on any other candidate at this stage could only sabotage his work. In addition, to import the leader of the militants and to nominate him in this manner drove the small but hard-working core of party members in Dublin West to distraction. The irony of the situation was that the non-militant members could loosely be described as supporters of Emmet. Who would he support now? Would he risk alienating the militants and their substantial voting power or would he let down his own supporters. This was going to be good!

Things began to go wrong with our plan quite early on. At my regular weekly meeting with Dick Spring on Wednesday 14 January 1988, I outlined the situation to him. I was horrified when he told me he was inclined to ratify Joe Higgins a candidate. More was to follow: on Wednesday 10 February a meeting was held between Joe Higgins, Mervyn Taylor, Pat Magner, Marion Boushell, and myself. The aim of the meeting was to resolve the problem in Dublin West. Early into the meeting it emerged that Pat Magner and Joe Higgins had already reached an agreement, privately, and without consulting me. It would allow Joe to contest the general election in Dublin West provided he follow certain guidelines including the exclusion of British militants from the campaign and an undertaking that their newspaper, *Militant Irish Monthly*, would give no advantage to one candidate over the other. It was a totally ludicrous arrangement guaranteed to beat Eamon Tuffy into the ground and I was having none of it.

Having failed to get the ruling body of the party to ratify Eamon Tuffy as the sole candidate, I decided that the problem must be resolved in a different way. With the full backing of the constituency officers and the advice of the party's legal adviser, I set about abolishing the branches where the militants of Dublin West nested. With their branches gone, they would be assigned to the limbo of 'membership at head office', where they would have no constituency membership or voting rights. They could, in theory, be assigned to other branches, but I had no intention of inflicting them on any other branch.

There would be no mistake on this occasion, and in September 1988 the three militant branches were abolished: Clonsilla, Ballyfermot and Palmerstown. But better was to follow. On the abolition of these branches at the AC meeting, the Labour Left members and their supporters staged a walkout. I could not believe my luck! I waited just a little while to make sure that they weren't returning and then signalled to the Chairman, Mervyn Taylor, that I wanted to bring up an item under any other business. Just before I did, I saw a twinkle in Pat Upton's eye as he anticipated my move. 'I propose that we hold our National Conference in Tralee', I said. Joan Burton was the only Labour Left member present to make the ritual proposal that Dublin be chosen. Dick spoke in favour of Tralee. Pat Magner said that the decision should be made in the presence of all the AC members, which I thought was the wettest thing I had heard in ages. The proposal was agreed and the stage was set for the final battle of the conflict.

After the meeting, Fergus Finlay took me up to meet the political correspondents in Leinster House. These are the famous 'Pol Corrs', in whose awe all politicians in the Oireachtas stand. I strongly criticised Emmet Stagg's behaviour in walking out from the AC meeting, especially considering the fact that he was Vice Chairman of the party. When the briefing ended, Fergus told me that he thought I might have gone out on a limb – he was right there. My comments were carried on the *Nine O'Clock News* that night and Labour Left and their followers howled in protest. I had attacked an elected officer of the party! I felt that I had done my duty; I was an elected officer too and had no intention of lying down under such criticism.

That night, the ATGWU had a millennium celebration in their hall in Middle Abbey Street (the millennium in question was to do with the founding of Dublin City). It was one of those awful, tedious affairs, listening to people who can't sing perform after others who can't act or tell jokes. To make matters worse, this was the leading anti-Spring union in the country, and their Regional Secretary, Charlie Douglas, had proposed the leadership motion at the last conference. His Deputy, Mick O'Reilly, was one of the leading Labour Left members in the country. When I got home to my flat, Mervyn Taylor was on the phone. He wanted to know how I could have done such a thing – attacking another party officer. I was quite unrepentant and, anyway, I believed that Mervyn was put up to this by Labour Left; Mervyn was not the type of person to make phone calls at midnight.

At the next AC meeting, Labour Left's moral indignation knew no bounds. I defended myself as robustly as I could and was well defended by my friends, including Billy Healy and Michael Kilcoyne. In particular, I remember Cllr Paula Desmond recount, tongue in cheek, how my comments had gone down quite well in Cork.

The leadership and policy commissions

The Conference of 1987 had established two Commissions to report back to the next Conference. The first and most urgent of these was The Commission on Leadership Selection, which was the agreed response to the motion intended to shaft Dick Spring. Liam Kavanagh, the Wicklow TD, was appointed as Chairman of this Commission. Under such steady leadership, all major hurdles were surmountable. I cast my eye around for a model on which to base a new system for election of the Labour Party leader by the general membership of the party. The model I arrived at was copied from my own union, the Irish National Teachers Organisation (INTO), for electing its General Secretary. It is based on the full membership taking part in a secret ballot. It was this system with few modifications that was adopted. It turned out to be a fair and democratic system, allowing all party members to vote in the election of their leader.

The other Commission was not to have such a happy outcome. It was the Commission on Economic Policy. This group met for the first on 10 March 1988 and was top heavy with trade unionists, including Charlie Douglas (ATGWU), Sam Nolan (UCATT), Tom Garry (FWUI) and Gerry Shanahan (MSF) as well as Flor O'Mahony, who was employed by the FWUI at the time. At the same time as this group commenced its proceedings, Dick Spring set up his own Economic Policy Group. This parallel group caused the greatest of tensions, as would be expected. For a while, it seemed that there might be two policy positions, one for each wing of the party! This ludicrous position was avoided only by the slowness of the official group's work. When it was completed, Fergus had to put the finishing touches, but the party leader's policy proposals were already in wide circulation. Both documents were merged for the 1989 Conference in 'Labour's Agenda'. I suppressed this unfortunate document almost as soon as it came out. It advocated house property tax and as we were heading into local elections at the time, I saw this as electoral suicide. The staff at head office were asked to be as vague as possible about the existence of the document. Unfortunately, some senior PD got hold of the policy and trotted it out every now and again. As we moved through the nineties, I was able to argue that the document, which was subtitled, 'An economic programme for the nineties' was now obsolete. The document was, of course, obsolete on the day of its publication!

Party finances at the end of the eighties

The 1987 general election had left an enormous burden of debt on the party. All during 1988, I was struggling with an overdraft of around £100,000. At that time, this was a huge burden and the strain of it told on us in head office, where the debt was handled. Envelopes, paper clips, even elastic bands were recycled. The frugality of our existence in Gardiner Place would have made de Valera proud! Once, there was not enough money to pay the wages of the small staff and I had to depend on the generosity of Bank of Ireland to cash our salary cheques. On another occasion, in 1988, the Revenue Commissioners commenced legal action against us for unpaid tax. This was only averted when I paid the bill out of my own personal funds. All this is, on the face of it, trifling, unless we place it in the context of the millions of pounds being collected and squandered at this time by the then Taoiseach Charlie Haughey. Each month, Sally Clarke summoned me to collect the leader's allowance in Leinster House. From this, a monthly allowance was paid to Dick Spring, Fergus Finlay and Sally. The rest was lodged into the party account. In January each year, the trade unions coughed up about £20,000 in affiliation fees. The rest was raised from the members, whose commitment at the end of the day kept the whole show on the road, and I never forgot it. During 1988, I issued an appeal to Dublin members to sign a monthly standing order in favour of the party and I raised almost £1,000 a month. When I suggested extending the appeal to the out-of-Dublin constituencies, Dick and Brendan Howlin vetoed the idea.

Far from being helped with finances, I found myself hindered on occasions. John O'Connor was a wealthy member of the party in my own constituency, Dublin South-East. An active party member, he was a barrister and civil engineer and had been one of the Labour Lawyers Group that had briefed the PLP for the divorce referendum. He is also the father of Sinéad O'Connor, the international singer. Early on in my career, John took me to lunch in the Unicorn Restaurant in Dublin and we discussed the state of the party and my plans for it. Of course, high up on my agenda was the poverty of the party; I wasn't going to let an opportunity like this slip. I was surprised and delighted when I received through the post a bank standing order from him to the tune of £100 per month. This was in 1989 and £100 per month really was a substantial and generous figure then.

Sinéad was impetuous, strong-willed, and prone to spontaneous actions. At the start of the Gulf War she burnt an American flag on stage. The following Monday, Dick Spring was on radio and, when asked about her actions, he roundly criticised them; he was always very pro-American. John was on the phone like a shot: 'I will take any criticism of myself but I will not let my family members be attacked, I thought Dick Spring was a friend.' It was fair comment I thought, so I telephoned Dick and asked him to telephone John O'Connor and mend fences. He refused outright. 'Family members of mine are getting ready to go to war', he said, referring I supposed to relatives of his wife Kirsti, who was American. It was over-the-top stuff and John received no phone call. Sometime later, the standing order was cancelled and John defected for a time to the PDs. With the election of Mary Robinson though, he returned to Labour 'never more to stray'.

But there were many things that could be done with very little money. During the summer holidays, I wrote a short history of the party and published it at my own expense. There had been a crying need in the party for such a book, as the only histories available were critical and undermining. Now I was able to supply my booklet, 'Labour from the beginning' to all enquirers, knowing that, for the first time, they would have a document that gave Labour credit for its many achievements. I also assembled a collection of portraits of former party leaders and displayed them in the meeting rooms of the Parliamentary Party. I excluded Michael O'Leary from this collection as he had dishonoured the position by deserting it to join another political party. Barry Desmond and Ruairi Quinn objected strongly and frequently to this omission, but I wouldn't give in. It was quite ironic anyway, as neither of those two gentlemen had been very vocal in their support of Michael when he was the party leader, as I had been.

Though frequently and regularly frustrated by the constant penny pinching and lack of money, I, like many of the party members and supporters, had a real pride in our self-sufficiency and independence. I also think that this meant something to the electorate; we were seen as a party on the ethical side of the spectrum. We were poor but honest and I think that is something to be proud of.

The political climate
(February 1987 to March 1989)

Though the Fianna Fáil Government was a minority administration, it had the security of the 'Tallaght Strategy', through which Fine Gael co-operated with it on certain economic strategies, especially cuts in expenditure. Ironically, it was these cuts, particularly in the health area, that proved the nemesis of the Government. Neither was Labour's performance in the Dáil likely to win it widespread support in 1987 and 1988. The former ministers were showing signs of withdrawal symptoms and they were not being replaced. Frank Cluskey was terminally ill during this period and Brendan Howlin had not yet come into his stride. In fact, the party's share of the vote showed worrying signs of stabilising at an appallingly low level of six or seven per cent. The Irish Marketing Surveys (IMS) Poll of July 1988 showed the party at seven per cent. The Market Research Bureau of Ireland (MRBI) Poll of May 1988 showed the party at the same miserable seven per cent. Such results could even lose us seats in the 1987 general election. The turnaround came with the expulsion of the militant faction. When this was signalled, in September and October 1988, the party jumped three percentage points. As Pat Upton put it: 'As soon as the public saw that we were going to clean up our act they were prepared to take us seriously.' From this time on, the party started to improve in the opinion polls, a situation sustained by a sharper performance in the Dáil.

I had commissioned a small piece of polling in 1988 in relation to the European Parliament elections, which were scheduled for June 1989. John Colgan, a Fine Gael Town Commissioner in Leixlip, had a small polling company and did a poll of the Dublin Euro Constituency. The results were much as expected. They showed that Barry Desmond would take a seat. In Leinster, Michael Bell, the colourful Louth TD, volunteered for the job in a difficult three-seater. In Munster, Eileen Desmond shared a platform with Michael Ferris, the South Tipperary Senator. Labour was on the floor as regards the European Parliament. We had lost all our seats in the 1984 election. The Socialist Group maintained its links with us, however, and gave us a seat in their bureau. This was filled for us by James Wrynn, the Party Financial Secretary, and during 1988 we were able to nominate a full-time employee of the group to replace Fionnula Richardson, who had reached the rank of Deputy General Secretary of the Socialist Group. Our nominee was Enda McKay, who beat stiff internal party competition for the job.

Each Labour candidate for the European Parliament was obliged to sign a party pledge promising allegiance to the party's principles and to the Socialist Group. Of great importance to us then was a commitment by the candidates to pay £1,300 per month into party coffers if elected to the European Parliament. MEPs were then, as now, scandalously overpaid and it was the least we expected. All candidates signed the pledge before the party ratified them as candidates.

The death of Dan Spring

During my travels around the country, I planned a major foray in the Munster rural constituencies for early September 1988. I would fit in a visit to Tralee to check out the Conference venue and to make arrangements. Dan Spring had been the Labour TD for Kerry North from 1943 until his retirement in 1981, when his son Dick took over. A big, tough man with a commanding presence and strong views, he was the epitome of the trade unionist Republican Labour tradition which had sustained the party through difficult times. On his election in 1943, he smuggled chains into the Dáil Chamber and chained himself to the seats in protest against Government inaction that had allowed the death of a Republican hunger striker.

On his deathbed now, I found him gentle and tender. I visited him as my first port of call in his house on Rock Street. Anne left us alone and I sat beside his bed while we discussed re-organisation. He was particularly worried about regaining the seat in next-door Kerry South. I stayed there for about half an hour and could have stayed longer but didn't want to tire him. In the front room afterwards, Anne explained their marriage to me in the simplest yet the most eloquent terms: 'We had a beautiful relationship.' I drove back to the Mount Brandon Hotel and Dick telephoned me 20 minutes later to tell me that his father had died shortly after I left. I felt that it was an extraordinary privilege to have been the last person outside the family to speak to this remarkable man.

The funeral, which took place on Friday 9 September 1988, was one of those memorable events the context and detail of which settle in the mind's eye forever. Dick's hands were agonisingly sore from the many hundreds of handshakes of sympathy he received in those three days. Thousands of Labour people attended from Kerry and from all over the country and his constituents, both supporters and not, flocked in their droves to say goodbye.

Building up the conference votes

The battle was now in full swing for the votes of the delegates at the next National Conference of the Labour Party, now set for the weekend of Friday 10 to Sunday 12 March 1989. A Committee was established to oversee the preparations to ensure a victory for the party leader's side. The committee was called the Communications Committee. When Emmet found out of its existence he called it 'The Hang Emmet Stagg Committee', which I suppose was accurate enough. The Committee only started its meetings in June, when a lot of the work had been done, but now the work was more co-ordinated and the detailed management of the event was gone through. The Committee met on a Wednesday night and comprised Sally Clarke, Fergus Finlay, John Rogers, Barry Desmond, Brendan Howlin, James Wrynn (the

Financial Secretary), Pat Upton, Anne Byrne, Marion Boushell, Dick Spring, and myself.

During that year, besides my work in the Dublin constituencies, I visited the rural constituencies. Everywhere I went I searched out and spoke with those loyal to the party leader as well as those who awaited his downfall. I was able to track and check the progress of Labour Left in this way.

In Mullingar, at a meeting in the ITGWU Hall, I told the members that in the past seven years the party had had three different leaders and four different general secretaries. I assured them that things had changed: the leader and the General Secretary were here for the long-term. My announcement was greeted with stony silence. The members in Longford-Westmeath at that stage generally supported Emmet Stagg, and were always in the anti-Dick Spring camp, but I didn't give up on them. By 1990 they had switched their allegiance.

I was particularly successful in Limerick East. Here I had been building up a warm relationship with the local organisation in the wake of its loss of Frank Prendergast's seat in 1987. I was preparing for the merger with Jim Kemmy's DSP. When I went to the local party on 23 September 1988 and told them of the difficult Conference ahead, they responded with great generosity. 'So what do you want Ray Kavanagh?' Frank Leddin asked. 'I want as many delegates to Tralee as you can organise.' That very Friday night, in the ITGWU Hall, Frank Prendergast and his members started to draw up lists that I was able to take back to Dublin.

Nor were the sitting TDs tardy about filling their delegations. I went time and again to Séamus Pattison TD for Carlow-Kilkenny to top up his already large delegation. He never refused. The same was true of Michael Ferris in South Tipperary. Though only a Senator at this stage, he had a formidable organisation. Between himself, Séamus Pattison, and Kerry North, approximately 300 delegates were accounted for. Of course, there were excesses on both sides, and Labour Left was organising actively too and I had to keep my eyes on them. In the Maynooth Branch, I noticed that Robert Gregory, the son of Lady Gregory, who was killed in the First World War, was signed up as a member, no doubt by one of Emmet's supporters with literary pretensions. Maybe it was a test of the literary knowledge of the General Secretary. On our own side, my good friend Vicky Somers had signed up her cat as a member of her Rathgar Branch! Emmet is reported to have said that during this time, if you lost two pounds (the cost of a year's membership) you were in danger of becoming a member of the Labour Party.

No to President Bush's inauguration

The new counsellor in the American Embassy, George Dempsey, got me an invitation to the inauguration of President George Bush at this time. Dick reacted very negatively, however, and, reluctantly, I had to turn it down. At least, I thought, I'm among that very select few who have refused an invitation to the White House for one if its most sought after events.

George Dempsey's appointment to the Dublin Embassy had signalled an important change in the type and calibre of representation from Washington. It had previously been distinctly third rate. The Ambassador at the time of my appointment in 1986 was the formidable Margaret Heckler, who had been Health Secretary, but she was sent here as a punishment for not bending the knee to Nancy Reagan. Worse was to follow: she was replaced by a Mr William FitzGerald, who was over 80 and seemed confused. Having George Dempsey around meant that one could be sure that some intelligent reports were getting back to Washington. This in turn must have some positive effect on American policy towards Ireland that was, at that time, lamentably hostile to the aspirations of the Nationalist community. Of similarly high calibre was his replacement, Dean Curran, but it was not until Jean Kennedy became Ambassador that Ireland's status as a Third World client state of the US was removed by the State Department. Policy towards the North changed radically and decisively.

Yes to Mo Mowlam's whisky

In the first week of October 1988, Dick Spring, Fergus Finlay and I travelled to the British Labour Party Conference in Blackpool. There we would meet up with Tony Browne, the International Secretary and Marion Boushell, the Deputy General Secretary, who had travelled separately. We took the ferry to Liverpool and from there Dick drove up to Blackpool in his Mercedes. Accommodation was very basic, we stayed in the Trafalgar Hotel, which featured canned everything for breakfast. The people were warm and friendly though. Dick was to address the traditional fringe meeting on Northern Ireland. More importantly, we were on a mission to get back into an influential position with the British Labour Party, as it was widely reported to us that the Workers' Party were moving in heavily on them, in particular in terms of attending their annual conferences, where invaluable contacts could be made. Kevin McNamara MP was the Shadow Northern Ireland Secretary and he gave us a great welcome. He introduced us to his Assistant Spokesperson, a certain Dr Mo Mowlam, who was bouncy, funny, relaxed and well briefed. I fell for her immediately. Kevin

McNamara was sincere and earnest, while Mo always seemed ready for a laugh. We were also briefed that Kevin's strong pro-nationalist views were out of favour with the leadership of the party and that he would soon be reshuffled, which seemed a pity for such a decent man.

This was the Conference at which Neil Kinnock laid out his vision of a Britain of co-operation and equality as against Margaret Thatcher's famous 'There is no such thing as society' remark. I was mightily impressed by his performance and therefore a bit deflated when Dick Spring remarked that he could never see Kinnock making Prime Minister. At this Conference, I witnessed a presentation to long-serving members for outstanding service which led me to introduce a similar award for our party at our next Conference. At Christmas that year, I was thrilled and surprised to receive two bottles of House of Commons Scotch whisky from Mo Mowlam! The whisky was delicious, but I must confess, tasted even better when Sally tersely informed me that it was intended for 'over here', meaning Dick's Office in Leinster House. But my name was on the gift box, so I had many toasts to Mo Mowlam that Christmas in my flat in Rialto. It was to be eight-and-a-half years before I met Mo Mowlam again, and under very different circumstances.

The Invasion of head office – 19 January 1989

This most remarkable and hilarious incident illustrates the intensity of the battle now raging in the party. On the morning of 19 January 1989, my Secretary, Marie McHale, telephoned me to tell me that Emmet Stagg had arrived in head office and, without any permission, had started to photocopy the financial records. These records indicate which branches have paid their levies and would therefore be entitled to attend the upcoming Conference. I had refused Emmet access to these records but he had obviously decided to take matters into his own hands. I immediately telephoned Dick Spring's Office and Dick himself answered the phone. By the time I arrived in head office I found Dick and Emmet sitting in the front office glowering at one another. Fergus Finlay was in the back office reading the paper. Upstairs, Angie Mulroy, who worked in the front office, was deeply distressed. Emmet had just barged in and started to photocopy the records. I went downstairs and told Dick and Emmet that I was going to call the Guards. At this stage, Fergus Finlay served tea to all involved, which was a nice little touch.

Later on that day, Mervyn Taylor telephoned me from Strasbourg in a state of agitation. He had been taken out of a meeting of the Council of Europe to receive a call from his wife Marilyn. Naturally enough, he thought that there was a major family problem. All that had happened was that Pat Gallagher of Labour Youth had telephoned her with an account of the incident. When I described it as 'an invasion' Mervyn in some exasperation said: 'Were there bazookas and grenade launchers?'

The Christmas party in Leinster House always provided a story or two and 1988 was no exception. The year ended with a bit of a laugh. Dermot Lacey, the future councillor and Spring supporter, in his jovial and good-natured manner said goodnight to Emmet Stagg at the end of the party with, 'I hope you have a good year ahead Emmet', to which Emmet, never stuck for a reply, laughingly answered, 'If it's a good year for me it won't be a good year for you!'

CHAPTER 6

THE BREAD AND ROSES
CONFERENCE

IN THE 1980s, Tralee's premier hotel was The Mount Brandon – now called The Brandon, it still retains that reputation. As the capital of the North Kerry constituency, where Labour had held a seat since 1943, Tralee was a fitting location for a National Conference of the party and the recently refurbished Mount Brandon was to be the venue for this historic meeting. When I had visited Tralee in September 1988, Anne Spring had succinctly summarised the tactics: 'We'll take Stagg down here, give him a good hammering, and send him home with his tail between his legs!' Well that was the plan, there or thereabouts. Dick wanted to promote his hometown and the Hotel, which were important parts of his constituency life. I suppose that in a way, I had been preparing for this Conference since I had become General Secretary, as it was to be the one to re-establish discipline within the party as well as the authority of the party leader. Labour Left and the militant faction were ready too, and it is a mark of the extent of their influence and strength in the party that they came so near to taking it over. Almost subconsciously, some leading party figures started to consider the results of different possible outcomes. Liam Kavanagh TD said to me that if Stagg won, he wouldn't resign from the party, but he would withdraw from any active involvement and just remain a constituency TD. Séamus Pattison TD made the mistake of telling Dick that he would be able to handle a Stagg victory, and that it would not be the end of the world. Dick was furious that the TD for Carlow-Kilkenny, whose delegates' support was so crucial for victory, had even considered such an outcome.

Pa Lowe was a Labour Councillor on Meath County Council from 1979 to 1985, when, with many other Labour councillors, he lost his seat. Nevertheless, he continued his political activism and was popular in his Meath constituency and throughout the party. Besides politics, his passion was horseracing, and he could speak for hours without break on either subject. His own branch of Longwood-Enfield would be represented at National Conference, and Pa himself was a constant attendee and popular figure at all conferences. He was a great storyteller and wit. Pa was in many ways typical of rural Labour activists; rooted in his community, his sport, his politics, his family and thoroughly enjoying them all. Emmet's failure to win the Pa Lowes of the Labour Party was a symptom of the upcoming defeat of his project. He telephoned Pa on that Tuesday night (7 March 1989) and Pa told him to stop his 'nonsense' and start learning a bit of loyalty to his leader. Emmet, whose Kildare base was quite close to Pa's, knew of the importance of his support. Emmet told him that if he didn't get support from Meath he would lose, and Pa told him that there was nothing surer. Emmet broke down and started to cry into the phone at this stage but Pa was unmoved: 'You'll have to start behaving yourself,' he told the Kildare deputy in his fatherlike but firm way.

I met Emmet later that night in the corridor of Leinster House outside his office. 'How many are ye going to win by?' he asked. 'Don't know', I said and walked on. In fact, Marion in head office had quite accurately calculated our strength among the various delegations attending Conference and we were quite confident of victory at that stage. Dick too was losing his cool. John Cooney, the political correspondent of *The Irish Times* in Leinster House at the time, was a constant thorn in his side. It was one of those relationships that was poisonous from the start and, indeed, doesn't seem to have improved much over time. Just outside the Dáil Bar, John encountered Dick and asked him what he would do in the event of a Stagg victory, Dick reached down to the stout Scotsman, removed his glasses and slapped him on the face. This did not go down too well with the other 'Pol Corrs'. It really wasn't a time of good behaviour or social graces!

The struggle between Emmet and Niamh Bhreathnach for the position of Vice-Chair was a proxy for the fight to control the party. It was also to launch Niamh on a path that would see her as Minister for Education in little over three years. She beat Emmet by 793 votes to 655, with the other two candidates, Joe Higgins, the militant leader, and Pat Moloney of Cork, coming in with low votes. Niamh had won on the first count. It was probably a more definitive victory than the defeat of the militants because, for the first time, it spelled out quite clearly that Dick's leadership was endorsed by the party. He had not been a popular leader among the party faithful up until then. Many thought he had come by the position too easily, almost by default, and his catapulting into Government just two short weeks after assuming the position gave him no time to get to know and bond with the grass-root members. Afterwards, in Dublin, he held up the results sheet and said to me: 'I'd like to frame this.'

A great contest also ensued for the election of 17 members to the AC, and we were taking no chances with the voting procedures. The Communications Committee had decided to tighten up the system to prevent double voting, or indeed multiple voting, and personation. Each delegate was to be marked with indelible ink that was visible only under an ultra-violet light. As the delegates got their voting papers, their hands were thus marked and each applying for voting papers had their hands checked for these marks. I had the task of getting the Standing Orders Committee to agree to this bizarre procedure. I expected a lot of opposition, but only Betty Dowling from Dublin South objected. The procedure produced what was probably the fairest internal election we ever held. Of course, it was again a great victory for Dick Spring's supporters, who won 11 of the 17 seats.

In the Conference Hall, the atmosphere was electric. It was overcrowded and the RTE lighting for the cameras added to the temperature – but it was the heat of the debate that fired the delegates. Conference had opened on Friday night with Chairman Mervyn Taylor's address in which he had asked for an end to 'infighting' in the party. Poor Mervyn! The delegates clapped and cheered wildly and then went on to do the opposite. It was almost a rallying cry to battle, which continued until close of Conference on Sunday at lunchtime, by which time Emmet's hope for control of the party or the militant's hope of remaining in it had faded.

On Saturday, all journalists were asked to leave while the Conference decided on the appeal against the expulsion of the three militant branches of Palmerstown, Clonsilla, and Ballyfermot. Emotions reached fever pitch and a delegate approached the platform to tell me that Brian Farrell of RTE was still in one of the wooden commentary boxes which RTE had built at the back of the hall. Sure enough, I looked down to the bottom of the hall and could see Brian's head peeking out of one of the boxes. Proceedings had to be interrupted as Brian was asked to leave. Mick Nagle and Colum McCaffrey eloquently but passionately put the case for abolition while PJ Madden, Tony Canavan, and Fiona O'Loughlin presented the appeals in equally passionate tones. But the party had had enough of the militant faction, of listening to its tired old slogans and suffering its dead hand pulling back the party from organisation and electoral success. The appeals were defeated by 757 votes to 518. The real meat of the Conference though, was to come in Motion 86 from Dublin West. This declared membership of the militant faction to be incompatible with membership of the party. An amendment from my own

Ballsbridge Branch proposed to insert this into the Constitution of the party. This device would allow for the expulsion of anyone judged to be a member of that faction. Emmet Stagg spoke against the motion, as did Michael D Higgins. We were a bit disappointed in Michael's decision to associate himself with the Trotskyites, but I suppose he was being true to his socialist principles of inclusion, or maybe he was just doing the left-wing thing.

When Dick Spring spoke to the motion he did so simply and directly: he put the proposal that the militant faction was a party within a party and that now they must choose. Many like myself had been waiting for a leader to make this statement for years and Conference roared their approval. The motion was carried by about two to one.

By the time the Conference ended, both the party leader and the party members had had their powers increased. The bureaucrats, the ideologues, and the voting blocks had diminished power. This empowerment struck a very responsive note in the party and soon this new feeling would be translated into political activity.

CHAPTER 7

BREAKING THE MOULD

THE MEDIA coverage from the Conference exceeded my wildest dreams. On Monday 13 March 1989, the front page of the *Irish Independent* read: 'Spring's Triumph as Left Routed'. *The Irish Times* headline was: 'Spring in Control as Stagg and Militant Defeated'. Even the *Irish Press* had to grudgingly give us the front page, albeit much less positively with: '250 Now Face Labour Purge' and 'Militants Shocked by Huge Defeat'. The odd thing was that we had not planned our next move at all. I had done a count of all the militants in the party and had come up with a maximum number of 530. Obviously, all we had to do now was to expel their leaders and the rest would follow. There was no mad hurry though, now that the constitutional provisions were in place, we could leave the actual mopping up until autumn/winter. It would be nice to enter the new year as a militant-free zone.

The European elections were just around the corner and we were sure to make reasonable inroads, winning in Dublin and perhaps Leinster and Munster. Our candidates were picked and I had ordered the posters. After the European elections we would finish off candidate selection for the next general election. I was intent on running candidates in all Dublin, Leinster and Munster constituencies. In the following election, we would then be in a position to contest all constituencies in the country. That was my plan, based on a now strengthening and disciplined party. It was not to be however. Charlie Haughey upstaged us all and called a surprise general election. His gamble, however, didn't pay off and actually changed Irish politics in a fundamental way. Fianna Fáil was about to abandon its core principle of opposition to participation in coalition government.

It was the opinion polls that led to this disaster for Fianna Fáil. Since their introduction into Irish politics in the seventies by Brendan Halligan, Labour's then General Secretary, opinion polls were treated as the infallible source of wisdom for all politicos. Now their limitations were to be shown all too clearly. In April 1989, Fianna Fáil registered 50 per cent (excluding 'don't knows') in an IMS survey. In February, the MRBI poll showed them at an astonishing 54 per cent support level (excluding 'don't knows'). These figures made it tempting for the leader of a minority Government to go to the country. An excuse was needed and the Dáil promptly provided one. On his return from a successful trade mission to Japan, Taoiseach Charlie Haughey found the Dáil preparing to vote in favour of a Private Members' Motion submitted by Labour's health spokesperson Brendan Howlin TD.

The Motion called for an allocation of £400,000 for haemophiliacs who had contracted the AIDS virus. If this were voted through, warned Mr. Haughey, he would call a general election. Many just couldn't believe that he would carry through on his threat, but I thought he might. He was a gambler and a supreme opportunist, and this looked like a lucky break. The course of modern Irish history would have been changed considerably if he'd decided to continue the Government for another three years, as his term was not due to expire until March 1992. But Charlie could not resist the chance of pulling a fast one. The Private Members' Motion was carried and on 25 May he called a general election to coincide with polling day for the European Parliament on June 15 1989.

The death of Frank Cluskey

In May 1989, Frank Cluskey finally succumbed to the throat cancer which had been diagnosed shortly before the 1987 general election. He had undergone radical surgery and the ugly scars were hidden initially by a scarf and later by holding his hand in front of his throat, an act that only brought more attention to them. On the night before the operation his consultant was horrified to find him sitting up in bed smoking a cigarette. 'Whatever harm they've done, they've done, this one can't cause anymore damage', he reassured the consultant.

His leadership of the party had not been a successful one for him, culminating in the loss of his own seat in 1981. His appeal was on a different level; it came from the sincerity of his socialist vision and in particular his commitment to the poor and to marginalised sectors such as children, single mothers, and prisoners. His funeral was a remarkable affair given the diversity of the mourners, who came from all walks of life.

The health cuts election

Almost as soon as the campaign began, the Government started to get into trouble. The fact that this election was unnecessary really was a sticking point for many, but it was the health cuts and increased waiting lists for hospital admission that offended large section of the public. The Taoiseach Charlie Haughey compounded matters by giving a disastrous radio performance on the *Pat Kenny Show*. In response to the question: 'Taoiseach, were you aware of the impact of the health cuts?' He responded 'No'. I suppose he could hardly have replied 'Yes', but anyway he was immediately pilloried as an uncaring Taoiseach, which was fair enough.

As the campaign started, I decided to undertake a whistle-stop tour around the constituencies, especially those who were experiencing some difficulties, and give a national semblance to our campaign. On Friday 26 May, I travelled to Nenagh for the Tipperary North Selection Convention. John Ryan, defeated in 1987, had retired. Could he now be coaxed back as a candidate? The constituency had found a replacement candidate in Johnny McLoughlin, a senior official in CIE, who lived and worked in Limerick. Under normal circumstances, he would be an excellent candidate, but now he hadn't been given the time to establish himself, whereas John Ryan was still held in deep respect and affection.

I decided to approach John and try to convince him to run. Andy Callanan guided me to his house and then hid under a wall so that I could walk casually up to the house as if led there only by fate. John and his wife Ena welcomed me with their usual courtesy and took me into the sitting room, where I proceeded to present my case, which was that, basically, only he could win back the Labour seat in North Tipperary. Ena wasn't too impressed, but I could see a chink in John's armour. I rehashed my arguments and put them again. It was now about six o'clock and the Angelus bell rang on the television. John, a devout person, stood up to say his Angelus. 'What the heck,' I thought, 'its time to take up religion, it might be worth a Dáil seat.' I jumped to my feet and belted out an Angelus that would have made the Angel Gabriel proud. Then the miracle occurred, a reward no doubt for my piety. When he finished his Angelus John said: 'I've changed my mind, I think I'll give it a shot.' Such is the power of prayer! I rushed out of the house as soon as I decently could, back to Andy who was still at the wall. We had to make arrangements for the Convention to accept John Ryan, but more importantly for Johnny McLoughlin to withdraw and show a united front. Johnny was furious at the turn of events and his supporters, who had been involved in some premature celebrations about his selection, turned on me. In the lobby of the Ormond Hotel, the group prepared to overturn my plan. I held my ground and eventually it was Johnny's own graciousness that brought agreement.

Unfortunately, just as this meeting was breaking up, John Ryan and Ena entered the hotel. One of Johnny's supporters shouted at John Ryan that it was time for him to go – now I had a distressed John Ryan on my hands. He said he had now changed his mind, he wouldn't run, he was not wanted! I managed to get John into a bedroom upstairs, where I could talk to him privately. Luckily, help had arrived in the personages of Senator Michael Ferris from Tipperary South and Billy Healy, both of whom ministered to John. It took an hour and a half before harmony was restored. Meanwhile the Convention, scheduled for 8.30 p.m., had assembled downstairs. The delegates were restless, but nevertheless they waited. It was not until ten o'clock that the group left the upstairs room. John Ryan was given a rousing reception by the 70 or so delegates present when he announced that he would accept the nomination. He was followed by Johnny McLoughlin, who announced his withdrawal from the race and his support for John Ryan. I gave a huge sigh of relief. After the Convention, one of the members warned me never to set foot in Nenagh again. How exciting!

(L-R) Michael Ferris TD, Senator John Ryan, Dick Spring TD, and Michael Moynihan TD at the launch of the 1991 local election campaign. Fergus Finlay is visible in the background.

On Monday night, I went to Limerick, where a difficult situation awaited resolution. I wanted to merge our party there with Jim Kemmy's DSP, but was nowhere near agreement. To hold onto our negotiating strength, we had to contest the election, though we knew that Jim Kemmy held the left-wing seat and that there wasn't a second one going. Naturally enough, the Convention was unwilling to send a lamb to the slaughter. I was at the pin of my collar trying to convince them to contest, but it is in situations like this that those years of laying the groundwork comes into play; I had been a frequent visitor and knew most of the people in the room. Finally they agreed to contest. The candidate was to be Declan Leddin, who in his early twenties was to be our youngest candidate of the campaign. The party there was still very hostile to a merger with the DSP. At that very meeting, I brought up the subject, as I usually did at meetings in Limerick, to get people used to the idea. 'My relatives are buried in the graveyard over there,' one delegate roared, 'if Jim Kemmy returned to the Labour Party, their bones would rattle.'

A cushy number?

The next day was Monday, and I moved onto the Clare constituency. I always believed that Labour could win a seat in the county, as it had a great tradition of independent representation at county council level. Directed by Flan Honan, my best contact in Clare, I now headed for the door of one of these independents. He was the jovial Cllr Tom Brennan, who represented Ennis on the County Council. He had been in the Labour Party for a short time, but left after some obscure disagreement. He lived in an immaculately kept, beautiful bungalow at the edge of town. His wife told me that he was in the garden and, sure enough, there he was tending his plants. It's hard enough to approach a stranger without any introduction. I had been following his career and felt that I knew several things about him, but it still didn't allow for a total stranger to walk into your garden on a May night and say: 'Excuse me, would you like to run for Labour in the general election?' 'Tom,' I said, 'I'm Ray Kavanagh, the General Secretary of the Labour Party.' He looked up from his watering can, and I knew from the smile in his eyes that there was something coming. 'Are you?' he said. 'That must be a cushy number.' We stayed talking for almost an hour. He had a good sense of humour and would have made a great Labour candidate and TD but he didn't bite. I asked him on at least one other occasion but Labour was not to have a Dáil candidate in Clare until Moosajee Bhamjee took up the challenge in 1992.

The only Convention I hadn't taken personal care of was Dun Laoghaire, and that turned out a mess. Barry Desmond was unable to influence the

Convention, which had chosen two candidates to contest, thereby splitting the vote and eliminating whatever chance we had of holding onto the seat. Each of the two would have been a fine candidate on their own. They were Cllr Jane Dillon Byrne and Flor O'Mahony. Flor had contested Dublin North-Central since 1981 and had an excellent chance of winning there, but had none, unfortunately, in Dun Laoghaire. Furthermore, Niamh Bhreathnach, who had some profile as Vice-Chair of the party, was rejected by the Convention and as Spring's candidate this reflected badly on him.

The health cuts dominated this election and they were the key to Labour's success. The Government never developed a strategy to avoid blame over the health cuts. Fine Gael and the PDs had agreed a pact for the campaign but it never took off; the PDs just can't hack it in opposition and they headed for a hammering.

The Euro elections of 1989

The European Parliament election campaign coincided with the general election. In Dublin, everything went well. Barry Desmond had a small but dedicated team around him, and he was well known and respected by the electorate. He won the seat rather comfortably in the end on the elimination of Trevor Sargent, the Green Party candidate. Proinsias De Rossa of the Workers' Party swept the boards however; his stylish poster showed him in an Armani overcoat with the slogan 'A breath of fresh air'. In the Leinster Constituency, Michael Bell was making a significant impact, but in the middle of the campaign, in response to a press query, he said he would never rule out a coalition with Fianna Fáil. It was a very strange statement considering his absolute dependence on Fine Gael transfers to be elected. Liam Kavanagh telephoned me to ask me to issue a statement on the subject. I never did, leaving it with Fergus, who did one on behalf of Dick. I wonder if it would have made any difference considering the outcome. Michael Bell was defeated only by the narrowest of margins; ten votes on the first completion of the ballot. On the eleventh count he had 75,239 votes as against 75,249 for Jim Fitzsimons of Fianna Fáil.

In the Munster Constituency, Eileen Desmond's campaign collapsed upon the calling of the general election. Her Director of Elections, Toddy O'Sullivan TD, had to head off to defend his own seat in Cork South-Central. The other candidate, Michael Ferris, was also a Dáil candidate. His Dáil bid was successful, but he made little impact in the European elections. In Connacht-Ulster our candidate, Ivan McPhillips, polled 1.59 per cent of the vote, which was a brave effort by a new candidate in very barren territory for Labour.

The end of single party government

The calling of the 1989 general election proved to be one of the major miscalculations of Charlie Haughey's career. Going into the campaign with over 50 per cent support in the opinion polls, he emerged with 44.15 per cent of the vote for the Fianna Fáil Party. This was sure proof that polls taken during the lifetime of a Government do not necessarily reflect opinion when an election is called, much less the standing of a party during the progress of a campaign. The situation can be further changed as issues emerge and develop during the campaign. Fianna Fáil lost four seats on their 1987 performance and were unable to form a Government on their own. Fine Gael gained four seats in a reasonably good performance. The Workers' Party gained three seats and now had a very respectable total of seven seats. The PDs lost eight of their 14 seats and ended up with six, while the Green Party made its first Dáil gain with the election of Roger Garland for Dublin South.

The new Government now formed in what was a dramatic change in Irish political culture. Fianna Fáil now commanded just 77 seats, six short of that magic number of 83, which gave an overall majority – but that was not going to stop Charlie Haughey. Conveniently, the PDs had six seats, which when added to the Fianna Fáil total, made the necessary number. It wasn't as easy as that of course; Charlie Haughey needed to use his immense prestige in Fianna Fáil and his absolute control over the soul and mind of the party to make it break what many of its members considered to be a 'core value'. In the PDs too, especially in their non-former Fianna Fáil element, there was strong resistance. It took a lot of swallowing of pride to enter Government with the man they had painted as the arch-villain of Irish politics, Mr Charles J Haughey, but the PDs proved themselves to have strong stomachs indeed. The American Embassy's fourth of July party occurred during the crisis. I met Geraldine Kennedy and her husband David there. Geraldine had just lost her seat for the PDs in Dun Laoghaire, and I got the distinct impression that another election, in which she might regain her seat, would be welcomed. I think many other defeated PDs felt the same.

Labour increased its vote by over three percentage points, which was the highest increase of any party. It increased its seats by a net three, winning five new ones but losing the seats formerly held by Frank Cluskey and Barry Desmond. Workers' Party candidates Eric Byrne and Eamon Gilmore won these seats, so they were not lost to the left. John Ryan did not make it in

Tipperary North, in spite of polling 22.81 per cent; the second highest Labour vote in the country, second only to Dick Spring. Dick headed the poll in Kerry North and this perhaps helped him to put the memory of the close result in 1987 behind him. New seats were won for us too: Sean Ryan won in Dublin North; Michael Moynihan returned to the Dáil after his 1987 defeat in Kerry South; Michael Ferris won in Tipperary South; Gerry O'Sullivan won in Cork North-Central; and Brian O'Shea won his seat in Waterford. All in all it was a very credible result, which was enhanced by a European Parliament gain by Barry Desmond in Dublin and victory in the Senate Elections for Pat Upton, Joe Costello, John Ryan, and Jack Harte. Now Dick Spring had a parliamentary team behind him that would become an effective weapon to harass the new Government. For me, the party had recovered much of its morale and self respect and certain constituencies had shown themselves to have winnable seats at the next election. It was a great result.

The PLP met on Thursday 22 June 1989, the first item being the election of the Chair. Incredibly to me, Michael Bell, straight from his splendid performance in Leinster, was dropped and Toddy O'Sullivan replaced him. It was a narrow margin but the credit or blame, depending on whichever side you were on, was given to 'The Munster Mafia', as the PLP members from that province were called. I thought it was a cruel and senseless demotion myself, and only found out about it when I walked into the room. Michael was very hurt, as he expected only praise for his brilliant electoral performance. He had spent the previous few days at the recount and felt that if he had spent it lobbying the PLP he would have beaten off the challenge. The meeting endorsed a report I submitted, holding forth the possibility of a legal challenge to the Leinster result based on the closeness of the result. The party was still broke, though spending had been kept to an absolute minimum during the elections. We had spent £90,021 on the European and general elections and had raised around £70,000 (approximately £20,000 of which came from the trade unions).

On Saturday 15 July a party member asked to meet me in Bewley's of Grafton Street in Dublin at 9.15 a.m. There he gave me a cheque for a thousand pounds to pay for the appeal to the courts. I was very impressed by such generosity. 'It would be a shame,' he said, 'to lose a possible seat in the European Parliament because of the lack of a few bob!' It wasn't to be however; we took the Appeal to the High Court where it was dismissed and the result stood, but I suppose it had been a long shot anyway.

The same meeting decided to nominate the leader of the Labour Party as Taoiseach and to vote against all other nominees. I think we can trace our good performance in Opposition between 1989 and 1992 back to this date.

The depression and inertia of 1987–89 seemed to have lifted and the new Parliamentary Party seemed possessed of an energy and confidence previously lacking. In the Dáil chamber, Dick Spring forced Charlie Haughey to drop his pretension to remaining as Taoiseach after his defeat in the vote for that position. Instead, he became Acting Taoiseach. In ways, it doesn't seem like a major victory, but it was the start of a period of very effective harassment by Dick Spring at a time of ineffective Fine Gael Opposition.

Barry Desmond was to cause us more difficulty before the year was out. He had signed a pledge to give £1,300 per month to the party, but now, when the time came to cough up, he turned shy and there was a serious altercation between him and the Financial Secretary, James Wrynn, as the correspondence on the subject indicates. Barry maintained that the other members of the PLP didn't contribute a proportionate amount of their salaries and wanted their contribution to be increased and his own to be decreased to £600 per month. But he had signed a pledge to pay and I considered it dishonourable of him to try to get out of it now. James stuck to his guns and Barry eventually did pay up, but it was a mean little incident which need not have occurred, and proof that generosity does not necessarily accompany wealth.

The expulsion of the militants

We still had the big problem of finding a way to expel the militants in a fair and equitable manner that would stand up in a court of law, if challenged. Working in head office in Gardiner Place, I often walked down O'Connell Street during my lunch break. In September 1989, on one of these pleasant walks, I spotted some militants selling copies of their newspaper *Militant Irish Monthly* outside the GPO. I bought a copy and was delighted to see that some of the leading 'millies' had penned articles in that edition. 'Would that be sufficient to expel them?' I asked John Rogers. 'No', he replied, but I was not satisfied with this. I went to Niall Connolly, our legal adviser, who assured me that the articles would be sufficient evidence for expulsion. So I proceeded along those lines in the expulsion process, and from then on I was guided totally by the legal advice of Niall Connolly and it didn't let me down once.

The expulsion procedure started at a meeting of the AC on 27 October 1989 and would be continued at three other meetings. Within six months, the militant hydra had been decapitated. After more than 20 years of infiltration, conspiracy, and parasitism the Labour Party had at long last been handed back to its members.

Here is an example of the widespread benefit of the militant expulsion. On Friday 6 October 1989, I received a phone call from a Sean Maloney in Letterkenny, Co. Donegal. He was an ITGWU shop steward in the hospital. He was reporting to me on the coverage in the local paper about the expulsion of Anton McCabe, a one-time Donegal resident. Donegal North-East was then a militant stronghold, and Sean appreciated what we were doing. On further investigation, I discovered that Sean had been an independent in the local elections and that he still harboured ambitions in that direction – just the person we wanted. After playing a full role in the subsequent Presidential election, I invited Sean and his wife Sally down to our 1990 Christmas Party, where they met Dick Spring. In January, I went to Letterkenny and we got rid of the militants. Later on in the year, Sean won a seat on Donegal County Council for us, and a year later became a member of the Senate, the first Donegal person to hold Oireachtas membership for Labour in 65 years.

The funeral of Brendan Corish

Brendan Corish was the leader of the Labour Party from 1960–77. He was TD for Wexford, elected first at a by-election in 1945. He was a handsome, gentle and considerate man whose popularity transcended the Labour electorate. I had many wonderful conversations with him before his death in early 1990. His theory on the unity and cohesiveness of the 1973–77 Government, in which he served as Tánaiste and Minister for Health and Social Welfare, was that ministers left their party affiliations outside the Cabinet door. I have to say that I didn't feel too comfortable with the idea of one Labour minister lining up with Fine Gael ministers against other Labour ministers. He spoke fondly of Brendan Halligan, who had been General Secretary during most of his period as leader. 'He was my handler', he confided jokingly.

His funeral on Monday 19 February proved to be a great magnet for Labour members all over the country. I travelled down the night before, as had Dick Spring and Fergus Finlay. After a few drinks with the local members, we went for dinner. During the meal, I mentioned my surprise at the fact that Brendan Corish had not been offered a state funeral in spite of his being Tánaiste. Dick explained that this honour was reserved for former or serving Presidents or Taoisigh. 'In that case,' said Fergus addressing Dick, 'you will have one.' 'Why?' I asked, genuinely mystified. 'Because, of course,' said Fergus, 'he will have been Taoiseach by then.' There was a certain embarrassed silence around the table. I wondered how anyone could be unaffected by such flattery if it was constantly being dished up – I hoped that Dick could.

Merger with the DSP

With the militant problem effectively solved, I could now bring the work I had been doing in Limerick to a head. For the previous two years, I had been assiduously attending to every problem that might arise in the case of a merger between our party in Limerick and Jim Kemmy's DSP. No detail was left to chance, as the loss of members from either organisation due to the merger, would, in my opinion, defeat the whole purpose of the arrangement. A very important part of this work was the building up of strong personal bonds between the members of both organisations and myself. This involved scores of trips to Limerick in the period of 1987–90 and marked the beginning of many friendships that have lasted, in particular my friendship with Jim Kemmy, which ended only with his untimely death in 1997.

The AC appointed Niamh Bhreathnach as a negotiator and I took her down to Limerick to meet the Labour members at a meeting in the ITGWU Hall on O'Connell Street. It was one of those 'roaring and shouting' meetings that was an important part of the talks. 'Let them get it off their chests' was my motto. The meeting began and Niamh said the usual few words about how happy she was to visit Limerick – then the ructions began and the allegations flew. Jim Kemmy was painted as the archfiend. No deed was too low for him. One member related in a shocked tone that Kemmy had accused an honest man of stealing blocks from Limerick Corporation to build a wall outside his house. Most devastating of all, a member roared that Kemmy had alleged that Mick Lipper, the former TD, had fathered a child in Waterford! I had heard it all before and enjoyed the theatre of it thoroughly. Poor Niamh was in a different category; they didn't carry on like this in Blackrock. She took it all in good humour though and we had a great laugh going back in the car.

Jim Kemmy's group was less dramatic in their dealings with me, but I clicked with them instantly. There was an enormous amount of small print to be worked out, as I wanted an agreed list of all local election candidates in the country to be decided in advance. I wanted no possible source of conflict for the future. The DSP had two fine candidates in Dublin at local government level: Michael Conaghan and Eamonn Maloney. Later, both were to become Labour councillors. By early 1990, the agreement was nearing completion and Dick was able to visit and give his blessing to the talks. I met him there on 5 March 1990 and afterwards drove him to Dublin. It had been a great meeting, held in Jim's headquarters in the Mechanics

Institute in Hartstrong Street in Limerick. Getting the agreement of the existing Labour Party in Limerick was based on their being given fair access to contest in the forthcoming local elections, and their loyalty to the party. I think they understood that I would always be an advocate for them if something went wrong. The attitude of the former TD, Frank Prendergast, was remarkable. The agreement held little for him, yet he supported it wholeheartedly in the interests of Labour.

The merger ceremony was to take place on May Day 1990 in Buswells Hotel, near Leinster House in Dublin. In the morning, we had our traditional wreath laying service, which was followed by a reception given by the new union SIPTU. This union had resulted from the merger of the ITGWU and FWUI on 1 January. In the afternoon, the merger of Labour and the DSP took place. The small room in Buswells Hotel was crowded for the occasion. Many DSP members had travelled from Limerick and around the country to join with the press to fill the room. Dick was in bad form: 'Where's the document?' was all he said during the event. Afterwards, the few Labour people who remained, mixed with their new comrades. The merger gave the party a new TD in Jim Kemmy and a new councillor in Jan O'Sullivan. The bitterness that had existed between the two parties now evaporated. There was not even one single resignation in the wake of the merger. In the following year, at the local elections, the Limerick Labour Party was to produce the best results for us in the entire country, winning five out of the 17 seats for us on Limerick Corporation.

CHAPTER 8

WOULD YOU LIKE A DRINK OR A TRANSFER?

THAT YEAR, 1989, was ending well for the Labour Party. The enlarged Parliamentary Party was performing well in the Dáil with a new confidence and clear focus. Dick Spring was really coming into his own and his harassment of Charlie Haughey and Fianna Fáil rarely failed to strike home. In the constituencies, organisation was improving to a level that had never been achieved before. Jim Kemmy was on the verge of rejoining and the next target would be Declan Bree and his small but highly effective organisation in Sligo-Leitrim. Furthermore, the Workers' Party, after its brilliant performance in the general election, when it gained seven seats, now found it had nowhere to go and the collapse of the Communist states in Eastern Europe only showed up the bankruptcy of its ideological outlook. 'It was,' said Billy Healy from Killenaule prophetically at an AC meeting that autumn, 'a party with a murky past and no future.' Labour Left was still around and Emmet Stagg was still as active as ever, but he was now more of an irritant than a threat. He was constantly involving himself in conferences on 'left unity' with other characters of the Irish left, after which there would be a statutory press release attacking his own party leader and 'coalitionists'. Meanwhile, all left-wing political activity was centred on the Labour Party.

The Presidential election was next. Labour had never contested in its own right, but now we had an opportunity staring us in the face. Fianna Fáil made it clear that Brian Lenihan, Tánaiste and Minister for Foreign Affairs, would be their candidate. He was a friendly, outgoing man who was impossible to dislike. In a serious error of judgement, he went on the *Late Late Show*, then hosted by the master of the airwaves Gay Byrne. Gay was always considered to be a Fianna Fáil supporter, but what transpired turned out to be a real sickener. All the worst aspects of Fianna Fáil cronyism and the 'You scratch my back, I'll scratch yours' type of politics which the decent voter finds objectionable were trotted out. The high-point of the show was when Ronnie Drew, prompted by Gay, told a story of a young Guard being threatened by a government minister, presumably Brian himself when he was Minister for Justice. Seemingly, some high level Fianna Fáilers were drinking in a pub after hours when it was raided by the local Guard who was then invited to join in or be transferred from his job: hence the phrase 'Would you like a pint or a transfer?' Gay thought this was hilariously funny, but many of us thought otherwise, especially Dick Spring. It brought out all his anti-Fianna Fáil feelings. He was genuinely infuriated by the show and told us that the show in itself was sufficient reason to take on Fianna Fáil in the Presidential elections.

Inside the party there had been a certain amount of cynicism about the office of President. Since its inception it had been the preserve of elderly Fianna Fáil men who had performed well in their professions, usually that of Cabinet Minister – with the exception of the first President Douglas Hyde. It was a dull and boring office. Many in the Labour Party, including myself, felt that the best thing for the country would be to abolish the job altogether. Like the Catholic hierarchy, the GAA, and the *Irish Press*, it was just another Fianna Fáil dominated institution symbolising banana republic status for the country. But now a mood arose in the party – closely connected to the increase in morale and discipline – that craved a contest. At the PLP meeting of 6 December 1989, Deputies Sean Ryan and Séamus Pattison both brought up the issue. On the Communications Committee, the debate was taking place. The problem was to find a candidate who was capable of taking up the challenge and who would have the confidence of the party. Many names were discussed: John Carroll, the former General Secretary of the ITGWU; Justin Keating, former Cabinet Minister; and Noel Browne, former Minister for Health and standard bearer of the left were all mentioned. I favoured Noel Browne. I knew he was an uncontrollable maverick, but likewise was aware that he had a lot of support outside of the party. Ruairi Quinn agreed, but it was not to be. Dick looked at me with his special glare when I made the suggestion and said: 'Have you read his book and what his says about the Labour Party?' I thought it best to shut up for a while.

Mary Robinson was an obvious choice, but she had left the party in 1985, ostensibly over the Anglo-Irish Agreement. Relations since then between her and Dick had been non-existent and I didn't see much hope of reconciliation; but this is where John Rogers proved his worth. As a fellow practising barrister, he had a connection with Mary Robinson that others didn't have and on 14 February 1990 he visited her in her Dublin house at Ranelagh, with the proposal that she should become Labour's Presidential candidate.

On 22 March I drove Dick down to the Longford-Westmeath constituency, where we were to spend the day on a reorganisation drive. On the way down, I had to drop him into the Four Courts. When he came out he said rather nonchalantly: 'Oh, incidentally, we have a candidate for the Presidency, Mary Robinson has agreed to run.' I was thrilled. I had admired her all through my political life and was very disappointed when she had resigned from Labour. She was the type of candidate that left-leaning liberals like myself just loved. Getting the party onside was another matter. Emmet Stagg now had an issue that he could get his teeth into. Noel Browne was an icon of the hard left and a struggle was about to ensue.

First of all, Dick brought his proposal to the PLP. Again he outlined his opposition to the Fianna Fáil monopoly of the Presidency and their treating of it as a sinecure. He was looking at the concept of a working Presidency. Let the president justify his/her existence and form a partnership with the Senate in a forum that would represent the marginalised and those currently underrepresented. The theme would be 'A working President'.

Dick received what he thought (and what I thought) was the approval of the PLP to invite Mary Robinson to run as our candidate on the proviso that he contact Noel Browne and explain the situation to him. All hell now broke loose as Dick announced to the media that the PLP had endorsed his choice of Mary Robinson as a candidate. Emmet Stagg announced that he would take legal action if she were nominated as she was not a party member. In any case, he threatened to not sign her nomination papers. This was a sore point as 20 members of the Dáil or Senate were needed to nominate her and this was exactly the Labour total plus Jim Kemmy.

I learned later that it was the only time during the campaign that Mary Robinson had second thoughts about running. The whole process had been handled very badly. The procedure was all hatched over in the Sally Empire and I was only brought in when things started to go wrong. If the proposal had gone directly to the joint AC–PLP meeting, the intervening row could have been avoided. Trying to short circuit party procedures had backfired. I hoped Dick had learned a lesson from this. The PLP met three weeks later and endorsed my minutes of the previous meeting. These indicated that the PLP had given Dick a mandate to invite Mary Robinson to run as our candidate. So intense was the party infighting that Brendan Howlin wondered if the campaign had been undermined even before if had started. Certainly it had been a mess. Michael Taft and Cllr Frank Buckley had joined in the fray bringing Labour Left in behind Emmet's position.

Choosing the candidate

A joint meeting of the PLP and AC to nominate Labour's candidate took place on 26 April 1990. On the Sunday before, Gerry Barry of *The Sunday Tribune* had done a ring around of AC members to see how they would vote in the Noel Browne vs Mary Robinson contest, which is how the choice was being perceived. We were horrified when we found that our stalwart, Jackie Culhane of Kerry North, was mentioned as being in the Noel Browne camp and I was dispatched to change his mind. I invited him to lunch in the National Gallery before the meeting. We were to be joined by Tipperary AC member Billy Healy, with whom he was also friendly. I had been so busy that I hadn't given much thought to the venue. It was a self-service restaurant. 'What kind of a place is this?' asked Jackie. 'Is it a serve-yourself sort of place? I'm not very impressed Ray.' He waited until the end of the meal and, looking at me quizzically, said: 'OK I'll vote for her.' Billy Healy started to laugh; he had enjoyed the torture that Jackie had put me through.

The joint meeting took place on Thursday 26 April and sure enough there were just two nominations; Mary Robinson, proposed by Dick Spring and seconded by Niamh Bhreathnach and Noel Browne, proposed by Michael D Higgins and seconded by Henry Haughton (a Labour Left supporter from Swords). Mary Robinson's nomination was carried by 32 votes to 11. There was one abstention, Mervyn Taylor, who wasn't going to offend either side. Mary Robinson then set off on her historic tour of the country.

She started in Limerick where, in the presence of her old friend Jim Kemmy, now a Labour Deputy, she launched her campaign in the Glentworth Hotel. Jim later told me a hilarious story about Mary's clothes, which happened at this occasion. Mary was a good-looking woman and always dressed modestly rather than in high fashion. Left-wing women were all inclined to be a bit dowdy in those days. Jim, however, was totally scattered about his dress sense. He was too absent-minded anyway; sometimes he would leave the house with his shoelaces untied. Patsy Harrold, his partner, and Margaret O'Donoghue, his secretary, did what they could for him but it was an uphill struggle. As often as not, Jim would have a bit of his enormous belly sticking out from his open shirt or some food from a recent meal attached to some part of his attire. But this didn't stop him lecturing Mary Robinson, the bluestocking Trinity Professor, about her dress sense. He sat her down after the launch and said to her in his gruff voice: 'Now Mary, if you want to win this one you'll have to tidy up your act a bit.' He boasted to me about this after the campaign, claiming complete credit for the transformation in Mary Robinson's appearance during the campaign!

Mary Robinson after her makeover in 1990.

There was an election committee part nominated by Dick Spring and part nominated by Mary Robinson. Dick nominated Ruairi Quinn to chair the Committee and Fergus Finlay, John Rogers, and myself as members. Mary nominated Bride Rosney, Peter McMenamin, Nick Robinson (her husband), and herself onto the Committee. Ita McAuliffe, Anne Byrne, and Anne Lane were seconded as assistants to the Committee. I was anxious to get on with the work, but even from the time of the first meeting there was an obvious tension between Fergus Finlay and Bride Rosney. Bride, a native of Kerry, was a powerful woman and Principal of the Rosminians Secondary School in Drumcondra. A close associate of hers described her as follows: 'If Bride wants to adopt you, you really have no choice in the matter. One Monday morning you will open your door to take in the milk and there she'll be parked outside. "I'm going to make you Chairman of your union, a TD or whatever", she will say, and then move in, leaving only when she has accomplished her mission.' I took to her immediately. I like women who can be decisive.

Nick Robinson was a big-framed man, very loyal to Mary and very committed to the campaign, but far too posh for the rough and tumble of an election campaign. Peter McMenamin was Deputy General Secretary of the Teachers Union of Ireland and later became Bride's partner. I knew him for many years; in fact he was one of the first friends I made when I joined the Labour Party. In this campaign, of course, he was a Robinson partisan first of all.

The campaign was slow enough to take off as nothing like it had been tried in Ireland before, but we had one tremendous asset in Mary Robinson herself. She was truly a person of her time. The country was changing from the gombeenism that epitomised it from the foundation of the state. A young population was educated, liberal, and confident. They found in Mary Robinson someone who could reflect their own confidence in themselves. This was particularly true when Mary glamorised herself with the help of Brenda O'Hanlon. Brenda had been a Public Relations Executive with Wilson Hartnell and worked full-time on the campaign in the office at Merrion Square. She was another tough cookie. Anita Geraghty, my solicitor, told me that she had introduced Brenda to Mary and that they took to one another immediately. Bossy Brenda soon did the famous Robinson makeover and Mary changed from being an elegant, plainly dressed woman to being a glamorous and heavily made-up icon. It took me a while to get used to it, being accustomed to the plainer version of female in the Labour Party, but the public loved it from the start and it soon caught on. From then on, all female candidates, not only Labour ones, have been more aware of the need for dressing and grooming. There was some criticism, unfortunately leaked to the *Phoenix* magazine, that we had allocated £4,000 for clothes during the campaign, an unprecedented move then. But Mary Freehill put it all in context for me at a party in her house on 28 July: 'If a man spends £10,000 on a car, everyone will congratulate him, but if a woman spends even less on clothes she is criticised.' After that I became a supporter of Mary Robinson's clothes allowance.

The campaign headquarters was in the basement of the Manufacturing, Science, and Finance Union (MSF) at 51 Merrion Square in Dublin 2. The official opening was on 20 July, when we held a reception for the press and some key supporters. The office was staffed by Brenda O'Hanlon, who assumed the role of Office Manager; Angie Mulroy from Labour Head Office, who was invaluable in liaison with the Labour activists around the country; John Gogan, a sort of a freelance campaigner who helped on most days; as well as a number of volunteers. One such was Brigid Murphy, who had been Secretary to President Douglas Hyde back in the thirties.

Brenda and Angie, both strong-minded women, were at loggerheads from the start. 'I think we have a problem with attitude here', sniffed Brenda in her superior tone, 'Yeah,' said Angie, in her Dublin accent, 'your fuckin' attitude.' Each morning, the Campaign Committee would meet at 8.00 a.m. and the battle would ensue. Brenda announced that these would be 'breakfast meetings', where we would take our decisions over coffee and croissants. Against my better judgement, I left my flat without breakfast for the first time in fifteen years. On arrival in Merrion Square, I found no sustenance, only Nick Robinson eating a single scone. He must have seen the hunger in my eyes as he offered me half of his scone, which I greedily accepted.

The meetings were mainly about the supremacy of Bride versus the supremacy of Fergus, and I think Fergus may have come off second best in that one. Everyone had their own work to do, which they did without complaint. Mary Robinson announced that she would go wherever she was sent and to me seemed the most compliant and hard-working of candidates. I don't think she complained about anything during the long and exhausting campaign, but then she had a fierce protector in Bride.

There were many problems of co-ordination, many rows and misunderstandings, and quite a bit of jostling for position, especially when, after September, it appeared that we might win. Overall, Bride was the big boss and looked after everything. In the background, Eoghan Harris advised Mary on strategy. He also produced one of the best Party Political Broadcasts yet made in this country. It is still used by media students as a superb example of the art. From Labour head office we distributed the stylish poster of Mary Robinson, 'A president with a purpose'. They were stacked in piles, metres high in the reception area. We allocated them by height to the constituencies. Each constituency was allocated 18 inches high of posters and '18 inches', said Marion Boushell, 'was enough for anyone, even in the Labour Party!'

Mary Robinson had been travelling around the country since her nomination, but her real tour began on 20 October in her hometown of Ballina, where she was rapturously received. Poor Brenda! She arrived in Ballina wearing a fur coat and was barred from the proceedings for this major breach in political correctness; she had to sit in her hotel room all day, wrapped, no doubt, in the offending fur coat. Anyway, even I found it hard to have sympathy for someone who couldn't pronounce Ballina. She emphasised the second syllable as in the third syllable of Crossmolina. She'd obviously never heard of the place before. Mary left her tour only to appear on the *Late Late Show* with Nick on 2 November.

It seemed possible to win right from the start as we offered such an attractive alternative to Fianna Fáil, but things began to mount up in our favour when Fine Gael, and in particular its leader Alan Dukes, misread the situation badly. Having promised a candidate of substance, he failed to convince either Garret FitzGerald or Peter Barry to run. It was then put to him that supporting Mary Robinson's candidature would be acceptable to the Fine Gael rank and file. He persisted in nominating a candidate and Austin Currie was chosen, a decent candidate but the wrong man for the job. From then on, it looked as if Mary would be in place to receive not only Fine Gael transfers but also many votes that would otherwise have been Fine Gael number one votes. This was put to me very strongly by many in the Fine Gael Party, including Councillor Martin Lynch, who approached me directly on the issue.

Furthermore, the Fianna Fáil campaign started to crumble with freelance journalist Jim Duffy's revelations of Brian Lenihan's previously denied telephone call to the President in 1982 concerning the dissolution of the Dáil. The Government was a Fianna Fáil–PD Coalition and when Brian Lenihan was caught out, the Taoiseach called for his resignation. This caused consternation in Fianna Fáil, as Brian was their most popular minister. When he refused to resign, it looked as if a general election might be called to sort out the whole mess. At this stage, I took my place on the Robinson Bus; no TD could be spared as a Dáil vote to topple the Government could take place at any time. As it happened the Government survived.

To add to Fianna Fáil's problems, Padraig Flynn, the then Minister for the Environment, attacked Mary on the *Saturday View* radio show, casting aspersions on her commitment to her family. This merely assisted her in mopping up every floating vote in the country.

On Wednesday 31 October I joined the bus in Kilkenny in the absence of Séamus Pattison, the Carlow-Kilkenny TD, who was needed in the Dáil. Totally committed to a Robinson victory, he told me that he would laugh with joy for a week when it happened. He was also interested enough to monitor the progress of the campaign and was sharp enough to get on the phone shortly after some press release had described her as being 'above politics' to have it corrected to 'outside politics' – Séamus was proud of the profession of politics. The crowd that had assembled outside the Town Hall where the bus was to pull up was excited and emotional in a way that political crowds rarely are. There was a sort of magic in the air. Mary alighted from the bus and mingled with the crowd, and it was as if everyone present knew that history was in the making. As usual, I went and spoke to some people. One old man with tears in his eyes told me that he had been waiting all his life to vote for someone like this.

We went on to Graiguenamanagh, Co. Kilkenny, where the local band waited on the outskirts of the town to greet the candidate. This was great Labour territory and local Councillor Michael O'Brien had organised this welcome. But the experience and political professionalism of Mary Robinson showed. She marched confidently behind the band and when the people came to their doors or out of the shops, she was there with extended hand to greet them. Handshaking, smiling, saying a few words – she was the consummate politician on her way to victory. I spoke to Labour members everywhere who were confident of victory in a way that they had never been before.

In Carlow, we visited a sheltered workshop. Here the pupils had their photos taken with Mary. I stayed well out of it, at the back of the crowd. With me were Carlow Councillor Michael Meaney, who had recently had a back operation, and Nick Robinson. Michael proceeded to explain to me all the intricacies of his operation. 'Would you like to see the scars?' he asked, and without waiting for an answer, he unbuckled his trousers, dropped them to where only the cleavage of his bum cheeks stopped them from dropping completely, and pushed up his shirt. All the while the photographers were snapping away. I'll never forget the look of horror on poor Nick Robinson's face. I suppose he had never seen a councillor's cheeks before! Anyway, he took off like a bat out of hell and I was left to admire Cllr Meaney's wonderful scars – just another of the many dubious pleasures of being General Secretary of the Labour Party.

The counting of votes was on 8 November in the Royal Dublin Society's Main Hall in Dublin. I was in charge of assembling the tally for the Robinson Camp. At the start of the morning I tallied the votes from Dublin North-West, as the promised tallymen had not turned up. It was amazing and exhilarating to see the Robinson No.1 votes tumble out in such quantities. Mark Little of Labour Youth was tallying votes from Dublin South-East. His eyes lit up in incredulity when he told me that Mary Robinson was getting 75 per cent of the votes in Sandymount. It was a rout for Austin Currie. In a box in Ballymun that I tallied, Dustin the Turkey, a children's TV character of the time, beat him on first preference votes. I made the mistake of telling an RTE journalist who wanted to use it on the *One O'Clock News*. I asked her not to, as it would have been too humiliating for Austin Currie. He would have a bad enough day without that.

At my Central Tally Station I had a map of all the constituencies in the country and when Mary arrived I was able to show her the clean sweep. She had won outright in the cities of Dublin, Cork, Limerick, Galway, and Kilkenny and in counties Kildare and Wicklow. The Lenihan surplus elsewhere would be more than negated when Austin Currie was eliminated, the vast bulk of his transfers going to Mary.

The Fianna Fáil vote held up well with Brian Lenihan getting 44.1 per cent of the vote. I'd always considered this election to be a sort of a referendum on the type of Ireland people wanted – a new, modern, outward-looking European country à la Robinson or more of the same à la Lenihan. The results squared up pretty well with this: in the anti-amendment campaign of 1983 we got 33 per cent of the vote, we got 36 per cent in 1986 for Divorce and 39 per cent in 1990 for Mary Robinson. A new Ireland emerged that day in the RDS that was liberal, inclusive, confident, and outward looking. We were present at an historic moment for the Irish people and we knew it. As the President-elect addressed us and said goodbye to her supporters my eyes filled with tears. It had taken a good few years to get to this position in Irish society.

Prelude to the presidency

In the period between Mary's election and inauguration (8 November to 3 December), there was a lot of tidying up to be done. A fundraising event in the Burlington Hotel was organised to pay off the debts and it was a swish affair. Mary was now the height of fashion and I had to kick myself every now and then to remind myself that she had received 39 per cent of the vote and not 99 per cent. It was only a few months since we had struggled to find 20 people to bother coming to meet her in the Community Hall in Rialto in Dublin. Over the next few years, it was impossible to find anyone who admitted voting for Lenihan or Currie, such was the aura around our first woman President. We had no trouble selling the £100 tickets to our fundraising event organised by Brenda O'Hanlon and Anne Byrne in the Burlington Hotel. It had been cleverly marketed by Brenda as, 'The Prelude to the Presidency'. At that price, there were very few people from the Labour Party, but it was a fundraiser and I suppose we were glad to get the money.

That night Mary was resplendent. In her speech, which was one of the last that Eoghan Harris helped her with, she paraphrased the words of Pope Leo X when she said: 'God has given us the Presidency, let us enjoy it!' Glenda Jackson, the British Labour MP, and Niall Tobin were guests of honour. Glenda stayed in a suite in the hotel and commented on its luxury and comfort in a way I found so down to earth for such a major film star, who must have been used to far more luxurious surroundings. Nevertheless, she laughed her gorgeous throaty laugh when I told her that everyone in Ireland lived in such surroundings. I sat beside Paul Brady, the singer/songwriter who had always been a supporter of the left. Noeline Dunphy, the Labour Party Constituency Secretary from Carlow-Kilkenny attended with her sister Nina, who was a nun. We danced together and afterwards Betty Dowling, a retired worker from head office, told me that she never thought she would live to see the General Secretary of the Labour Party dance with a nun at a function for a left-wing woman President of Ireland!

The Presidential Inauguration took place on Monday 3 December in Dublin Castle. There was a row on the Election Committee as the Labour Members were excluded, but I wasn't too pushed; it was a stuffy and boring affair as I saw it on television. Instead, I headed for Kitty O'Shea's Pub in Grand Canal Street, where Kevin Duffy, the Deputy General Secretary of the Irish Congress of Trade Unions, had organised 'an alternative inauguration'. I wore a swallow-tailed coat that I had bought in a second-hand shop in the George's Street Arcade for £15. On it I wore the badges that I had kept from all my previous campaigns: 'Anti-Apartheid', 'Anti-Amendment', 'Divorce Now', 'Stuff the Jubilee', 'James Connolly Commemoration', but now proudest of all 'Mary Robinson'. A great crowd gathered during the day. There were a lot of Labour and trade union people who had taken the day off, and later on, Chief Justice Liam Hamilton dropped by. A great day was had by all.

In the evening, there was a reception in Dublin Castle. On my way there in my car, I was stopped by a Garda in Lord Edward Street. 'You'll have to wait awhile,' he said, 'the President's car is coming up Parliament Street. That's her car now.' 'Her car', what a beautiful pair of words. After the reception, I went with Dick, Fergus, Sally Clarke, Pat Magner, Anne Byrne, and Gregg Sparks to a restaurant in South Great Georges Street, where we had a meal and a good old-fashioned bitching session about Robinson, Rosney, and O'Hanlon until we were joined by the Lord Mayor of Cork Frank Nash, and his lovely wife, Maria. It had been a wonderful campaign. Even though Mary Robinson had run as 'a candidate outside of politics', she was widely perceived to be a Labour candidate. Until then, the Labour Party had never won a national victory.

He who laughs last

The next scheduled elections were the local elections, where we had some catching up to do. We would be able to gain great benefit by association with the Robinson Presidency. One big negative feature of the campaign, which I had never experienced to such a degree, were the hateful rumours circulated about Mary Robinson's personal life. She was rumoured to be separated from her husband for years, her private life was held up to mockery and false accusation. Her husband, Nick, was included in all these. Ita McAuliffe, who handled her incoming correspondence in Leinster House, found some of the mail so offensive that she binned it immediately and wouldn't even pass it on to Mary's Secretary, Anne Lane. The comments of Padraig Flynn about Mary Robinson's 'new-found interest in family', and the dangerously provocative comments by Fianna Fáil TD, John Browne, of Wexford, that she might open an abortion referral clinic in the Park, fanned all these. Of course, some of us received added satisfaction from the victory as it drove Fianna Fáil crazy. My own favourite barman, Jimmy Kennedy, the Manager of the Long Hall in Georges Street, gave me a particularly special scowl: 'Its always the same,' he said, in a fairly accurate analysis of the result, 'it's everyone against Fianna Fáil.' Séamus Pattison could certainly laugh heartily for a week!

The 'Red Ball'

Dick Spring was now a national hero and it was time to exploit his new-found celebrity status. For many years, Declan Bree and his organisation 'The Independent Socialist Party of Sligo-Leitrim' held an annual dance grandly entitled 'The Red Ball'. Dick agreed to attend with me. We would talk to a delegation from Declan's party first and then attend 'The Ball'. It was held on Friday 7 December on a freezing cold and snowy night. Dick drove up in his Volvo and we had an argument even before we set off – but we made it up on the way. It was a great success and laid the groundwork for a merger a year and a half later. This one too would be planned with care and attention to detail. There was another Dáil seat to be won here. I always believed that Declan Bree could win a seat in Sligo-Leitrim if he expanded his appeal to that wider electorate that can vote Labour.

Dick was closely questioned about the extradition of IRA prisoners to Northern Ireland at the meeting. This was always a tricky one with a Republican group like the ISPSL, but he did not concede any treatment other than the due process of the law. If his answer was not exactly as they expected, at least they knew they were in the presence of a straight talker and that always goes down well. 'The Ball' was very unball-like with the usual tinned soup followed by chicken and ham, but the guests were warm and friendly and I took to them immediately. Dick left as soon as he could after the speeches and drove to Tralee: an arduous journey at the best of times, but a dangerous and foolhardy thing to do in the middle of a snowstorm. Declan Bree and his General Secretary Pat Fallon visited me in my hotel, the famous Silver Swan, the next morning, and we discussed how their party would fit in with Labour and retain as much autonomy as possible. In late morning, I got the Sligo to Dublin train and arrived home many many freezing hours later.

The new alliance: Dick Spring TD shaking hands with Ald. Declan Bree on the merger of their respective parties in 1992.

Fergus Finlay was very much concerned that we make the most of the Robinson victory. I didn't share his concern I must say; I believed that credit for it was going to come our way and that a 'soft sell' approach was required. Nevertheless, there was much tidying up and modernisation required in the party. Its structures had not been radically overhauled since the sixties and they were cumbersome and slow. For all that, they were very consultative and representative, so it was very important not to throw out the baby with the bathwater. But there was a great mood for change and for the next step forward in the party and in its ruling body, the AC, which expressed such sentiments as soon after the Presidential election as its meeting of 16 December 1990. By the next meeting – 23 January 1991 – these radical proposals were ready.

CHAPTER 9

ROSES ARE RED,
COUNCILLORS ARE TOO

THE FIRST meeting of the AC in 1991 was a joint meeting with the PLP held in Jury's Hotel in Dublin's salubrious Ballsbridge. It was here that the modern image of the 'nineties' Labour Party was formed. The rose was adopted as the party's logo. It was the design used by the Swedish Labour Party, which was now going on to better things, and its copyright had been purchased by James Wrynn, the Financial Secretary. Many, including myself, regretted the passing of the old starry plough that was so filled with symbolism and Labour history. It was James Connolly's flag, carried by his union the ITGWU and by its militia The Citizens Army in the Rising of 1916. The starry plough was to be retained for ceremonial purposes. Emmet Stagg said that it was the one item of the day's proceedings that he felt sure he could have overturned if he had called a vote. Many in the party, including Anne Spring, continued to use the starry plough, as did Declan Bree and his constituency when they joined the party. Nevertheless, the new rose soon became a popular symbol and was very quickly accepted by the general public as Labour's symbol. The meeting also agreed in principle to a new constitution for the party, though this would have to be agreed by the Party Conference, which was scheduled to meet in Killarney later on in 1991.

The party leader addressed the meeting on 'Strategies for Party Growth', but little of significant change on the policy front emerged. This was a good thing, as it left the party time to develop in its areas of traditional strength and credibility: health, social welfare, and the environment. It was very important for me too, as it always fell to me to reassure the troops that the essence of the party would not be tampered with. Some of us felt a bit queasy about the concentration on image rather that on substance. Giving voice to my feelings exactly, Sean McCarthy, a Kerry AC member and former President of the Teachers Union of Ireland, paused over some of the promotional material on his way out of the meeting and said to me, 'Its all very Third World stuff, isn't it?' Overall though, the situation was very positive indeed. The party was closely associated in the public's mind with winning the Presidential election. More importantly, it was associated with Mary Robinson, who was now going through a time of unprecedented popularity getting a satisfaction rating of 90 per cent and portraying an image of modernity and style.

Valentine's night in the Áras

As a 'thank you' to her campaign committee, Mary Robinson invited us to Áras an Uachtaráin on 14 February 1991. It was a beautiful occasion and a waiter wearing white gloves served us with drinks. The President gave each of us a framed drawing of the Four Courts as a souvenir, on which she wrote a little personal dedication. It was a nice touch.

She took us on a tour of the building, which seemed a bit dilapidated and run down. In the picture gallery, my partner, Kathleen Gill, rubbed her finger across the top of a picture frame. When she withdrew it she showed me the film of dust. Kathleen was the Housekeeper in the Nurses' Home in St Vincent's Hospital. She wasn't too impressed.

National conference 1991

National Conference that year (1991) was to be held in Killarney, in the Kerry-South Constituency. Michael Moynihan, the sitting TD, was a sprightly 73 years old, not that this caused him a moment's hesitation about contesting the upcoming local elections. The succession problem though, was acute. The obvious choice was his daughter, Breeda Moynihan-Cronin, who had so far refused to commit herself. An acrimonious Local Government Selection Convention – at which her father failed to be selected for the Killarney electoral area, the base of the Dáil seat – changed her mind. In response to the insult to her father and the endangerment of the Dáil seat she threw her hat in the ring and allowed her name to be added as a candidate and went on to win the seat. The Selection Convention, which I chaired, had been a tense affair. The sitting Councillor, Michael Gleeson, had a reasonable chance of retaining the seat and going on to become the next Dáil Candidate. The zeal of his supporters in shafting Michael Moynihan sealed his fate however. Michael, who had given his lifetime to winning the Dáil seat, having first contested in 1954 and not winning it till 1981, had built up a following, particularly within his own generation, of tough, hardened political fighters. They were not going to let their man be snubbed. At the Convention, they held their fire; in fact Bernie O'Connor and Vince Follin sat on either side of Michael and held him in his seat by each putting a hand in his jacket pockets to prevent him from rising to address the meeting, in spite of provocation. After Breeda's selection, this elite group swung into action behind her providing her with an organisation as efficient and loyal as her father's.

The Killarney Conference was to be a showcase for the party in the run-up to the local elections: a vehicle for the local party to display itself (and make a few pounds out of the delegates). The media spotlight would be on a party that having won the Presidential election was now clearly going places. There was the new constitution to pass and, most importantly for me, there was the promotion of our local government candidates. If I could arrange 30 seconds TV coverage for them, it could make the difference between victory and defeat for those in marginal seats.

Labour Left showed itself as still being a force to be reckoned with inside the party, even the election of Mary Robinson had not convinced them of their folly. They put on quite a show in opposing the new constitution, which they maintained, with some justification, would remove decision-making powers from the members. Michael D Higgins had described the new document contemptuously as 'a county managers constitution'.

The constitutional proposals that were to come into place two years later, involved the breaking up of the existing ruling body, the Administrative Council, into two bodies: a small Executive Committee and a much larger and more representative General Council. The abolition of the AC would certainly make my job much easier, as handling the new bodies would be much less problematic. The General Council would be too large and cumbersome to be a decision-making body and the Executive Committee would be too difficult to be elected to for its members to take any controversial initiatives. Nevertheless, it was important for the momentum of change to proceed. Finbarr O'Malley, a bright young lawyer from the famous O'Higgins political family (Kevin O'Higgins, the assassinated Minister for Justice was his granduncle, and Chris O'Malley, the former Fine Gael MEP, was his brother) had drawn up most of the document.

I concerned myself mainly with the local election candidates, ensuring that as many of them as possible would speak during the environment debate, which would go out on live television. It was a major logistical nightmare, but one that I enjoyed and think was of great assistance to the candidates. This was Jim Kemmy's first conference since his resignation from the party back in 1972. How different he found it! The politically correct, highly motivated, and good-humoured crowd seemed light years away from the fractious mob of the seventies. He thought so, but it wasn't the case at all; far from being light years away from that we were just two years away from the bloody Tralee Conference. In addressing the Conference, he referred to Michael D Higgins' remarks that he had found it relatively easy to achieve office inside the party, up to and including the position of Chairperson. Jim said that unlike Michael D, it had taken him years. 'Of course,' he said, 'unlike Michael D, I travelled via the scenic route.' He was referring to his election as Vice-Chairperson of the party. Seemingly, Sam Nolan, a leading member of Labour Left, had been asked to contest the position by Pat Magner and had refused, so I received the summons from Sally commanding me to ask Jim Kemmy to go for the position. I thought it was a bit insulting to ask a man of Jim's status in this way, but I went into his office and put it to him. 'Did they send you?' he asked perceptively, looking me straight in the eye. 'Of course they did', I answered and we both laughed. I think that was the moment our friendship set.

Conference was a great success. It was good humoured, good natured and united. It was a terrific showcase for the local elections to be held in June 1991. The militants appealed their expulsions and their appeals were dismissed; the new constitution was approved; Niamh Bhreathnach became Party Chairperson; and Jim Kemmy became Vice-Chair. Dick made another innovative-style speech, during which actors in the audience contributed. Most of all he announced to Conference that Labour would from now on be 'leading the Opposition' and aiming to be the second largest party in the state. Needless to say, he got a rousing reception.

At National Conferences, it is traditional to give a special welcome from the Chairperson to any civic dignitaries who attend. During our Killarney Conference, we held the Mayoralty of Cork and Wexford. We got a message from Cork North-Central to remember to welcome Frank Nash, the Lord Mayor of Cork, and not to forget the 'Lord' bit. Shortly afterwards, we got a message from the Wexford delegation. We were to make sure that if we mentioned the Mayor of Wexford, under no condition were we to call her the Lord Mayor, she was just simply the 'Mayor'. The person in question was the beautiful and vivacious Helen Corish, niece of the former party leader and Tánaiste, Brendan Corish. She was an independent-minded person who refused to tow the line in Wexford; in fact she opposed the proposal to adopt the new constitution. Her failure to be nominated by her local party later that year led to her running as an Independent candidate and she was elected to Wexford County Council.

The greatest leader

This Killarney Conference was our most successful one during my period as General Secretary. We came out from it ready to take on the world in the cause of Labour. Outside the Hall, Una Claffey of RTE interviewed members for a conference *vox pop* and that much sought after soundbite. She got it from Councillor Ned Brennan of Killenaule in Tipperary. 'What do you think of the leadership of Dick Spring?' she asked the canny sixty-something-year-old Ned. 'I think he is the greatest leader we have had since James Connolly', Ned replied.

Local elections 1991

County Councils and County Borough (City) Councils elected in 1985 lasted until the elections held in June 1991. Urban District Councils and Town Commission elections were postponed for even longer: until 1994. This period, 1985–91, was the time of the great controversy in the planning process, particularly on Dublin County Council. The whole area in Dublin County that surrounded Dublin City was under the control of one vast local authority called Dublin County Council. It had 78 members and was the second largest elected assembly in the state, having fewer members than the Dáil (166) but more than the Senate (60). Much – but not all – was revealed more than ten years later by the Flood Tribunal. Basically, the system worked like this: there was a plan for the development of the area called the Development Plan, which had been agreed by a previous Council. The councillors could change parts of this plan by agreeing a motion called a 'Section Four'. This mechanism enabled councillors to change the designation of land from agricultural to building use, thus increasing its value many times over.

The dogs on the street knew that the planning process was questionable, but no one could prove it. This was partly because many of the money transactions were in cash. For the small band of Labour councillors (8) on the Authority, it was a very frustrating and maddening time. Perceived by the general public to be honest brokers, they were nevertheless powerless to do anything about it. Mervyn Taylor TD, who was a member of Dublin County Council at the time, told me that he often wondered why he bothered at all. He showed me the agenda paper for that Council meeting. It had 47 'Section Four' motions and he told me that no other business would be taken. This was the Council whose life the Government extended by a year until 1991. It took the courage and initiative of two private citizens, Michael Smith and Colm O'hEocha to gather the evidence that would lead to the establishment of the Flood Tribunal, which investigated planning in the Dublin County area – but that was not until 1996.

With new-found confidence and discipline in the party we were heading for a very happy election. Furthermore, our association with the Robinson Presidency was most beneficial and would be shamelessly exploited by our candidates. Many of them produced the famous 'candidate standing beside President Mary Robinson' photo on their promotional literature. A number of our candidates had effectively been in the field since before the disastrous 1985 campaign. After that election, I had conceived of the idea of the Labour 'Representative', i.e. the defeated candidate would do the representative work of a councillor, styling him or herself as 'The Labour Representative' on literature, at meetings, or wherever, thus achieving a certain status and recognition. So all in all we were well prepared, even without the additional bonus of 'the Robinson factor' and the increasing exasperation with the Fianna Fáil element of the Government.

The PDs were doing well, albeit in a marginal and niche sort of way as they never again entered double figures in opinion polls or elections. They were seen as moral watchdogs in the Government, keeping Fianna Fáil away from the excesses it would reach if in power alone. Mary Harney, as Junior Minister at the Department of the Environment, had taken on the vested interests of the coal merchants when she had banned smoky coal in Dublin. Looking back now, it seems an obvious step, back then it was a courageous and progressive one. Each winter, Dubliners were literally choked with fumes from coal burning fires, and those with respiratory illnesses, as well as the elderly, suffered dreadfully and still no Government acted until the Harney ban. Fine Gael, with their new leader, John Bruton, was still recovering from the Tallaght Strategy and the debacle of their presidential campaign.

The Workers' Party had run out of steam. The collapse of the Communist regimes in Eastern Europe had deprived many of them of the moral certainty that they'd had since their foundation; anyway, Labour's advance deprived them of the room to grow. But that was not all, after the 1989 general election, their enlarged Parliamentary Party of eight members was about to split with the rest of the party. This was an inevitable outcome of its parliamentary success; no Parliamentary Party wants to be told what to do or how to behave by another body inside its own party. There was some talk that Pat McCartan, their Dublin North-West TD, would join Labour just then, but he declined the offer. It was a big mistake for him; he lost his seat in the following general election. The overall view then was that the major beneficiaries in the elections would be Labour and the PDs. As it turned out, the Workers' Party also made a modest gain of 0.6 per cent.

The major loser was Fianna Fáil, down a whopping 6.6 per cent, while Fine Gael lost 2.5 per cent of the vote. For Dick Spring personally, this election was a great success, both externally with regard to the increase in Labour seats and internally as it strengthened his prestige within the party. It was the last local election in Ireland in which the TDs contested for council seats on a large scale. In the next election, most TDs would shun this dual mandate. Dick Spring himself contested in the Tralee electoral area and headed the poll. Controversially, he took no running mate, leaving himself open to criticism for failing to extend Labour representation. All the Labour TDs contested these elections and all were elected, with the exception of Michael Moynihan in the Killorglin electoral area in Kerry South, to where he had moved hoping to expand Labour representation out of its stronghold in Killarney town. The candidates associated with Labour Left fared poorly; it was the day of mainstream Labour. Emmet Stagg's Kildare Constituency actually lost two seats, returning three councillors. The great success was in Limerick where the party became the largest block on the City Council. In Dublin, the party moved up from two seats won in 1985 to 10 seats. In overall terms, the party won 90 seats as opposed to 58 in 1985, an increase of 55 per cent, while the vote increased to 10.63 per cent.

After local election victory in 1991, Sean Kenny signs the register as Lord Mayor of Dublin. (L-R) Mairéad Kenny, Sean Kenny, the City Steward, Ray Kavanagh and Angie Mulroy.

Election lessons

Elections are an end in themselves; Labour's new influence on local authorities enabled it to achieve many significant goals. Most spectacularly, its gain of 32 seats returned it to a position of influence in local government. In Limerick, Jim Kemmy and his group were able to abolish the dreaded water charges. But for political parties, local elections have a wider significance related to the party's ability to contest the following general election. In particular, elections display the ability of individual candidates to get elected, and conversely, those unable to get elected to local authorities realistically stood little chance of getting elected at the following general election. In this way, local elections can serve as something akin to 'primaries' in the US.

It was now time to take the results into account. An example of this was the party's decision to drop Dr Billy Tormey in Dublin North-West. As early as the night of the Count, I discussed the matter with some constituency members, who were enthusiastic about the project, as Billy had been a difficult as well as an unsuccessful candidate. In fact, I discovered over the years that these two characteristics often go hand in hand. The case of Billy Tormey is important, not in itself, but rather as an example of the pitfalls and difficulties facing anyone trying to reform a candidate list and apply common sense to a political organisation. It is a warning against introducing 'a list system' – where the party makes 'a list' of candidates and being elected would depend on how highly placed on the list you are – which many maintain would reform our electoral system. On the contrary, such a system would allow rich and influential people like Billy to be nominated by their parties ahead of candidates chosen by party members. Billy Tormey was a consultant in Beaumont Hospital, and as such did not require the resources an ordinary candidate would need from a constituency organisation; Billy could just pay all election costs himself. He was very friendly with Fergus Finlay, Anne Byrne, Pat Magner, and Sally Clarke and through them had direct access to Dick Spring. His failure to be elected in the local elections of 1991 was the last straw for me. He had also been defeated in the local elections in 1985 and in the general elections of 1987 and 1989. I really could see no political future for him, especially after the 1991 defeat when the political wind was in Labour's favour. Furthermore, a superb replacement had presented herself.

Róisín Shortall had come into my office early in 1991 to discuss the possibility of her contesting in the Drumcondra local electoral area, one of the two that comprised the Dublin North-West Dáil constituency. A teacher in the school for the Deaf in Cabra, I was very taken by her sincerity and charm. But there was much more, behind the big blue eyes I sensed a steely determination to win. I told her that she should contest the local elections and that she would have the time of her life; we had a bit of a laugh. She did, and was elected on her first outing. This was the kind of candidate the party wanted, so full of sincerity, passion, and intelligence, and I was delighted when she decided to continue and contest the Dáil nomination against Dr Tormey. Of course, the members chose her over Billy Tormey, when left to their own devices Labour members can be trusted to make sensible political choices.

These events caused uproar in the Sally Empire, where the consultant was the golden boy, but I refused to give in and to intervene on Billy's behalf as I could have done. I was even brought to lunch in the Mont Clare Hotel with Dick and Fergus, (a rare occasion) but I remained unconvinced that Billy could offer anything over Róisín. Niamh Bhreathnach too, to her credit, refused to use her powers to add him on as a candidate, which as Party Chairperson she shared jointly with the party leader. Dick, in all fairness, did not unequivocally insist on Billy's selection.

The affair dragged on right up to the general election, with Billy Tormey telling me arrogantly that he would be put on the ticket and that I knew it. In March 1992 I was hospitalised and detained for a few days. Without my vote on the Organisation Committee, a motion to recommend his addition as a candidate would be carried. I discharged myself early from the hospital. I rarely enjoyed anything so much as the look of exasperation I caused when I walked into the room where the Organisation Committee was held and helped thwart the attempt to foist Billy onto the ticket. After his failure to be added on, Billy contested the general election as an Independent and he was defeated again, after this he contested the Senate elections, where he suffered a further defeat. Since then, he has contested the 1997 general election and the 1999 local elections and, hardly surprisingly, has lost in these elections too. He is now heading for a Guinness Book of Records entry as the world's most defeated candidate! Even after his automatic expulsion from the Labour Party for contesting against an official party candidate, he continued to enjoy the support of an inner circle in Labour, just as Róisín Shortall was excluded from such support. The whole incident was, in my opinion, living proof of why a list system would be a retrograde step for Irish politics. Because of the nature of our society, it would lead to a level of cronyism and jobbery difficult to achieve at the moment. At least under the present system, members of political parties can exercise enormous powers in the choosing of candidates.

Three in a row

Counting the local elections, the 1989 general election, and the Presidential election, this was the third success in a row, so it was now reasonable to expect that Labour would increase its level of representation at a general election. Nothing succeeds like success, and it seemed that every day after these elections the party was growing from strength to strength. Events were soon to bear out this trend.

CHAPTER 10

THE BANANA REPUBLIC EXPOSES ITSELF

IN SEPTEMBER of 1991 the *Sunday Independent* published a story concerning the former Irish Sugar Company, Súicre Éireann. This company had a major place in the Irish psyche, being central to the policy of successive Governments regarding the support of indigenous industry as part of all 'Buy Irish' campaigns. Journalist Sam Smyth revealed the goings-on in that company in and around the time of its privatisation in 1991. It was a story of enormous amounts of money changing hands between a small group of top people in the company, all of course paid for by the consumer. The story was sensational and deeply disillusioning for those who had faith in Irish industry. Shortly before privatisation, Súicre Éireann had bought the remaining shares in its distribution company 'SDH'. These shares were owned by members of the management of SDH. Where did they get the money to buy these shares initially? From a subsidiary of SDH. And who authorised this loan? Súicre Éireann of course. During the course of one year these men had made a profit of £3.2 million. It was the start of a veritable cloudburst of scandals that was to emanate from the establishment at the start of the nineties.

Next to follow was the Telecom Affair. The site of the former Johnson, Mooney and O'Brien bakery in Dublin's Ballsbridge was sold in 1989 for £4 million. The public was shocked to learn that just a year later, the state telecommunications company, Telecom Éireann paid £9.4 million for the site. One of the wealthy owners of the company that owned the site was Dublin northsider Dermot Desmond, a close associate of the Taoiseach, Charlie Haughey. Mr Haughey distanced himself from this controversy and subsequently the Chairman of Telecom, Michael Smurfit, resigned.

Another bombshell of this time concerned the former teacher training college in Carysfort, Blackrock, Co. Dublin. Part of it was bought by wealthy Dublin northsider and businessman Pino Harris for £6.5 million. The site was then sold on by him just six months later to University College Dublin for £8 million, all provided by the taxpayer.

These scandals weren't confined to the business community. That most impregnable of Irish institutions, the Catholic Church, was shaken to the core when *Irish Times* journalist, Andy Pollock, revealed that Dr Eamonn Casey, the charismatic bishop of Galway, had had an affair with an American woman and had a son, Peter, from this liaison. Bishop Casey would have been considered to be on the left of the Irish political spectrum and his stance against American Imperialism in Central America was deeply appreciated. His being found out and his subsequent resignation and flight marked the beginning of a decade that saw the influence of the Catholic clergy wane to its lowest point in the twentieth century.

The other major scandal to dominate this remarkable period in Irish life concerned the beef industry. As with the questionable practices in the planning area, the beef industry was awash with rumour of shady practice for years. We were told of gigantic tax dodges, abuse, and double payment of European Union grants; of workers being paid in shares to avoid tax and mislabelling and misdating of meat products. Of course, nobody in Ireland could prove any of this and no newspaper or TV programme could cover this story true or false. All was changed when ITV's *World in Action* programme covered the story and a plucky young journalist called Susan O'Keefe came to public attention. This was in May 1991, and Dick Spring immediately took a high profile on the issue calling for a public enquiry. This call was echoed by the PDs, who forced an enquiry on the Government.

There was a question about political contributions from Ireland's premier beef baron Larry Goodman to Fianna Fáil, and the sole member of the Tribunal Mr Justice Hamilton investigated the question of contributions to all political parties. In this context, I was called to give evidence and was happy to confirm that the Labour Party had received no contributions from Larry Goodman. I was rather surprised that I was not asked about contributions to individual politicians. This is where I believe most of the trouble arises.

Contributions to parties are accounted for and are used to pay the enormous debts incurred by election campaigns. Contributions to individual politicians on the other hand, did not then have to be accounted for at all, and in any case, such contributions would inevitably put the politician under an obligation to the donor. Years later, the harmless report of the Beef Tribunal was to play a major role in setting the scene for the fall of the Fianna Fáil–Labour Coalition. It had already caused the downfall of the Fianna Fáil–PD Coalition in the year after its publication.

All these scandals of the early nineties set the backdrop to Labour's increase in the polls. We were not implicated in the business scandals, nor were we perceived to be: Mr Haughey and Fianna Fail *were*, and with much justification. Since the sixties, mixing business and politics was synonymous with the 'mohair suit brigade' of which Mr Haughey was the chief surviving example in his party.

The country and western Taoiseach replaces 'The Boss'

When Charlie Haughey was finally driven from power by elements in his own party, the irony was that the coup that replaced him was led by ministers of his own making. The general public, unaware of the intricacies of internal Fianna Fáil feuding, would have been unable six months previously to identify his successor, Albert Reynolds, as anything other than a Haughey loyalist. The major difference, and that of those closest to him like Brian Cowan, Máire Geoghegan-Quinn and Attorney General Harry Whelehan, was that if he was not exactly anti-urban or anti-Dublin, he was very definitely the face of rural Ireland in the party. Thus emerged the nickname that stuck to Albert Reynolds for his two years and ten months as Taoiseach. First used by the satirical radio show *Scrap Saturday*, Mr Reynolds became known as 'The country and western Taoiseach'. The *Scrap Saturday* team even had a song to go with the title.

General election preparations

In the 17 months between the local elections of 19 June 1991 and the general election of 27 November 1992, the party prepared relentlessly for the general election that we were all sure would bring us great gains.

In the Dáil, Dick Spring relentlessly harried the Government, particularly the Fianna Fáil element. He was proving to be one of the great anti-Fianna Fáil leaders of the generation and they knew it, responding to his attacks with bitter invective. But the public loved it. The PLP met across the road from Leinster House in another Government building called Kildare House. The meetings took place every Wednesday while the Dáil was in session. In June 1992, I accompanied Dick from Kildare House in the short walk across the road to Leinster House. As we approached the gates, we saw a group of about 15 middle-aged ladies. When they saw Dick Spring they spontaneously burst into applause. It was a magical moment. The public had found its foil to corruption and cynicism.

Stagg resigns from the PLP

For Labour Left there was to be one final but significant death rattle. In spite of the recovery of the party, it still remained a fixture within, having its adherents on the AC and in the PLP, where Emmet Stagg represented its view. Labour Youth, in which I always maintained an active interest as a source of new candidates and an indication of the health of the party, had been removed from their control with the appointment of Dermot Lacey as Youth Officer in 1990. At this stage, Labour Left seemed to be more of a nuisance than an actual threat, with ritual denouncements of the 'leadership conspiracy' to bring the party into coalition.

The party was shocked then when Deputy Emmet Stagg resigned the Whip at a meeting of the PLP on Wednesday 19 February 1992. He claimed at the meeting that his resignation was due to the consistent ignoring by the leadership of the 1987 'Report of the Commission on Electoral Strategy', which ruled out coalition 'except in the case of grave national emergency'. In particular, he objected to an interview that deputy leader Ruairi Quinn had given to the *Sunday Tribune* in July 1991, though this had been a year previously!

To resign because of something that might happen just made no sense, argued Mervyn Taylor; furthermore, any new political group that might be formed now would in all likelihood be headed by Pat Rabbitte, who was a former Workers' Party TD, and he was on record as saying that he had no principled objection to coalition. This comment somewhat let the cat out of the bag. The Workers' Party had just broken up dramatically with six of its seven TDs leaving to form an as yet unnamed party. They'd had enough of the old democratic centralism of the Workers' Party. They were, of course, recruiting like mad.

Emmet now assembled his constituency members in Kildare and expected them to stick with him. He was shattered at the result of the constituency meetings. Kildare has a proud Labour tradition, having been the constituency of William Norton, who had been party leader from 1932–60, and its members took their loyalty to the party seriously. Three members took verbatim notes of these meetings for me and I was able to collate these and pass them over to Dick Spring's office. Some members, led by Ned O'Rourke of Monasterevin, had formed a 'shadow' constituency executive to come into place when Emmet made the final break, and the recruiting of Jack Wall of Athy as an alternative candidate was discussed. It seemed as if Emmet's apostasy had been rejected by his own constituency.

There seemed to be great indifference to his plight in the greater party, as if this moment were inevitable. Only Mervyn Taylor seemed genuinely distressed at Emmet's defection, but Mervyn was always worrying in case the sky would fall down. His anxiety was impersonally enough expressed as nervousness about the effect a split would have on the party. It looked as if Emmet was heading for the wilderness, and yet it was his own decisiveness that saved him.

On Wednesday 25 March I was having an after-lunch cup of coffee in the Dáil bar with Pat Magner. We were standing beside the coffee machine at the far end of the room and were in a position to see who entered the bar. Emmet soon walked in and came straight over to us and said: 'I've told the Superintendent that I don't want Michael Taft in the house again.' We were flabbergasted; he had banned this chief aide and Labour Left Secretary from Leinster House. So it was all over. We spoke to Emmet as if the previous six weeks had never occurred. A week later, appropriately on 1 April, he submitted a letter to the PLP asking for re-admission. His request was agreed to without discussion, and in another week Emmet was cheekily contributing as if nothing at all had happened.

However, I was taking no more chances; on Thursday 30 July 1992, I chaired the Kildare Selection Convention in the Johnstown Inn. I received a warm reception and there was no opposition when I announced the intention of the party to run two candidates. The second candidate was to be Jack Wall, a fitter from Castlemitchell who lived in Athy and was former Chairman of the GAA County Board in Kildare. Jack started his address to the delegates with this unforgettable line: 'The first thing that I want to make clear to everyone here is that I'm a Dick Spring man.' I didn't expect any more trouble from Emmet after that. Nevertheless, Emmet was unflappable and we had a few convivial drinks together after the meeting with John McGinley, his Constituency Chairperson, and David Moynan, his Secretary. He even introduced me to Cllr Patsy Lawlor from Naas, a former Fine Gael representative and now Independent. Patsy was one of those who found Fine Gael too left wing, but like many of that ilk, she was just bursting with personality and colour. Kildare has been a quiet place for the Labour Party ever since.

Paddy Bergin bows out

One of the great characters to emerge from the Labour Party since the forties had been Paddy Bergin. A Carlow man born in 1913, he started his working life in the Sugar Factory there and had led one of its first strikes. He stood for the Dáil unsuccessfully in 1948. When he moved to Dublin he became National Organiser for the party, and was appointed to the Senate by William Norton in 1954. I knew him from my early years in the party. In the seventies, he gave a series of Labour history lectures to the members. He told me of a priest in Carlow who had preached from the pulpit that a man had not done an honest days work unless he dropped to his knees with exhaustion when he came home in the evening. When I expressed outrage at such exploitation he was quick to correct me. 'It wasn't the priest's fault,' he said, 'he was the son of a big farmer.' Oddly enough, another contemporary of Paddy's held the same view of the clergy's innocence in all this and he was Frank Edwards, the Communist schoolteacher from Waterford who similarly corrected me. Paddy Bergin also told me that during the infamous 'Mother and Child Scheme' controversy in 1951, when Noel Browne resigned from Cabinet, the Labour leader William Norton, who was Tánaiste and Minister for Social Welfare in that Government, had completely believed Noel Browne when he told the Cabinet that he had the approval of the hierarchy for his scheme. When this proved to be untrue, Norton was very unsupportive as he felt that he had been misled.

Paddy's funeral was on 19 April 1991. On May Day of that year, we held a celebration in the Labour History Society's Museum in Beggars Bush in Dublin. Paddy had been a founder member of the Labour History Society and so appropriately the day was dedicated to his memory, with the Secretary of the Society, Charlie Callan, delivering a eulogy. Also present were members of the Bergin family, including his sons Emmet, the star of the RTE series *Glenroe*, and his other son Patrick, who is an international movie star. I was reminded of Paddy's reputation as a womaniser and told Vicky Somers of Joe Birmingham's remarks about Paddy's ever readiness 'to tip a cat goin' out through a skylight'. She looked at me mockingly with her big eyes and then at the gorgeous Bergin brothers. 'I wish his sons had some of his habits', she said.

CHAPTER 11

ELECTION COUNTDOWN

THE OPINION Polls were very favourable and inclined us to further optimism. The IMS poll of July 1991 gave us 14 per cent of the vote (excluding the undecided) and a Landsdowne poll published 6 October 1991 gave us 13 per cent. Better still, an MRBI poll taken 9 and 10 October 1991 gave us a heady 15 per cent. The next 12 months were to be a wonderful race against time to get the candidates and the materials in place. Each constituency had to be dealt with methodically, while the election essentials were prepared at the same time. As for our policies and campaign, these had been handed to us by the Government and its scandals; we were to be the ones to clean up politics, a job we relished. Labour always had a certain high view of its own probity; we alone were unaffected by the planning scandals and we would restore standards in public life. Given the almost daily traffic in these now filling the Irish media, raising standards did not seem such a daunting task.

Fianna Fáil too seemed intent on making some gesture towards popular feeling and in February 1992 Charles Haughey resigned as Taoiseach. This man, who had held Fianna Fáil in his stultifying grip, was forced out in a series of bizarre events commencing with an interview by former Justice Minister Sean Doherty on a late night RTE programme *Nighthawks*. Mr Doherty alleged that he had passed transcripts of tapped telephone conversations onto Mr Haughey in 1982. Mr Haughey was Taoiseach at the time and he had denied knowledge that the phone tappings were taking place. Considering the amount of water that had flown under the bridge since then, one might be forgiven for thinking that Mr Haughey might survive this one as well. But no, in true soap opera fashion it was this story from the murky past that was to bring him down.

The truth of the matter was that his own party was waiting for an excuse to dump him. He was now an embarrassment to them and, above all, they did not want him leading them into the next general election in which ethics were bound to be a major issue. Instead of the lordly art-loving Haughey, they chose former showband promoter and Longford businessman Albert Reynolds; and so the era of the country and western Taoiseach began. Shortly after he came to power, Mr Reynolds fired most of the ministers appointed by Haughey; it was to be his most popular move. It was all downhill after that; even his appointment of the popular RTE correspondent Sean Duignan as Government Press Secretary didn't seem to help. His express dislike of his partners in Government, the PDs, meant that the Government was living on borrowed time. He had referred to the Fianna Fail–PD Coalition as 'a temporary little arrangement'. His feelings for the PDs were more than reciprocated; they considered him and his wing of Fianna Fáil to be somewhat uncouth and incapable of the efficient modern Government of which they considered themselves to be the paragons. The armed peace remained in Cabinet until the Beef Tribunal brought the whole house of cards tumbling down, but that was not to be for another nine months.

Working the constituencies

Those constituencies where we held Dáil seats were considered safe enough for us. All our TDs were hard-working and most had fought, gained, and held their seats against tremendous odds. They would have it a bit easier this time round, but I hoped that some of the more comfortable would take running mates. We had six TDs in this category: Séamus Pattison in Carlow-Kilkenny, Mervyn Taylor in Dublin South-West, Emmet Stagg in Kildare, Jim Kemmy in Limerick East, Brian O'Shea in Waterford and Liam Kavanagh in Wicklow. Very few Labour TDs feel confident enough to take on running mates; the primeval fear that a running mate will prove to be more popular than the sitting TD haunts them. Nevertheless, three of the six took running mates. The ever-generous Jim Kemmy had Cllr Jan O'Sullivan as his running mate, Mervyn Taylor had Cllr Eamon Walsh, and Emmet Stagg had Jack Wall. It was, of course, true to say that Emmet's acceptance of a running mate wasn't altogether voluntary. The other three felt that circumstances or strong local reasons precluded them from being accompanied on the ticket.

Some constituencies were listed out as areas where we might be very hopeful of making gains. They included Dublin South-Central where Pat Upton was already a household name. Both himself and Joe Costello had been elected to the Senate after the 1989 general election, and so had certain access to resources and publicity that they used assiduously. Joe was in the neighbouring Dublin Central constituency and had been building up the Labour vote since he first contested in the local elections in 1985. He had a terrific organisation and was soon to restore the party's fortunes in a constituency that had been deserted by its last Labour TD Michael O'Leary in 1982. Joe was from Sligo and played a significant role in recruiting Declan Bree to the party. He was a secondary-school teacher by profession and was President of the Association of Secondary Teachers (ASTI) in 1990–91. Joe and Pat, as Senators since 1989, enjoyed a certain seniority in the party; they ranked along with our three Dublin TDs who comprised the Dublin Oireachtas Group: Ruairi Quinn, Mervyn Taylor, and Sean Ryan.

The Dun Laoghaire constituency had been left in a mess after Barry Desmond's departure for the European Parliament. Niamh Bhreathnach now had to get herself selected. Flor O'Mahony, one of the Labour candidates in 1989, had quit the scene leaving only Cllr Jane Dillon Byrne, the colourful and long-serving representative from Monkstown. Barry Desmond wasn't on speaking terms with her and so I took it upon myself to explore the situation with her. It seems strange that I should have had to do this, but relations in the Dun Laoghaire constituency were very strained indeed. Jane is also somewhat colourful and exotic in her dress sense. Tony Brown, the International Secretary of the party, once said to me: 'In the morning, Jane gets up and goes into her living room, grabs a curtain that takes her fancy and wraps it round herself, then proceeds to the kitchen where she finds a utensil that she likes and places it on her head. Then she is ready to face the world.'

At that time, jokes about the northside of Dublin were in vogue and Jane had a great sense of humour. I told her the one about the difference between a Northside and a Southside woman: 'A Northside woman has fake jewellery and real orgasms, with a Southside woman it's just the opposite.' Quick as a flash she said: 'Well, I'm originally from Drumcondra and these are real jewels.' I took her to lunch to convince her not to contest the nomination in favour of Niamh Bhreathnach. As it turned out, Jane paid for the lunch, ordered wine to go with it and told me that she had gotten such a sickener in the 1989 general election that she had decided not to contest again anyway. Nobody had asked her intentions since and it was just assumed that she would go again. We had a great lunch, it was in the Royal Dublin Hotel and Jane was on a break from Dublin County Council business. At this time, Dublin County Council headquarters were in O'Connell Street and the hotel was next door. On the other side of the County Council offices was Conway's Pub, now famous as the venue of the open bar for councillors paid for by developers. I always thought that it was a pity that Jane never made it to Leinster House. She certainly would have brightened up the place.

Sean Kenny had been a long-time contestant in Dublin North-East. Originally from Galway, he was a systems analyst with CIE, who had taken to politics in the capital. I had first met him as a fellow contestant when he was elected to the City Council in 1979. He has fought each general and local election since then. Before the Presidential election of 1990, he considered stepping down, and, with his agreement, I approached John Rogers to see if he would be interested in the constituency. John declined and Sean quickly changed his own mind, going on to hold his council seat again in the local elections. He was one of the two Labour councillors to be elected in the 1985 local elections and as such had a certain claim to the mayoralty of Dublin when next it was in Labour's gift. Furthermore, it would considerably enhance his profile as a Dáil candidate. It was an old political rule in Dublin that the mayoralty was worth 1000 votes in the year of an election. Anyway, Sean Kenny would make a fine Lord Mayor and so it was after the 1991 local elections.

(L-R) Senator Pat Upton, Barry Desmond MEP, Cllr Joan Burton, Cllr Sean Kenny and Cllr Eithne Fitzgerald during the 1992 election campaign.

The election of Sean Kenny as Lord Mayor of Dublin 1991–92 was in some way part of the reason for the magnificent result in his constituency in the general election when the party won two seats. Sean had actively sought a running mate in Tommy Broughan, a secondary teacher from Coolock, estimating quite astutely that this would damage Pat McCartan, the sitting

Workers' Party TD, whose strength lay in that part of the constituency. Pat McCartan lost his seat and Sean Kenny and Tommy Broughan were both elected. Theirs was not to be a happy co-habitation, but whatever about their intense rivalry, their work rate was phenomenal.

The Dublin West Constituency was a mixed bag of social classes and landscapes. Beautiful Lucan, with its picturesque village and stately homes, shared TDs with working-class Clondalkin, with its unemployment blackspots. Leafy middle-class Castleknock, full of neo-Georgian estates unimagined by the Georgians, stood cheek to jowl with the budget housing of Mulhuddart and Blanchardstown. Joan Burton, an accountant and Labour Left supporter, was selected to contest here. When I announced this at an AC meeting, Dick Spring said: 'Tell her that's as far west as she's going.'

Laois-Offaly was my native constituency and the party was lucky to have a young, articulate, and well-connected candidate in Pat Gallagher. He was one of the few candidates more associated with Emmet Stagg and Labour Left than with Dick Spring, and it took a special meeting with Dick Spring to convince him to run for the local elections in 1991. After that though, he was clearly marked out for a Dáil victory. His base was Tullamore, the populous county town of Offaly, where he was manager of Tullamore Community Training Workshop. As if all this wasn't enough, his father was a GAA County Selector and his granny had been the Dispensary Doctor in nearby Kilcormac! His Achilles' heel was that half of the constituency comprised County Laois. However, his strength in Offaly carried him to victory. After his election, he became quite supportive of Dick Spring, so much so that he was nicknamed 'the mini-minister' by his colleagues. He never lost his sense of irreverent humour though, about the airs and graces of office.

During 1991 and 1992, I accompanied Dick Spring on constituency visits. One of the most successful of these was on 20 February 1992, when we toured extensively in North Tipperary. In the evening, Dick and John Ryan, who was then a Senator, addressed a meeting of members and supporters in Nenagh numbering about 300 people. Then, as now, people ranted about politics being unable to attract people 'as it used to'. Here in North Tipperary, and again and again around the country, we showed that with the right organisation, leadership, and attitude, politics could still touch a vital chord. Sadly, there was animosity between Dick Spring and John Ryan, based on some ancient feud. In fact, the more I tried to bring them together the worse it seemed to get, and yet they never said a bad word about one another in public. It was that bitter private contempt that destroys unity and comradeship. A pity, I always thought.

Westmeath was a new constituency; it had been part of Longford-Westmeath since 1948. It had a strong Labour tradition based on the Irish Transport and General Workers Union (ITGWU). The party had aspirations to win a seat there with Jimmy Bennett as recently as 1981. Since then, the party had fallen on hard times and was unable to put forward even a token candidate in 1989. Now it had changed radically. I had attended many meetings here in the years since 1989 and determined that the constituency would never again be uncontested by Labour. Senator Helena McAuliffe-Ennis had left us to join the PDs in 1986, but had now returned with a vengeance. On 5 February 1990, her sister Ita, who was Administrator of the Dáil Secretariat, arranged a meeting between us. Helena was at this time a PD councillor. We met in the Country Shop Tea Rooms in Maynooth. Yes, Helena wanted to come back, but only on condition that Labour took the council seat from which she intended to resign. Under no condition could she bear the PDs holding onto it, such was her contempt for the party with which she'd had the briefest of flings. We were delighted of course, and Mark Nugent of Rochfordbridge, a Worker Director with Bord na Móna, stepped in. I thought that Helena would have been more than slightly embarrassed about her escapade with the PDs, and perhaps have kept a low profile for a while, especially given the venom with which her defection was greeted. But this was not Helena.

On 22 March of that year (1990), Dick Spring and I did an extensive constituency tour of Westmeath, visiting Derrynagrenagh Bord na Móna works and finishing up in Ballinacarrigy. This village was the stronghold of Cllr Willie Penrose, who had been elected along with Helena to represent the area on Westmeath County Council in 1985. They had been bitter rivals. Yet it was here that Helena chose to address the party in the first major outing since her return to the fold. The hall was full on this sharp spring night, and without the slightest embarrassment she stood up and addressed the members and supporters who six months previously would have had her guts for garters. She even berated the PDs for their right-wing policies! She really was most brazen; one could not but admire the woman. When the meeting was finishing, our host, Willie Penrose, with a dose of political incorrectness that is his hallmark, said: 'I'd now ask the women to leave the room and get the tea ready.' I thought that women's lib would have reached Westmeath by then. Quick as a flash Dick Spring asked: 'Can no men down here make tea?' There was a bit of an embarrassed silence before the tea-makers went out and prepared some delicious tea and sandwiches for us.

It was now Monday 27 July 1992, and I was chairing the Selection Convention for Westmeath in the Greville Arms Hotel in Mullingar. After all our work, Willie Penrose was refusing to accept the nomination as Dáil candidate and the convention was in an ugly mood. The party had never been so well organised in Westmeath and they sniffed victory; it seemed that just as they did, the favoured candidate had turned shy. There was nothing for it but to select another candidate and wait and see if this would make him change his mind. He told me that he would run if the party promised him a Senate seat in the event of his losing. I told him that this was out of the question: the party was not in a position to see what the situation would be after the general election, and couldn't favour one candidate over another beforehand. The frustration of the meeting was eloquently expressed by Fidelma Bennett, the Moate delegate, who demanded that the party contest the election. Despite calls for a recess, I managed to keep the meeting on the rails. There is always a danger in a situation like this that an unsuitable candidate would be picked just for show, but the meeting held its head. The Convention went ahead and selected poll-topping Cllr Michael Dollard from Mullingar. Addressing the meeting, Michael expressed his reluctance to accept the role of candidate, but said that if he did, people would have to realise that he was a pedestrian and that if they expected him to attend meetings they would have to provide transport. At this stage many delegates hid their faces in their hands with embarrassment.

On Wednesday 11 November 1992, just a fortnight before polling day in the general election, Willie Penrose telephoned me in head office. He had changed his mind; he would give it a shot. I asked if he had straightened this out with Michael Dollard. He had indeed. 'Tear away and best of luck', I said. This is how Willie Penrose became Labour's Westmeath candidate in the 1992 general election. He went on to win a seat in this three-seater constituency: a remarkable achievement by any standard.

We had briefly held a seat in Longford-Westmeath in 1927, but we had never had Dáil representation in nearby Cavan-Monaghan. Here, the prospective candidate had been recruited by John Rogers. She was a beautiful 25-year-old solicitor from Castleblaney, and she had a terrific sense of humour. We headed up to Castleblaney as late as 13 October to meet her and she was irrepressible, dragging Dick Spring from one function to another at breakneck speed, never slowing down and never taking no for an answer. She was stylish, articulate, liberal, and daring – quite a contrast to our usual candidate. In the evening we had dinner with Brian Johnston, the Cavan County Manager, who was a friend of Liam Kavanagh's dating back to the time when he was County Manager in Wicklow. It was unusual for county managers to be friends with Labour public representatives. They were usually mortal enemies. That night in the restaurant in Cavan town, however, we drank to Anne's political success.

Those constituencies where we had less support were also coming through now. In Cork East, after his successful first outing in the local elections, John Mulvihill from Cobh was now preparing to run in the general election. The neighbouring constituency was Cork North-West, at that time the most conservative constituency in the country. In the recent Presidential election, it had the dubious honour of being the only Dáil constituency in the country that had voted Austin Currie ahead of Mary Robinson. Bill Cashin of Kanturk, a maintenance engineer at Mallow Hospital, had decided to run. I'd put a lot of time into this constituency and Bill was an enthusiastic and able candidate, but we just couldn't break in. He had failed to be elected in the local elections. This constituency, against my best efforts, had been uncontested by Labour in the 1987 and 1989 general elections, and I always put this down as the reason for our failure to make more progress later on. Once electors have switched their allegiance to other candidates or parties, it is very hard to get them back.

Cork South-West is the most beautiful constituency in Ireland. It stretches 100 miles across from Cork City to the Kerry border and all along a sea coast full of romantic and dreamy harbours and inlets, studded with picturesque towns like Kinsale, Courtmacsherry, Clonakilty, Bantry, Glengarriff, and Castletownbere. On 5 and 6 December 1991 I went on an extensive tour of the constituency with Dick Spring, Gerry O'Sullivan (the Cork North-Central TD), Toddy O'Sullivan TD and Pat Magner. To make the enormous trek across the constituency we had to stop off every few miles. Sally had placed ads in the local papers and those who replied were invited to these meetings. In Brinny, we visited the pharmaceutical factory of Sheering Plough. We stopped off at Kinsale, Bandon, Dunmanaway, Skibbereen, Skull, Ballydehob, Bantry, Castletownbere, and Allihies.

I had kept up a reasonable contact with members in the constituency, though we hadn't had a TD since Michael Pat Murphy retired in 1981, but the warmth of our reception belied the sparsity of Labour members on the ground. Our only councillor was Michael Calnan of Dunmanaway, and he had organised a meeting for us in the Castle Hotel there. It was more of a pub than a hotel and we met the locals in the room upstairs. They were full of enthusiasm to get things going again. The local characters were out in full force. In Bandon, former Labour Town Commissioner Corney Looney demanded that no Labour money go to the Mary Robinson campaign as punishment for her refusal to stop in Bandon during her national tour. In the same town, a group of boys from the Grammar School came to our meeting, full of curiosity and goodwill.

The natural beauty of the area attracted a large expatriate community that we believed we could win, as it would be liberal and progressive. The constituency had a vibrant Church of Ireland community that we thought would also look favourably on the Mary Robinson-style Labour Party. Add all this to the traditional Labour vote, and we would not be far from a Dáil seat, we thought. So all in all we were quite confident about the situation there: but who would run? John Rogers had a candidate. Gregg Casey was young, good humoured, eager, and, of course, a solicitor. He hailed from Bandon, and though a native, had spent much time in Dublin. At weekends he often visited Allihies, a small and idyllic sanctuary at the far end of the constituency, where the 'laid-back' could commune with the elements.

Another possible candidate was Bambi Cotter from Bantry, where she ran *The Bread Shop*. She was sexy, glamorous, stylish, charismatic, and bubbled with enthusiasm. As a businesswoman, she had been involved in the Chamber of Commerce and seemed to have a large number of contacts all over the constituency. The sitting councillor Michael Calnan also showed an interest. He was an inveterate organiser and when he set his mind to winning the candidate selection he was unstoppable. In the general election he did extraordinarily well, gaining over 11 per cent of the vote; a very decent showing, but far from a Dáil seat. On the strength of his showing, he went on to win a Senate seat.

It had a tragic aftermath though, as Bambi Cotter was to die in a road accident in July 1994. The Volvo car in which she had been travelling outside Inishannon had overturned, crushing her. On Wednesday 6 July 1994 her funeral took place in Bantry and I attended to say goodbye to the TD who might have been. It was an enormous funeral; people had come not only from all over West Cork, but from all over the country, to pay tribute to this vibrant woman. I wondered all day long what would have happened to her, what would have happened to the party in West Cork and what would have happened to the Dáil seat if we had picked her as our standard bearer.

Five years later I attended a function in Dublin's Mansion House at which both Michael Calnan and Dick Spring were present. 'Do you remember that meeting in Clonakilty?' asked Michael Calnan. He referred to a meeting tucked into the recesses of my memory, which I was sure nobody but myself had remembered. It was on Friday 12 June 1992, which was a beautiful summer night. I had travelled to Cork and had dinner with my friends Pat and Dennis in Briar Hill before travelling on to Clonakilty. The meeting was a constituency one for all of Cork South-West in O'Donovans Hotel and Dick Spring was to attend, as was Michael Calnan, who was Chairman of Cork County Council at the time. As the start of the meeting dragged on, I could feel Dick's patience start to slip. Scheduled for 8.30 p.m., the meeting did not start until almost 10.00 p.m. We were not only joined by our members from Cork South-West, but by a member from one of the city constituencies, Cork North-Central, who insisted on having his say. I was all in favour as I felt that listening to members, however off the wall, was a small price to pay for their work and loyalty – but this guy did go on and on. He was followed by one of our stalwarts, Gerdie Harrington from Castletownbere, whose style of oratory involves a lot of shouting and stabbing the air. I suppose that at this stage Dick had had enough; he turned on me and growled, 'Ray, take some control over this meeting.' There was nothing I could or would do, some people had traveled a round trip of 100 miles to attend this meeting, and I wasn't going to cut them short.

What I didn't know, and what Michael Calnan told me in the Mansion House so many years later, was that Dick Spring had then turned to him, scowled and said, 'You're supposed to be Chairman of the County Council, do something about this meeting!'

There were 41 constituencies at this time and we were really stretching ourselves to contest in so many. It had always been my ambition to present a Labour candidate in each of the state's constituencies, but I thought that that was something for the general election after next, when the party's resources would, I hoped, be considerably enhanced. Nevertheless, we were able to carry a few extra passengers at this election. This was possible so long as the situation didn't get out of hand and drain scarce resources from areas where there was a real chance of winning. So when Jim Nolan of Arigna contacted me about running in the Taoiseach's own constituency of Longford-Roscommon I was delighted to let him off. He had contacted me in 1989 about running in Cavan-Monaghan, but he had to collect the nomination papers from head office; a little test I had set him to justify his candidature – he failed. This time we asked for a poster-quality photo and he caused hilarity in head office when he sent one up of himself and his dog. Ita McAuliffe managed to edit out the dog, saving the voters of Longford-Roscommon a very confusing poster indeed.

The death of Jimmy Tully

Jimmy Tully had been TD for Meath from 1954 to 1957 and again from 1961 until his retirement in 1982. It was not, however, for his role as TD that he was most remembered, though that was distinguished in terms of his service to the people of Meath. Rather it was his term as Minister for Local Government from 1973–77, when he built a record number of local authority houses and, more controversially, executed the infamous 'Tullymander' that was an imaginative redrawing of the state's constituency boundaries. The redrawing was supposed to favour the ruling coalition of Labour and Fine Gael. Unfortunately, because of the magnitude of the swing in favour of Fianna Fáil, it did the opposite and contributed in no small way to that Party's 20-seat majority at the 1977 general election.

Andy Callanan, a member of Thurles Urban District Council, had told me that he had attended a meeting at the Minister's office, making representations on behalf on the Tipperary North constituency. Mr Tully had taken the delegation into a nearby room that had a map of the constituencies on the wall. 'Now boys,' said the Minister, 'you just tell me what you want.'

He died in 1992 at the age of 76 and his death evoked the traditional tributes from the PLP that met that morning. It was one of my first encounters with Jim Kemmy's rigid honesty. Many members spoke, all flatteringly of Jimmy Tully, his work, and his legacy. Though many were genuine, others of course came from members who had received many a tongue lashing from the abrasive Meath TD. But that is our tradition in Ireland: 'Never speak ill of the dead.' Then Jim Kemmy spoke. He mentioned that Jimmy Tully had been deeply conservative on religious and social matters. He said that he had seen him through the eyes of a young man in the sixties and seventies and had found him to be very difficult. He did, however, appreciate his very practical nature when dealing with the Departments for which he was Minister. There was a great silence in the room. I believe that Jimmy Tully, the harsh and practical realist that he was, would have preferred Jim Kemmy's blunt, almost Puritan honesty.

The party expands and strengthens

All this constituency re-organisation and general election preparation had been a mammoth undertaking: moving from one constituency to another, tracking each local problem, and following up on each request and then keeping in contact. Keeping contact with key personnel while back at the office, while at the same time making myself available at all times to any party member who wished to talk to me, now became more important than ever.

Dick Spring performed brilliantly in the constituencies, and particularly in the out-of-Dublin ones. Perhaps there was some residue of resentment stemming from the capital's rejection of the 1982–87 Coalition or perhaps Dick Spring being a country TD, and when reduced to essentials, just couldn't empathise with the urban members and supporters. Anyway, by autumn 1992 the organisation was in top shape and a considerable array of quality candidates were lined up.

The year 1992 had been a momentous time for me. I had travelled thousands of miles for the party and got to know hundreds of new people and enjoyed it all thoroughly. I had seen the strength and influence of head office grow within the party. It was a time of great optimism about the future of the party and, indeed, the country, which was renewed, modern and outward looking under the Robinson Presidency.

Summer of 1992

It was a quiet and warm summer. The Government was living out its time on death row. Albert Reynolds as Taoiseach sat uncomfortably with PD Leader Des O'Malley in Cabinet, while the electorate bided its time. Only the firing of so many Haughey-appointed ministers had brought Albert Reynolds any popularity, after that it was back to scandal time again. The X-Case, in which a fourteen-year-old girl was pursued by the state when she went to England for an abortion, showed in the most graphic detail a state that made criminals out of children, while its own supporters and friends lined their pockets with taxpayers' money. Fianna Fáil was harried, not only in the Dáil, but also in the workplace, the pub, and the social club. It was a party in hiding.

The PDs were feeling the heat of this unpopular Government and were looking for a way out. Labour alone was in the ascendant and was seen as being untainted by the scandals and as bright, new, and modern while we basked in the reflection of the first truly popular President in the Phoenix Park. Labour had shown that it could take on Fianna Fáil in a way that Fine Gael had failed to do. Because of this success, it was being vested with the role of Opposition to Fianna Fáil. It was building support from previous Fine Gael and Workers' Party supporters and disillusioned Fianna Fáil voters. Our candidates were picked, our constituency organisations were geared up, and before I went on holidays the poster design had been agreed by the PLP. When the election came, we would be more ready and able than we had ever been before.

CHAPTER 12

THE SPRINGTIDE AND THE FATAL MISTAKE

THE BEEF Tribunal had been set up on 31 May 1991 and it sat until it reported its findings in 1994. However, by winter 1992 the temperature in Dublin Castle, where the Tribunal sat, began to increase considerably when both Albert Reynolds and Des O'Malley gave evidence. That Mr Reynolds as Taoiseach should appear before a Tribunal was remarkable enough, but for him to accuse Des O'Malley, his fellow Cabinet member and Leader of the PDs, of perjury was spectacular. Much of the Tribunal's work concerned the business of beef baron Larry Goodman, and Mr Reynolds, referring to Mr O'Malley's evidence, said: 'He puffed up Goodman's claim for what I regard as cheap political gain. He was reckless, irresponsible and dishonest to do that here at the Tribunal.' With these remarks the Government fell. It had gone beyond the point where even an abject apology would save it. Anyway, Mr Reynolds made it clear he had no intention of apologising, but said that any suggestion that he did not talk to Mr O'Malley outside of the Cabinet was 'crap, pure crap'. Was the man intent on political suicide we wondered as we laughed all the way to the polling station?

More was yet to come, probably out of tiredness or nerves he announced on radio that the Minister for Social Welfare, Charlie McCreevy, was going to 'dehumanise' the whole social welfare system. When given a chance to correct his comments he just repeated them. After that, he was sidelined by the Fianna Fáil strategists. But it didn't matter; the damage was done. I was on my annual holidays in the Canaries when these exciting events started to unfold, but even there, they were all the talk of the Irish. On 4 November I hightailed it home. On the very next day, the general election was called. Polling day was to be 25 November, just three weeks later – the short campaign was always favoured by Fianna Fáil.

There were formal Selection Conventions to be held, though we expected no surprise results. In Wicklow, where I had hoped for a second candidate, Liam Kavanagh told me that the person in question, Cllr John Byrne of Bray, was away in America on a junket and therefore could hardly be selected. We contested 38 of the 41 constituencies, which was a very respectable number indeed. It was the highest number of constituencies contested by Labour for the 23 years since the watershed election of 1969. It had been my ambition to contest in every constituency, but now I would not spread scarce resources too thinly. When the members in Donegal South-West offered a candidate, I stubbornly refused and asked them instead to concentrate on the election of Sean Moloney in Donegal North-East. There was disagreement on the Election Committee, but few of them knew of the painstaking work of building up a good organisation around a candidate. It was not fly-by-night stuff to be decided after a flattering phonecall.

The committee meets in my office during the 1992 general election campaign.
(L-R) Marion Boushell, Greg Sparks, Ray Kavanagh, Barry Desmond, Sally Clarke,
Ita McAuliffe and Aidan McNamara. Missing from the photo are Fergus Finlay, James
Wrynn and Dermot Lacey.

We couldn't find a candidate in Clare in spite of having a small organisation there. Jo Walsh, who worked in Guinness Peat Aviation (GPA), the aircraft leasing company, couldn't get time off, as she was involved in an important

114

project. I asked six other members before they came up with a candidate. It was to be Dr Moosajee Bhamjee, a psychiatrist of Indian race who originally hailed from South Africa. I knew him through the organisation as an opponent of the militant expulsions, which had not endeared him to me. One attribute that marked him out as a good candidate was his brilliant sense of humour. This would be severely tested over the next five years. In truth, the party wasn't bubbling over with enthusiasm when I told them of Bhamjee's candidature, but as I pointed out to them, they had little choice. He had been nominated by the local organisation and as nobody knew him except me, they just had to take my word for it. As I pointed out to the General Election Committee, the people of Clare had elected de Valera and he was an American, and what was worse, they had elected Daniel O'Connell, and he was a Kerryman!

More abortion referenda

Polling day for the general election was also to feature another two referenda on the abortion issue. Back in 1983, abortion had been forbidden by a constitutional provision, but in March 1992, the Supreme Court had decided that abortion was permissible when a real and substantial risk of suicide of the mother was involved. With typical insensitivity and indifference to the rights of women, the Government sought to restrict this right while at the same time include a right to information and travel for pregnant women. All this had come about because of the Government's mishandling of the so-called X Case, in which a pregnant girl was dragged back to the country on foot of an injunction from the Attorney General, Harry Whelehan.

We strongly opposed the first referendum and supported the second. These were potentially explosive and divisive issues, but nonetheless of enormous importance to society. We published 100,000 leaflets on the issue and the electorate responded by rejecting the Government's new wording and endorsing the rights of travel and information. Even if nothing else was to succeed in this election, we had done a good thing in our stand on these issues.

The campaign kicks off

Straight away I ordered car stickers and lapel stickers, and the first 11 lots of posters arrived in head office on Friday; not bad going considering the election was called on the previous day. We published a national poster that would be displayed in all constituencies. Naturally enough, it was of Dick

Spring and it was no surprise that it was in big demand for the first time ever. Very early into the campaign, the canvassers were reporting back to me on the positive reception his name was given. Now, just as the candidates had used Mary Robinson as a 'stand beside' in 1991, they suddenly stood beside Dick Spring on their literature photos. It was then that Fergus came in with his masterstroke 'Dick Spring for Taoiseach', and why not, even if it was to be that newest of species, 'a rotating one'? It grabbed the headlines and our members loved it. Labour hadn't seriously aspired to that office since 1927.

1992 General Election Press Conference. Joan Burton speaks to Emmet Stagg. Both are soon to become junior ministers while Róisín Shortall is in the background.

The Party Manifesto was divided into two parts, allowing for two launches. Both were held in the Riverside Conference Centre on Sir John Rogerson's Quay. The first dealt with ethics in Government and the second concerned justice in economics. They were remarkably traditional as far as Labour's policies had been for the previous 20 years, but what had changed was the climate. At the first launch, on 13 November, Mervyn Taylor asked me how many seats we would win and I really thought I was putting my head on the block by saying that I thought we would win 26. By the look on his face I think he thought I was quite mad. By the time of the second launch, on 18 November, Fianna Fáil had announced that they would restore 100 per cent mortgage relief to first-time buyers. I asked Emmet Stagg if this was dangerous for us; after all, the recent mortgage increase was coming across as a huge issue on the doorsteps. 'If Fianna Fáil announced a grant of £1,000 for every man, woman, and child in this country it wouldn't help them now', he replied. He was right, it was a week before polling day and Fianna Fáil had lost its credibility. It now descended to desperate measures and its PR company, Saatchi and Saatchi of London, resurrected the issue of house property tax. This was from the old policy document of the eighties that I had put into permanent cold storage, but it made no difference at all to the electorate. The Election Committee, however, did panic a bit.

But we were ready for every eventuality, partly because we now received financial contributions in a volume that had never been available to us before. Our campaign was comprehensive and we assisted our candidates in the constituencies more than ever before. For the first time ever, a Labour leader used air transport; we hired a plane to take Dick Spring from Kerry to Donegal, where Sean Maloney was craving his assistance for the last hours of his tour. We covered all the angles that a modern election campaign should, and yet we displayed modesty and restraint, which I believe was appreciated by the electorate. Our literature, posters, lapel stickers, press conferences, and TV and radio broadcasts were top of the range and all performed within a modest budget of £120,000, which was a minuscule amount beside the millions spent by Fianna Fáil. Yet business was generous to us in this election, in a volume that it had never been before, giving us about £113,000, while the unions gave us almost £32,000 and private individuals sent a number of small donations amounting to about £6,000. The point in all this was that contributions could by no measure of means be accounted as enormous or compromising, and this was in an election that even the dogs in the street knew that we would come out well from, most likely as members of a new government.

Of course, many of these business contributions were eachway bets. I received a substantial dollar cheque from the well-known impresario Noel Pearson. I smiled as I read the endorsement. The cheque was made out to Fianna Fáil! I sat back and waited and sure enough before the day was out I received a phone call from a man describing himself as Mr Pearson's Personal Assistant. A 'girl' had made a terrible mistake, he said. The wrong cheque had been put into our envelope. I assured him that it was all right I wouldn't take offence. Then he really got melodramatic: 'The girl's job could be on the line if this was discovered. Could I oblige and have the cheque returned to be swapped with the one made out to us?' Of course I did so, and was not at all surprised to find that the new cheque was for a considerably smaller amount than the original one made out to Fianna Fáil.

As the close of nominations approached, it became crucial to keep our heads. The candidate strategy had been worked out over several years and had strong backing in the various constituencies. It was based mainly on a single candidate strategy aimed at concentrating the vote behind a single candidate, thus increasing his/her chances. There were two candidates in four constituencies, but this was achieved by exhaustive negotiations. There is little point in running second candidates in my opinion where there will not be a unified campaign. Nothing is more destructive of a party's unity, or of its candidates' chances of success, that to have two candidates bickering with one another. Then on the Saturday before close of nominations I received a call from Dublin North.

The night before, Dick Spring had telephoned after canvass. The call went through to the upstairs room where the canvassers were congregating and they all gathered round to hear what the party leader was saying to their candidate, Sean Ryan. They couldn't believe it when they heard him broach the subject of a second candidate. Sean had finally won a seat in 1989 after working on it for over a decade. The next most senior person in the constituency was Cllr Bernie Malone, but it was not her who was to be added, rather an outside person close to Dick Spring. The constituency was about to explode. They asked me if I could do anything about it. I brought it up at the General Election Committee meeting and it appeared that Fergus Finlay knew all about it, but Barry Desmond had been kept in the dark. Well we blew that one out of the water. It could actually have impacted on the whole campaign and lost us many potential seats.

It seemed as if the scandals had lifted a cloud from the people's eyes and that for the first time ever they were receptive to our policies. Of course, the strong leadership of Dick Spring, who became the symbol of integrity during the campaign, and the contrasting weak leadership of Albert Reynolds, kicked into play also. It was a conjunction of factors, not the least of which was the advanced state of readiness of the party and the quality of our candidates. Polling day was on Wednesday 25 November and it was a doubly lucky day for me; an offer I had put on a house near the South Circular Road was accepted on that very day. Polling day is a bit of a lull after the storm, but on this occasion we knew that the storm would restart when the results came in. First of all we had the referendum results, and then the results from the constituencies. Tommy Murtagh, a member in

Dublin South-Central, had been coming in to me for years with the best bookies' prices at election times and placing the bets for me. I bet on 26 seats, more than the party had ever received before. It was Saturday before the enormity of our victory had realised. Tommy Broughan's winning of a second seat in Dublin North-East had brought our total to 33. It was a triumph. Fianna Fáil had lost 9 seats and Fine Gael 10, Democratic Left (a new party formed from the split in the Workers' Party) had won 4 seats. The PDs had gained four and were up to 10 seats.

The numbers now had to be matched to an incoming Government. The magic figure was 83, after the election of a Ceann Comhairle. There were 166 seats in the Dáil and we had 33, Fianna Fáil held 68, Fine Gael had 45, the PDs had 10, Democratic Left had 4 while the independents held 6 seats. The party was ecstatic; this was its finest hour. Since its foundation, it had never exceeded 22 seats, which it achieved in the June election of 1922 and again in 1965. Dick Spring, the leader who had delivered this victory, was riding on the crest of a wave. He could do no wrong in the eyes of the members. This was a unique position for a Labour leader, who always has a questioning, thoughtful, and occasionally quarrelsome membership. But this was not so now. I think that the unquestioning authority that was now given to Dick Spring was to be a cause of the major problems later on. When people delegate their judgement to others, some very strange things can happen. Sean Ryan, the Dublin North TD, was to ask me later how we fell for the idea of a coalition with Fianna Fáil, and I could only answer by reminding him of the atmosphere then and that if Dick Spring had asked the PLP members to jump one by one out of the windows of the Shelbourne Hotel they would have queued up in an orderly fashion to do so.

The first meeting of the new PLP was held on the following Tuesday, 1 December 1992, in the Shelbourne Hotel. It was a major press event being covered by television as well as by the print media. The mood was highly congratulatory at first, until Jim Kemmy asked that 'a real meeting' take place. Then followed an analysis of the political situation. Eleven of the deputies spoke of involving Democratic Left in any government arrangement. Only Liam Kavanagh spoke of taking in the PDs. Many spoke of the strength of the anti-Fianna Fáil sentiment that had elected them. Some mentioned the inclusion of Fianna Fáil in any discussions, but only to increase the bargaining position of the party; it was not considered as a serious option. There wasn't even one advocate of coalition with Fianna Fáil at the meeting. How then did it come about that six weeks later, when a motion in favour of forming a government with that party was put to a delegate conference of Labour in the National Conference Hall, not one TD voted against the proposal? The situation on 1 December was clear enough; discussions were just starting. Between then and the next meeting of the PLP, the decisions were made. The Fine Gael–Democratic Left option most favoured by the party was dropped.

This is how it happened: the next meeting of the PLP took place on 14 December and Dick Spring asked for a mandate to open serious discussions with Fianna Fáil. All members, as well they would, expressed total confidence in Dick Spring and his mandate to negotiate as he wished. Coalition with Fianna Fáil was another matter. Confusion reigned, nobody wanted to be disloyal to Dick Spring, all wanted to express confidence in him, yet even then, when the deal with Fianna Fáil had effectively been done behind their backs, few of the Labour TDs believed that Dick Spring would lead them into a Coalition with the party they had opposed so strongly. After all, Dick Spring had been at one with them when he said in the 'No confidence' debate in the Dáil on 5 November, slightly over a month before, '…it must surely be considered amazing that any party would consider coalescing with (Fianna Fáil)'. The story of those few days is even more remarkable than fiction.

First of all, there was the isolation of Dick Spring from his party; access to him was now restricted. The limited socialising in which he had engaged now stopped completely. I was used to meeting him weekly, but now had to book my calls with him. I wasn't too upset just then as I was up to my eyes in getting our candidates for the Senate general election together. However, the neurotically secret nature of negotiations was beginning to have a serious effect on the solidarity of the party. Pat Upton, now the TD for Dublin South-Central, who had played such a crucial role in Dick Spring's survival in the late eighties, was now dropped from Dick's inner circle. He telephoned Dick's Office and was not put through. He asked that Dick return the call. It was not returned and for the rest of his life Pat deeply resented his treatment during these important days. Jim Kemmy, perhaps the clearest minded of them all, was left to rot in Limerick, but then he was never in favour. Jim was far too blunt. It seemed as if Dick Spring and Fergus Finlay intended to do it all by themselves with others in assisting roles. This attempt at centralisation was to have the most extraordinary consequences.

The immediate aftermath of the election saw talks commence with Democratic Left. Many in Labour believed this to be the right thing to do ideologically, but also the right thing to do from an opportunistic point of view. As a left-wing party, it would be dangerous to leave Democratic Left in opposition; it could revive its fortunes at Labour's expense. The party had returned only four TDs, and like many left-wing parties, they were in two factions. Party leader Proinsias De Rossa was bitterly opposed to Labour, and he was supported by Liz McManus, the Wicklow TD. Pat Rabbitte, the member for Dublin South-West, and Eamon Gilmore, the Dun Laoghaire TD, were more pragmatic and craved a role in Government. Pat Rabbitte, always the provider of the soundbite, said that he didn't want to continue his career, 'doing out social welfare problems'. These talks were very important, but much valuable time was used up in preparing a joint document; it was not ready until 8 December.

Meanwhile, there was also some unfinished business to settle with John Bruton TD, the Fine Gael leader, and the remnants of the eighties 'monetarist' wing of his party that had humiliated the then young Labour leader in the 1982–87 Government. Particularly the jibe from Alan Dukes that 'Labour, once bought should stay bought'.

The revenge was enacted ritually with all the precision and cruelty of a Sicilian vendetta and was just as pointless. Finally, it was agreed that Dick Spring and John Bruton should meet. It would be on Sunday 6 December in the Constitution Room of the Shelbourne Hotel in Dublin. It was a full 10 days after the election. The day before, Barry Desmond was on the Saturday Radio Current Affairs programme *Saturday View*, hosted by Rodney Rice and with him was Nora Owen, deputy leader of Fine Gael. Barry, who seemed at that stage to be privy to the talks going on in the inner circle, announced that Dick Spring would 'put manners on John Bruton'. Thus was revealed the purpose of the Sunday meeting. If this was to be the content of the meeting between the two leaders then there was little political gain to be had from it. Fine Gael people were understandably very insulted and this radio programme is still embedded in their memories. The Sunday meeting took place with the anticipated antipathy. To add to the childishness of the whole affair, Fergus Finlay, Labour's Press Officer, and Peter White, the Fine Gael Press Officer, sat outside the room trading insults at one another.

While Fergus and Dick Spring were having such juvenile fun going round town insulting Fine Gael, those who sought a coalition with Fianna Fáil were busy: contacts were made between Ruairi Quinn and Brian Lenihan that opened up negotiations. When the document agreeing a joint programme with Democratic Left arrived on Wednesday (9 December), it was sent to Fine Gael and the PDs, who were so unbelievably scattered that they didn't get around to replying to it. On the following day (Thursday), it was dispatched to Fianna Fáil. They had been waiting for it, and within four hours had returned a response – perhaps a response that had been prepared even before the document formally arrived.

Insults over, Dick Spring met John Bruton and Des O'Malley, the leader of the PDs, in the Dáil, supposedly now to work out the details of the new government. Labour absolutely insisted that it be given a share in the position of Taoiseach for two years of the Government's life. Also, it was an absolute that the Democratic Left Party be part of the government. This was on Monday of the same week. Further talks followed on Wednesday. On the lunchtime news, Barry Desmond announced that talks between Labour, Fine Gael, and the PDs were about to begin. But he was wrong, and was very quickly contradicted. By now, Barry had been frozen out of the inner circle where those favouring a coalition with Fianna Fáil now held the whip hand. When the response of the Fianna Fáil Party arrived on Thursday, surprise, surprise, they had agreed to everything. The party that had opposed the divorce referendum in 1986 now favoured divorce; the party that had restricted contraceptives to married couples, now advocated availability of contraceptives for all. They were even in favour of gay rights – you just had to admire Fianna Fáil for sheer brass neck.

Dick and Fergus were now trapped. There was no denying the attractiveness of the Fianna Fáil response; after all, it was just a rehash of the Labour general election Manifesto. It was as if Dick had returned to his office and found one of those 'While you were out' messages left there. It would have read:

Dear Dick,

While you were out we decided to form a coalition with Fianna Fáil.

Regards,

Ruairi and the boys

P.S. You're to be Tánaiste under the new arrangement, congratulations!

To add to the surreal nature of the fiasco, Fine Gael and the PDs now took insult and withdrew from talks; their timing was as inept as their whole handling of their side of the talks. They left just at the time when they could have taken Dick and Fergus out of the hole they had dug for themselves and propelled their respective parties into government. Their reasoning was that they would not be involved in competing negotiations! Of course, they hadn't even replied to the document sent to them on Wednesday. As Fianna Fáil had agreed to all Labour's policies, all that had to be decided on was the spoils; the number of ministerial and junior ministerial seats, the number of Senate seats, who was to be Attorney General etc. This is where Fianna Fáil comes into its own. A strange thing happened now, as the proposals that had been absolute positions with Fine Gael, like the rotation of the position of Taoiseach and the involvement of Democratic Left in government, were dropped like hot potatoes. Most baffling of all, Albert Reynolds, the most unpopular Taoiseach in the history of the Irish State, was to remain on. But first of all, the PLP had to be squared. The fatal meetings of the PLP were held on Monday 14 December, both before and after the Dáil resumed. On that day, Albert Reynolds failed to be re-elected as Taoiseach and submitted his resignation to President Mary Robinson. He remained on as acting Taoiseach and the talks detailing the arrangements with Labour got under way.

That same day, Sean Treacy, the Independent TD for South Tipperary, was elected as Ceann Comhairle. This was partly as a smokescreen to indicate that a non-Fianna Fáil coalition was still possible. It was amazing how many in the media fell for it. The meetings of 14 December were watershed ones for the party and for Dick Spring. He was uncharacteristically emotional at the final meeting. The second meeting was the crucial one and it commenced at 7.30 p.m. and lasted till 10.10 p.m. The early meeting concerned itself with the technicalities of the proposals for Taoiseach; all nominees for the position would be beaten to allow negotiations to continue. Dick Spring did say that the party had the responsibility to form a government and that the meeting must continue in the evening to assess the situation. As the adjourned meeting started, he asked for the authority of the meeting to start 'serious' discussions with Fianna Fáil. He found it remarkable that Fine Gael had not even produced a document on a possible government programme. Questioned about the Fianna Fáil document he said that it was so compatible with Labour's own Manifesto that we could have drawn it up ourselves – I think he may have hit the mark there without even knowing it.

Brendan Howlin outlined the contents of the Fianna Fáil document. Michael Ferris and Tommy Broughan expressed a fear that talks might give 'the kiss of life' to the discredited Fianna Fáil leadership. Jim Kemmy, as would be expected, was more blunt: 'You are supping with the devil,' he told Dick Spring, 'Fianna Fáil is the party of jobbery, corruption, and land speculation.' Róisín Shortall asked that Fine Gael be approached again and asked for a document. She was supported by Séamus Pattison, who reminded the meeting that the electorate had voted for change. Now the meeting began to develop the flavour that was to be its trademark for the rest of the twenty-seventh Dáil, i.e. very gently at first but getting more noticeable as the evening wore on, the meeting polarised between those favouring a coalition with Fianna Fáil and those opposing. Brendan Howlin, Mervyn Taylor, and Emmet Stagg lined up behind the Fianna Fáil option. They were greatly assisted by the crass remarks and behaviour of the PD Leader Des O'Malley, who had said that 'Michael D Higgins would go mad in Government'. Even members who had at times been critical of Michael D inside the party weren't going to take that. It had become obvious during this period that neither Des O'Malley nor John Bruton had a clue how to conduct negotiations.

The one item all speakers agreed on was that Dick Spring would have their total support in his negotiations. This was a fateful day for him: he was to lead the Labour Party for less than five years more. For him, this was the last meeting at which he would have the full support of the entire PLP. At the end of the meeting, he expressed gratitude for the trust he was being given, in a tone that was full of sincerity, almost to the point of sadness. It was indeed a sad moment as it marked his separation from so many of his colleagues, some of whom had been his strongest supporters. From now on, until his resignation, he would be dealing with a deeply divided PLP.

Northern Ireland has since been mentioned as a reason why the Fianna Fáil option was chosen. This is the sum total of discussions had regarding Northern Ireland at the meeting of 14 December. Liam Kavanagh asked, 'What about Northern Ireland?' and there was no reply. The matter was not raised again. Pat Upton did not speak at this meeting, which was unusual for him. I spoke to him about it afterwards: he said that he was too shocked to make a contribution when he realised that the leadership had already agreed to go into coalition with Fianna Fáil. He was the first member of the PLP, apart from the negotiators, to figure out what had happened. From this date on, it was war in the trenches, of varying degrees of intensity, between the pro and anti-Fianna Fáil factions in the party.

The honeymoon ends

It had been two and a half weeks since the election and now everything was changing rapidly. The high regard in which the party had been held was vanishing. The springtide was ebbing rapidly.

Head office was in the eye of the storm, and on one of these days we had 104 telephone calls of complaint about our plans to enter government with

Fianna Fáil. I passed them all over to Dick's office. One morning, Angie was in early and the phone rang, when she discovered that the caller was another complainer, she announced that she was the cleaning lady and that no member of staff had arrived for work yet. The PLP was to meet twice more before the new government was formed, but from now on the opposition to the formation of the Labour–Fianna Fáil coalition was solidifying, though it had no leadership.

At the meeting of 22 December, Dick Spring said that as far as negotiations with Fianna Fáil were concerned, they were so compliant on policy matters that he felt if he asked for a return to the Commonwealth they would agree. I believe that at this stage he was completely committed to the option of coalition with Fianna Fáil, especially given their willingness to concede on every policy issue important to Labour. Fergus Finlay, on the other hand, was never committed to this strategy in my opinion, which made his role as adviser to Dick Spring and his extreme influence over him very dangerous to the continuation of the arrangement. At this stage, the plot to enter Government with Fianna Fáil could have been overturned by the concerted action of the TDs, the majority of whom opposed such an arrangement, but they had no focus and no leader to make such a move. Many of them were living in hope of a position in the new Government and thus were not going to rock the boat. Others were just getting used to the idea of being TDs. Just a few were genuinely supportive of the idea, without any vested interest in their own preferment; these included Pat Gallagher of Laois-Offaly, and Eamon Walsh, who was elected along with Mervyn Taylor in Dublin South-West. I was still busy on the Senate campaign. I had very little contact with Dick; in fact his only intervention was on behalf of Anne Gallagher to give her an easier Senate panel to contest than I had suggested. I switched her from the Cultural and Educational Panel to the Industrial and Commercial, where the quota is lower.

As sure as success follows success, we were to do well in the Senate elections. We gained an extra seat, bringing our total of elected senators to five. This, together with the four we would have from the Taoiseach's 11 nominees, our one MEP, and our 33 TDs, would give us a PLP of 43, an enormous number by former standards for the Labour Party.

The final meeting of the PLP before entry into government was stormy and difficult and presaged, in more ways than one, the fractious period ahead. It was held on Thursday 7 January 1993, just three days before the party Delegate Conference to decide the issue. The first of the many scandals to hit the Labour–Fianna Fáil Administration broke the week before the Dáil was to sit to elect a new Taoiseach and Government. The allegation was that one member of the state's legal team in the Beef Tribunal, Mr Gerry Danaher, had threatened a member of Des O'Malley's legal team, Adrian Hardiman (who was later to become a Supreme Court judge). There was also a subsidiary allegation that confidential documents relating to Des O'Malley had been copied and delivered to Fianna Fáil headquarters. Dick Spring was distinctly nervous, but indicated that no evidence had as yet surfaced to back the allegations. His nervousness, I think, was a premonition for him of the welter of scandals he would have to face when he did enter Government with Fianna Fáil.

The meeting had been called to discuss the Programme for Government, which was circulated at the start. However, it soon became evident that the meeting was to be dominated by the allegations. A cloud hung over the new Government even before its appointment. Sean Ryan, Joe Costello, Pat Upton, and John Ryan all expressed the gravest of reservations to the point of rebellion. Their view as expressed by Pat Upton was that they had received votes in the election on the basis of integrity: could they now support Albert Reynolds for Taoiseach until this was cleared up? The big question, which is still asked during all scandals involving Fianna Fáil in Government, was put by Derek McDowell, the new member for Dublin North-Central. 'Did the Taoiseach know?' This controversy was to end with an examination by the Bar Council and an appeal by Mr Danaher, after which he was declared 'to have breached proper professional standards'. It certainly breached the meeting of the PLP. When the Programme for Government was reached it was nodded through without discussion.

Conference endorses coalition

On 30 December I received the command from Sally to book a Dublin venue for the Delegate Conference, which under Labour's constitution must take place to receive a report from the party leader as to whether or not it would enter Government. I was asked to try the National Concert Hall. I had my doubts as to whether it would accept a political booking, but to my surprise we were welcomed with open arms: being on good terms with Fianna Fáil was to open many doors as I soon learned.

The Conference took place on Sunday 10 January 1993. Getting the delegates was the next problem. I was seriously worried for a while that we would not produce a sufficient crowd but was soon allayed in my fears when the TDs who hoped for office sought to outdo each other in the size of their delegations. Carlow-Kilkenny threatened not to come at all. Out of all the constituencies they seemed most hostile, but of course at the end of the day, we almost filled the thousand-seat capacity hall. There was a great feeling of camaraderie as this was the first meeting after our marvellous election result. The TDs were as nervous as hell – the hungrier for office, the more on edge they were. I too was living on my nerves, these conferences are minefields; hundreds of things can go wrong every minute. I took charge of the speakers' list. I intended to let alternative speakers for and against address the floor.

At a conference in the National Concert Hall in 1993, the platform party enthusiastically vote to enter a coalition with Fianna Fáil.

Niamh Bhreathnach was Chair of the party and as such she would open Conference. I insisted that she do a rehearsal with me beforehand. I was lucky I did, she tripped on the way to the speaker's podium at the rehearsal. If that had happened during the Conference itself it would have brought the house down and with it, in all probability, Niamh's nascent ministerial career. Marion Boushell was in charge of the front of house where the delegates were checked in. It was a lax affair in comparison with the usual strict regulations for attendance at Labour Conferences. Emmet Stagg, who had previously been a thorn in the establishment's side, was now a part of it. Marion never thought that she would see Emmet's Secretary, David Moynan, given control of a check-in area, which he was – the poachers had turned gamekeepers.

My formula for getting alternate speakers for and against the motion was not meeting with much success. I just couldn't get enough speakers to speak against the motion. The delegate from Drogheda, Pat McDaid, pulled a fast one on me by telling me he would speak against the motion, which guaranteed him a speaking slot. Of course, when he got up to speak he gave a ringing endorsement of the Programme for Government, of Dick Spring, and of everything that could possibly influence Michael Bell's choice as a minister. Suzie Byrne said that she would eat her hat if Fianna Fáil introduced gay rights, but the main anti-coalition speaker was Paddy Costello from Mullinavat, Co Kilkenny. It must have taken considerable guts as no TD spoke against. In fact, the Conference was to ringingly endorse the proposal and especially its proposer Dick Spring. I had lined up Moosajee Bhamjee to speak, knowing what a hit he would be with the crowd. After he agreed to speak, he promptly dropped his head and went to sleep on the platform. I woke him up two slots before his own to give him time to pull himself together. Thinking that his wake up call was for his immediate slot at the podium, he rushed up, out of turn and was given a rapturous welcome. He was a natural performer and soon had the Conference eating out of his hand. He told the audience that the people of Clare had elected enough cowboys in their time and at the last election they had decided that it was now time to elect an Indian.

A total of 91 delegates offered themselves as speakers and we were able to accommodate 42 plus Dick Spring and Niamh Bhreathnach. In all, 37 spoke in favour of the Motion to enter coalition with Fianna Fáil (including Spring and Bhreathnach), five spoke clearly against and two speakers were unclear in their contributions. All trade union speakers spoke in favour. The proposal to enter Government with Fianna Fáil was carried by over 90 per cent of the delegates present and the platform party applauded wildly. Kirsti Spring, who sat near Dick on the platform, turned to her husband and was heard to say: 'See you in five years, Dick.' It was a sad little ending to such an important day and as clear an indication as possible of the personal sacrifices made by politicians' wives and husbands.

CHAPTER 13

THE PARTNERSHIP YEARS

IT WAS Monday 11 January 1993, the first morning after the Delegate Conference that decided that Labour would go into coalition with Fianna Fáil, and it felt like a different party. I was prepared to give it every chance and to be positive about the outcome, though it would not have been my choice at all. Recent history had shown that Fianna Fáil could not operate a coalition arrangement and anyway we had sought a mandate for change, not a continuance of Fianna Fáil-led Government. For years I had condemned the anti-coalitionists in the party because they refused to accept majority decisions. Now it was my turn to accept a decision that I believed to be bad for the party. Shortly after my arrival at work that morning, I got the news that nine members of the Cahir Branch (South Tipperary) had resigned in protest at the decision of the Delegate Conference to enter coalition with Fianna Fáil. This was not going to be easy.

The first day

On Tuesday, the Dáil met and elected Albert Reynolds as Taoiseach, receiving all the Labour Party's 33 votes along with 67 votes from Fianna Fáil and two independents: Neil Blaney from Donegal North-East and Johnny Fox from Wicklow. At this stage, Padraig Flynn had resigned to become a European Union Commissioner, thus avoiding much embarrassment for Labour, as we would have found it difficult to sit in Cabinet with him because of his personal attack on Mary Robinson on radio in 1990. I went over to Leinster House at lunchtime. It was a bright sunny winter's day and at the Kildare Street entrance I met Niamh Bhreathnach, resplendent in her brand new power suit. She had been getting in some last minute shopping and was weighed down by four Marks and Spencers' plastic carrier bags. I relieved her of the bags. 'A minister can't be seen entering Leinster House like a bag lady', I told her. 'Oh no one has told me anything about that', she confided in me unconvincingly. On the plinth outside Leinster House, a TV crew filmed prospective members of the new Government as they entered the House. At lunch I met Sally Clarke: 'I saw you on the *One O'Clock News* carrying plastic shopping bags into Leinster House', she said disapprovingly. 'Sorry about that Sally', I replied contritely. In the Dáil bar itself, stood Michael D Higgins and his wife, Sabina. He looked worried, 'Nothing can go wrong now, Ray?' He nervously asked. 'Nothing at all', I replied. In fact, the Cabinet line-up of Labour members had been published in that morning's *Irish Times*, setting a pattern of communication through newsleak that was to be a trademark of this Government.

By lunchtime, the Dáil Bar, the Restaurant, and their environs swarmed with TDs, their families, and supporters. Even the rawest deputy on the Fianna Fáil–Labour side secretly longed for the surprise call from their party leader to offer them ministerial office. The election of Taoiseach was a foregone conclusion with Fianna Fáil unable to believe their luck at being returned to power after an election in which they had lost nine seats. The Labour crowd was still intoxicated with the election results of the previous November and the 33 TDs it gave us. Now we would have six Government ministers and a Programme that was based on Labour's own. The negative aspects of entering Government with Fianna Fáil, whose rejection by the electorate was a major reason for our own success, and the leadership of Albert Reynolds, who had been the subject of every attack and the butt end of every joke, was blocked out. Like Scarlett O'Hara in *Gone With the Wind*, we would deal with that tomorrow, and tomorrow was another day.

But there was a detectable undercurrent, felt more keenly by those not swept along in the wave of excitement and by those whose expectations of ministerial office were on this day shattered. Liam Kavanagh, a minister in the previous Fine Gael–Labour Government was subdued and depressed. Jim Kemmy felt hurt and tricked. *The Irish Times* had asked his secretary, Margaret O'Donoghue, for his biography, acting, he thought, on information received from 'a Labour source'. He then realised that his name had been omitted from the ministerial list and believed that he had been set up by Fergus Finlay, who denied it. Kemmy had been leader of the Democratic Socialist Party before its merger with Labour and he had quite reasonably expected an appointment. Michael Ferris TD from Tipperary South, a fierce Spring loyalist, was surrounded by his family. When the announcements were made, he left Leinster House in dejection. All were gone by the evening, having melted away silently. Only Toddy O'Sullivan of Cork

South-Central, surrounded by supporters, railed against his rejection. It is a cruel system inflicting great pain and humiliation on those who do not receive 'the call'. But the mood of those remaining was high. Six ministers were to be appointed; the highest number Labour ever received.

The Irish Times had reported that Dick Spring was to become Tánaiste and also Minister for Foreign Affairs. This was more than a little perplexing for Labour members in that the Department of Foreign Affairs was new territory for us and not associated with our areas of traditional concerns. Ruairi Quinn was to become Minister for Enterprise and Employment, an area he was well tutored for, having been our outgoing Finance Spokesperson. Brendan Howlin was to become Minister for Health; a difficult task considering the size of the hospital waiting lists and the health cuts imposed by the outgoing governments of the previous six years, but a position of deep interest to the party. Michael D Higgins was to become our first Minister for Arts, Culture and the Gaeltacht, a position conjured up for him by Fergus Finlay, who always valued him highly in spite of their none too warm relationship. Niamh Bhreathnach, TD for Dun Laoghaire, was to become Labour's first Minister for Education. As a newly-elected TD and former teacher, she had beaten Eithne Fitzgerald, poll-topping TD for Dublin South, to the position of woman Government member (Labour had to appoint at least one women minister). Eithne was philosophical and said she didn't mind so long as she was given a 'meaningful' position as a junior minister when these were announced.

Mervyn Taylor became Minister for Equality and Law Reform. Dick Spring always had an almost filial devotion to Mervyn and had been very wounded when Mervyn had refused the position of Minister for Justice in the 1982–87 Government. Anyway, Mervyn had brought in his running mate Eamon Walsh. On this basis, and on the basis of his seniority, it would be hard to refuse him a position. Mervyn was 61 years old and he was not asked for any undertaking that he would contest the next general election. It was a major oversight that didn't surprise me. When the general election came around, Mervyn, then over 65 years old, decided not to contest. He had been threatening to leave politics since 1989 and not only was his own Dáil seat lost, but also that of his running mate.

In the evening I returned to the Dáil Bar after the appointments had been announced. The atmosphere was triumphalist and wildly optimistic. These new ministers would dominate the Government and give it a Labour complexion, especially considering the fact that there were six of them. With Dick Spring's leadership, we were watching history in the making.

Moosajee Bhamjee, the newly-elected Clare TD, was in party mood. Moving from group to group he joked about himself, his careers as psychiatrist and politician, about his never being in Leinster House before and his having to ring Labour head office to get directions to it. James Wrynn, the Financial Secretary of the party brought all who were willing back to his house in Ranelagh to party further. Brendan Howlin, now complete with state car and Garda driver, arrived with another load of guests. He left the driver sitting in the car outside and when asked why he didn't take him in for a drink, informed the shocked questioner that that was what he was paid for. As we start so do we continue.

Appointments of senior and junior ministers

Shock waves were felt throughout the party at the appointments. Liam Kavanagh, Labour's most experienced minister had been dropped completely. Jim Kemmy, who had been leader of his own small party wasn't offered even a junior position. Séamus Pattison, who had played such a crucial role in keeping Dick Spring in power at the 1989 Conference and was a former junior minister of the 1982–87 Administration, was likewise dropped. Toddy O'Sullivan, who had been a junior minister from 1986–87 was not offered any position, nor was Michael Ferris of Tipperary South. There was no minister from the northside of Dublin, where the party now held six seats, almost a fifth of its total. Experienced and senior people like Joe Costello and Pat Upton were overlooked. The opportunistic nature of the appointments soon showed itself. Of the 11 appointments, junior and senior, five would have been sponsored by Labour Left. It seemed as if these positions were being used as a method to remove any internal opposition in the party. The five junior ministers (ministers of state) appointed were Eithne Fitzgerald, TD for Dublin South, at the Department of Finance and the Office of the Tánaiste; Joan Burton, who was TD for Dublin West, at the Department of Social Welfare; Brian O'Shea, TD for Waterford, at the Department of Agriculture, Food and Forestry; Gerry O'Sullivan, TD for Cork North-Central at the Department of the Marine, and last but certainly not least, the unflappable Emmet Stagg at the Department of the Environment. I heard the senior team line up on Tuesday and I assumed that the junior appointments would bring balance, taking in those who were now bewildered and becoming embittered. They asked me rhetorically what they had done to offend Dick Spring.

Jim Kemmy was deeply wounded at his exclusion. He believed that he had been set up and fooled. His partner, Patsy Harrold, later told me that he had decided not to accept a junior post, but to be ignored completely was as humiliating as it was inexplicable. I think it was a great mistake and I felt sorry for Jim, whom I believe would have made a great minister. To make matters worse, each TD who did not receive an appointment was sent a letter by Dick Spring. The name of the recipient was not typed in but filled out in biro. The letter spoke of Dick choosing 'the strongest possible team', making a rather obvious implication about the TDs who received the letters. Rather than placating the recipients, this letter made them even angrier. Jim Kemmy even went to the trouble of replying to his. 'In the last few weeks I have learnt a lot about politics...', he wrote.

'Don't worry,' he said to me, as if I had been the injured party, 'we'll have some fun yet.' He predicted that the Coalition would last only half way into its term. On a cold Sunday night, 13 December 1992, I had attended the twenty-fifth anniversary celebrations of Cllr Ned Brennan's membership of Tipperary South Riding County Council in the Caman Inn in Killenaule. There, Billy Healy said the same to me. I thought they were both crazy. A Government with such a mandate from our Delegate Conference and such a majority in the Dáil must surely last its full term, yet its disintegration came about in the timescale Jim and Billy had predicted, lasting less than two years. But before this, there were many trials and battles and indeed many great achievements.

Ministers' relatives and the Tánaiste's Department

The nightmare began almost immediately. The party that had been the flavour of the month in November could now do nothing right. Each senior minister appointed a Programme Manager (so called as they were in charge of overseeing the implementation of the Programme for Government) and a Special Adviser. The programme managers, who were sort of 'super advisers', were paid over £40,000 per annum and the advisers somewhat less. At this time, TDs received about £34,000 per annum. I thought it was wrong to pay unelected advisers more than TDs. The junior minister could appoint one adviser and two drivers (the senior ministers had Garda drivers). In addition, the Tánaiste was given a whole new Department, which was to be the clearing house of the Labour side of the Government. In each minister's office, there was at least one further secretarial appointment. It was all a bit extravagant and a bit unnecessary. It was certainly out of line with the traditional frugality and modesty of Labour.

There was a public outcry, but in truth, many in Labour weren't too enamoured with these trappings, especially given the poor state of the country's finances at the time. The level of the pay was not the major issue, but rather the large number of advisers and their total cost. The cost of the Tánaiste's new Department was also an issue. Fianna Fáil were clever enough though, as one would expect; they accepted the programme managers and advisers, but the appointments to their own Departments were mainly civil servants, while Labour appointed party members or supporters. The attack then was on Labour, not on Fianna Fáil. To accentuate the issue many of the appointments were given to relatives of the ministers. This was just the type of public relations disaster that one would have thought that a system of advisers was invented to avoid. All the attacks came down on the head of Labour. There was no honeymoon for the Labour part of this Coalition. The critics were not confined to the enemies of Labour, far from it; these appointments did not go down well within the party. We had not been fighting jobbery in Fianna Fáil for the previous 60 years just to join in when the opportunity suited us. There was no action taken on this early blunder.

Inevitably, the ministers who had no part in it suffered as much as those who did. Niamh Bhreathnach, Emmet Stagg, and Gerry O'Sullivan had all appointed their daughters to jobs in their Departments. In vain did Noeline Dunphy, Constituency Secretary of Carlow-Kilkenny, protest that if Séamus Pattison had been given an appointment he would not have damaged the party like this. Sitting in the Dáil Bar the week that this controversy broke, I was having coffee with a group that included Cliona Ferris, Niamh's daughter, when Jim Kemmy joined us. I introduced him to Cliona, but the penny did not drop about her being the Minister's daughter. 'What the hell is Niamh doing appointing her daughter?' asked an indignant Jim. 'I don't know,' I mumbled and then said in as low a voice as I could, 'Cliona is Niamh's daughter.' 'Why didn't you tell me?' asked an embarrassed Jim, who was always courteous. It was the same with the other appointees. These daughters were far too decent for the situations in which they found themselves. All the blame rests fairly on their appointers. Gerry O'Sullivan's excuse was the worst of all: 'My daughter was on the dole and I wasn't going to put up with that', he told a PLP meeting too embarrassed to look him in the face. The three ministerial daughters, whom I knew personally, were very young women just starting their careers. None of them would have chosen politics. They were the victims of indulgent and embarrassing parents, who should have let them go off and find employment on their own, thus saving themselves and everyone else (including the Labour Party) a whole lot of trouble.

The PLP shapes up

When I think back to the bitterness and lack of trust in the first meetings of the PLP, I wonder how the Coalition lasted even as long as it did. The non-office holders decided to form their own group, 'The Backbench Committee', soon called the BBC for short. Here the ministers were excluded and members could discuss their grievances in private. It didn't last, in fact it made little sense to exclude the ministers, other than to make them uncomfortable, and enough of that happened at the full meetings of the PLP.

The only minister who seemed to be able to ride the storm was Michael D Higgins, in spite of the incredible difficulties of his brief, such as the building of an Interpretative Centre at Mullaghmore in the middle of the Burren, which was causing outrage to conservationists. Soon he would make the development of the Arts a distinctly left-wing project. At the PLP, he used his sense of humour to weather the storm, while all the other ministers were getting upset. 'And now for the Great Cultural Revolution', he announced as he first spoke as Minister. As for his brief as Minister for the Gaeltacht: 'No minister has even visited the office for three years, its like Miss Havisham's room', he announced in an animated fashion eliciting the first laugh from the PLP since the Government took office. There were quarrelsome meetings on 26 and 27 January and Dick Spring was so surprised at the level of antagonism that he remarked, 'Things are worse than I thought.'

The perceived briefing to *The Irish Times* before the TDs were informed caused particular ire. Pat Upton referred to the paper as the new *Iris Oifigiúil*, alluding to the official newsletter for Government announcements. I had never seen this phenomenon before, but when Pat made that allusion, the hair actually stood up on the back of Dick Spring's head. Michael Bell brought to the attention of the ministers that new cuts had been introduced by the new Minister for Social Welfare, Charlie McCreevy, during the negotiations with Labour. One can imagine the uproar this caused.

Sean Ryan warned of the Aer Lingus storm ahead, particularly in the light of a negative reply about extra funding made in response to a Dáil question by Brian Cowan, the Fianna Fáil Minister for Transport, Energy, and Communications. Jim Kemmy said that since gaining power the Government was going round like a headless chicken. Insult was followed by counter insult. There was heavy criticism of the difficulties ministers were having dealing with queries from Labour members and fury was expressed at letters received back from the Department of Education, signed by civil servants and formally addressing the TDs. Ministers were being given no time to settle in and establish their systems.

Toddy O'Sullivan fumed at the manner in which he had been informed that he would not be appointed to ministerial office. The party had forgotten its roots, none of 'the cloth cap brigade' had been appointed, nor had anyone with trade union experience. He had never been so insulted in his life. Trust had disappeared so completely that Pat Upton demanded that Dick Spring refute rumours that he was about to appoint Eric Byrne, the defeated Democratic Left candidate in Dublin South-Central, to the Senate. Dick Spring made a vain attempt to calm things down and said that he would give time to repairing personal relationships, but in his next breath said that if he was to do it all over again he would do the same. He defended Fergus Finlay and said that he was working for the party at half his value. This didn't go down too well with TDs who were earning considerably less than Fergus. Ministers appealed for support from the members, referred to the massive support the Coalition had from the Delegate Conference and in the opinion polls. The ministers were working night and day to get command of their briefs and were now besieged by a hostile media as well as a deeply antagonistic PLP. That none of this was foreseen by Dick Spring or Fergus Finlay was incredible to me. It was a total mess and Labour had not been in power for even a month.

Two more blows; the tax amnesty and Aer Lingus

Nothing illustrated the bind Labour was in more than the 1993 tax amnesty. It was agreed by the Cabinet on 25 March. This was to be the second such amnesty in five years. The theory was simple: let those who had hidden money from the Revenue Commissioners now declare it and they would be charged a mere 15 per cent penalty within six months of the amnesty. The morality of the issue was equally simple: those who had defrauded the state were to be let off in the interest of increased revenue. The 'Pay As You Earn' taxpayer, who had been carrying the state, would never enjoy such easy treatment. The ministers were very anxious to get their hands on the money to spend on such things as social services and the abolition of the 1 per cent levy imposed in the 1993 Budget. Pat Upton, as usual, explained it all: 'There was a concept of morality when I was last acquainted with it, that said that the end does not justify the means and this applies now as much as it did then. We are the party of integrity and ethics. How do we explain this? This is Fianna Fáil behaviour.'

The tax amnesty went through with spectacular success; but it was a disaster for Labour and is still pointed out as a moral low point of the Partnership Government. Though many in Fianna Fáil opposed the amnesty (even the Finance Minister Bertie Ahern), no blame was attached to them for agreeing to it. But then of course, they never portrayed themselves as a party of morality. As Róisín Shortall pointed out: if one person went to jail for defrauding tax, it would lend some credibility to the scheme, but nobody was sent to jail for this reason, not then, and not during the period of that Government or the next. It was not until October 2000 that the first jail sentence for tax fraud was handed down and that, ironically, during the period of a Fianna Fáil–PD Government.

The Aer Lingus issue was another critical problem for the party. It was a major issue in the general election campaign, especially in the Dublin Northside constituencies. Dick Spring had addressed a meeting in a hanger in Dublin Airport and promised funding to bail out the ailing company. Other candidates made even more extravagant promises. Few realised the disastrous state of the company until the party gained power. Another crucial feature was that the Minister for Transport, Energy, and Communications in charge of the affair was Brian Cowan of Laois-Offaly. This Minister was particularly unsympathetic to Dublin Labour TDs and their ailing company. A new management was moved in and the dreadful white elephant appendage to Aer Lingus, the parasitical Team Aer Lingus, an airline maintenance company, was phased out. All this was done in an atmosphere of mistrust, accusation, high handedness, and subterfuge. It ended in the expulsion of four of the six Labour Northside TDs from the PLP in 1994.

Events came to a head in June 1994 with Team now charging 30 per cent more than its competitors. The issuing of redundancy notices sparked a Fine Gael motion in the Dáil. This could have been weathered had not Minister Cowan, without Government approval, lodged an amendment supporting the new developments in Team. This was more than some TDs could bear, they were committed to supporting the craft unions that represented the Team workers.

An effort was made by Michael Bell, himself an experienced trade unionist, and Jim Kemmy, also an experienced trade unionist, to come up with a formula that would defuse the situation. The episode showed up the total lack of trade union expertise in the Labour Cabinet members. Dick Spring and Ruairi Quinn undertook to speak with Brian Cowan with a view to getting him to withdraw his amendment. I knew they were wasting their time; Brian Cowan would have no sympathy for such wetness. That day I had lunch with Sean Ryan, the TD for Dublin North, who stood to lose most from the debacle. He did not owe his seat to the victory of 1992 but to two decades of hard work in Fingal on behalf of the party. He had been elected to the Dáil in 1989. He asked me what I thought Brian Cowan would do when Ruairi Quinn approached him on the subject.

I knew Brain Cowan only slightly on a personal level, but extremely well as the TD for Laois-Offaly. I told Sean of the graphic language that Brian Cowan would use in refusing a lifeline to Labour. So it transpired: the Minister refused to withdraw his amendment and Sean Ryan, Tommy Broughan, Joe Costello, and Derek McDowell refused to vote for it. They were expelled the very next day from the PLP. I was deeply in sympathy with them even though I did not condone their failure to support a Government amendment. They had been caught up in the excess of their own honourable promises to the workers and unions, not that they got any thanks from either, though virtue is its own reward. The whole episode again illustrated the impossibility of working in Government with Fianna Fáil. All the bad news could be shoved onto the trapped-in junior partner. It was June 1994, just 18 months after entering Government and the future was bleak.

Not that it was all bad news by any manner of means. The difficulties for Labour were matched by some remarkable achievements. The punt had been devalued by 10 per cent on 30 January 1993 and later on that year a transfer to Ireland of £7.85 billion in European Union Structural funds started a growth pattern in the Irish economy that later became known as 'The Celtic Tiger'. Accompanying the growth was a consequent drop in unemployment that was over 300,000 in early 1993. The slow but steady take-off of the economy occurred as the Labour ministers took office. This was unprecedented. On all other occasions, Labour entered power to find a world recession taking place or just around the corner. Labour is very much a spending party and the increases in revenue allowed the ministers a scope in the area of expenditure that enabled them to introduce many initiatives. This coupled with the Fianna Fáil compliance on policy issues meant a rush of new Labour-influenced achievements. Brendan Howlin in Health was able to pump money into hospitals to reduce the waiting lists. He was able to introduce legislation liberalising contraception laws – even to the extent of allowing for the sale of condoms through vending machines – and to make a major contribution to services for the mentally disabled and introduce a hard-hitting Aids Prevention Programme.

Niamh Bhreathnach, as Minister for Education, was able to channel extra funding into her Department and signal her plans for major reforms. Her major initiatives were, however, to await the fall of the Fianna Fáil-Labour Coalition, as was Mervyn Taylor's in the Department of Equality and Law Reform. For Michael D Higgins, it was full steam ahead. He re-established the Irish Film Board and with the use of judicious tax allowances, turned Ireland into a major film producer. His establishment of the Irish language television station *Telifís na Gaeilge* did not happen until 1996, but the groundwork took place here. Emmet Stagg too was a major success and people in the party who had previously lined up to drown him out, now lined up as his greatest admirers. He was officially the Minister of State at the Department of the Environment, but soon gained the well-earned title of the Minister for Housing. He more than trebled the number of local authority houses built in his first year in office and threatened inept local authority maintenance departments with privatisation if they didn't improve their performance. He also brought in legislation compelling the use of Rent Books for tenants in private rented accommodation. Ruairi Quinn made May Day a public holiday in 1994, something that had been refused him in the Fine Gael–Labour Coalition of 1982–87. Joan Burton, as Minister of State at the Department of Social Welfare, presided over the biggest ever increase in Child Benefit: 26.6 per cent. Meanwhile, Eithne Fitzgerald in the Department of Finance had been given control of the National Development Plan, which would account for the spending of the Structural Funds.

Dick Spring in the Department of Foreign Affairs was in a senior Department, but one of little traditional concern or interest to Labour voters except its small section on overseas development aid. This he more than trebled during his period in Foreign Affairs. It was, however, for the remarkable events in Northern Ireland that he gained the limelight. Perhaps it might be better said that he shared the limelight with Taoiseach Albert Reynolds, and as we know the limelight is a difficult thing to share. As Minister for Foreign Affairs he had an important role in the Northern Ireland peace talks, as did Minister for Justice Máire Geoghegan-Quinn. The achievement was remarkable and has stood the test of time. It was John Hume's foresight that finally brought about the end of 33 years of slaughter. The leadership of Sinn Féin in the hands of Gerry Adams meant that a younger, more internationally-minded Republican movement was in place that would do business. The third member of the ménage was that superb maker of deals, none other than the Taoiseach Albert Reynolds. With these three ingredients a deal was possible, and with an American President actively aiding the process it was unstoppable.

There is no doubt in my mind either that war weariness in the IRA was a significant underlying factor in the whole process. The scheme was so enormous and ambitious that many even in the SDLP were sceptical about its chances of success. As part of my duties, I took it upon myself to attend the Annual Fundraising Dinner of the SDLP in the Burlington Hotel. In 1993, it was a dismal affair, full of pessimism and dark undercurrents about John Hume being 'past it'. It was also badly attended. In 1994 it was a sell-out and I witnessed the remarkable spectacle of Seamus Mallon apologising publicly to his leader, John Hume, for his lack of belief in his ability to deliver a cease-fire. Seamus Mallon went up considerably in my estimation after that and I rapidly dropped the rather condescending Labour attitude to him as a mere manifestation of Fianna Fáil in the six counties.

For Labour, the process was a strange mixture of worthiness and remoteness. The Northern Ireland situation never had the same resonance for our party as it did for the Civil War parties of Fianna Fáil and Fine Gael. For Labour, republicanism had a deeper meaning than mere territorial integration; it meant a reunion of the peoples of Ireland. Nevertheless, it was with considerable pride that it noted Dick Spring's role in the process especially considering that he had played a similar role in the 1985 Anglo-Irish Agreement.

A joint declaration was signed by the British and Irish Governments on 15 December 1993, known as the Downing Street Declaration. It recognised the key role of the Irish people in the affairs of Northern Ireland and sought to legitimise the Sinn Féin Party. The British Prime Minister, John Major, said that if the IRA rejected violence within three months then the British Government could engage in talks with them. This was the key. As a follow-up, the Irish Government removed Section 31 of the Broadcasting Act, which had denied Sinn Féin use of the airwaves. After much internal debate, the IRA declared a cease-fire on 31 August 1994 to be followed by the Loyalist Paramilitaries' cease-fire on 13 October of the same year. Since then, even with temporary breakdowns of the cease-fires, the violence has never returned to its pre-1994 levels. It has been a major work for peace; of all the achievements of the Partnership Government this stands out. Of course the widespread and much deserved adulation that Albert Reynolds received in all this did not go down too well in some quarters. Formerly attacked as an underachiever, he was now attacked for being 'a high king on a roll'. It was hard for poor Albert.

There were other major landmarks for this short-lived Government. On Thursday 24 July 1993 the Dáil removed the 132-year-old prohibition on homosexual acts. Many believed that Fianna Fáil could never get itself around this. Suzie Byrne had remarked at the Delegate Conference in the National Conference Hall: 'I will eat my hat if Fianna Fáil legislated for gay rights' – but it did happen. It was a major achievement in the so-called Liberal Agenda. Its progress through Cabinet was symptomatic of the enormous policy flexibility of the major partner. When proposed by the Justice Minister Máire Geoghegan-Quinn, it went through without any discussion whatsoever. In the Dáil the Bill passed without a debate or a vote, a most dignified entry into a liberal society. It had been included in the Joint Programme for Government but Mervyn Taylor, Minister for Equality and Law Reform, made it clear that it was a matter for the Department of Justice and not for him. The plucky Justice Minister had no hesitation in introducing it and rightly received many plaudits for her handling of the issue.

At Christmas in 1993 I was over in Government Buildings, those beautifully appointed offices which will always be remembered as one of Charlie Haughey's more positive contributions to the state. Sitting in the courtyard at the wheel of her state car was Eithne Fitzgerald, Minister of State at the Department of Finance. I went over to her. 'Eithne,' I said, 'you're the Minister, you're supposed to be the one that is driven around.' She laughed and said, 'You know I don't drink very much so I'm letting my driver and the people from the office have a few and I'll drive them home.' What a great attitude, I thought.

The year 1993 ended on a happy and optimistic note with the Downing Street Declaration and I thought that things might settle down at last. Even if it was chilly outside with the electorate, the prestige of Dick Spring inside the party remained very high. The PLP was beginning to settle down too, though I thought it would never recover from the bruising experiences of the mishandling of the entry into Government. I was wrong: looking back it seems that the tone of this Government had been set and that this tone was one of scandal from the Fianna Fáil side and of blame on Labour for putting up with it all.

Labour Head Office staff in 1993. (L-R) Dermot Lacey, Jackie Byrne, Marion Boushell, Ray Kavanagh, Pamela Foley, and Angie Mulroy.

The 'Passports for Sale' affair

In May 1994 the 'Passports for Sale' issue broke. It appeared that an Arab family, the Masris, had been given a number of Irish passports on foot of their heavy investment in CD Foods, which had been owned by Albert Reynolds. It astonished a general public that many thought had become immune to scandal. Dick Spring offered to examine the files in the Department of Justice to see if any wrongdoing had taken place. The PLP greeted this with exasperation, surely the Minister for Justice would hardly keep incriminating evidence on file about her Taoiseach in her own Department. Anyway, it happened and Dick Spring didn't find any evidence of 'wrongdoing' in the files as everybody in the country had figured out beforehand. It was this incident that gave rise to Michael McDowell's very damaging remark that Dick Spring was morally brain-dead. At this stage, however, Labour had its own troubles. The curse of Paddy Costello of Mullinavat, made at the Delegate Conference in the National Concert Hall, had descended on the party. He prophesied: 'If you lay down with dogs you'll get fleas.' True enough, things had now become particularly itchy.

The 'Minister in the Park' affair

On 25 November 1993 I was informed by a parliamentarian that a Labour junior minister had been questioned by Gardaí in the Phoenix Park in an place well known as a pick-up area for gay men going right back to Roger Casement's time in the early nineteen hundreds. The Minister in question was Emmet Stagg. It was a bit of a joke at first among Spring's people, but so many knew about it that it was soon leaked to the press. Nevertheless, it was the type of thing that one hoped would just go away. No offence had been committed and Emmet had turned out to be one of our best ministers. I had been his greatest enemy previously and now I saw him outperform senior ministers. He was also very happily married and had a lovely wife and family, whom I knew would be distressed if this type of thing were made public. There was no need for these good people to be hurt.

There is a strong and admirable tradition in the Irish media that allows a politician his or her own personal life and does not intrude. In this way, the Irish media was always far superior to the British and it is one of the aspects of our public life that I hope will continue. I put a lot of trust in this convention and it nearly worked; I think perhaps that at a different time it would have, but the air was redolent of scandal and when one died down another surfaced. I discussed the matter with Emmet in early February 1994 at the Leinster Euro Convention in Kildare and he was understandably a worried man. I told him that if he stood up to all this he would become a hero. Emmet, who is pale by nature, was sallow with worry. When I said this to him, whatever little blood left in his face drained away. But I had every intention of supporting him fully.

It all came to a head on the weekend of 6 March 1994 with newspaper reports about the mysterious 'Minister in the Park'. I think it could still have been weathered, but that was not to be Labour's way. On the same day, Pat Magner and Fergus Finlay advised Dick Spring to ask for Emmet's resignation. The twisted logic behind it was that in Britain when a scandal occurred in the John Major Government, the person in question was invariably given support for a number of days and then forced to resign by the hostile media. This, I was told, would damage the Government more. Emmet, being the plucky man that he was just refused to resign and called their bluff. Luckily for all concerned, including themselves, they hesitated to fire him but were on the point of doing so on Monday morning when I came on the scene. I was flabbergasted by what had occurred. The English model, which had been so frequently held up as being cruel and invasive, was to be followed. Whatever about the denizens of the Sally Empire, the Labour members would go mad at this news.

It took me a while to compose myself and figure out a plan of campaign. I spoke to both Pat Magner and to Fergus Finlay. I strongly supported Emmet and told them of the uproar his dismissal would cause in the party. The members just would not stand for it. I told them that I had spoken to Emmet that morning and he would not resign and that I would stand over my prediction. If he were dismissed, then it would be the end not only of the present Government, but also of the leadership of Dick Spring. This scenario, would, I thought, get a few knickers in a twist over in the empire.

I sat back and waited and soon my moral indignation wilted and my humour returned, so much so that when Ruairi Quinn rang to see what was going on, I was able to greet him with a 'Good morning Ruairi, Oh what a Gay day!' By the afternoon, the crisis had passed and people were queuing up to support the beleaguered Emmet. Included in these was Pat Cox, the Independent MEP who was trenchant in his support on the popular RTE programme *Questions and Answers* that night. Emmet found that he had many more supporters than were available at the top levels of his own party. Among those who wrote to him in support was none other than my old friend, Anne Spring, Dick's mother. He prepared to return to the Dáil Chamber in the same week, this would be a difficult experience as he would be under the critical gaze of his peers. It is a long walk down from the junior ministerial offices to the Dáil Chamber and it would be particularly harrowing that day. Emmet was surprised when a knock came to his door. It was Pat 'the Cope' Gallagher, the Donegal South-East TD and Minister for State at the Department of the Gaeltacht. 'Would you like me to walk with you down to the Chamber?' It was a kindness that Emmet deeply appreciated.

On Monday mornings, Jim Kemmy did clinics in the Pike Inn on the Ballysimon Road in Limerick. From there, he was interviewed for the *One O'Clock News* about the speculation in the Sunday papers. Jim called on the Minister in question 'to make a clean breast of it'. There was a despicable attempt to link Jim Kemmy to some sort of outing of Emmet by this remark. Jim, who was the most humane and liberal of politicians, didn't even know that Emmet was the Minister in question and that very day took the head off me for not letting him know. But I could envisage the scenario: fire Emmet and put the blame on Jim Kemmy. It was not to be, mainly because of the courage of the Kildare Deputy in facing them down. For that if for nothing else we owe him a debt of gratitude. The whole affair then blew over showing a new liberality in Irish society. Not only did Emmet hold on to his job, but he went on to be re-elected quite easily at the following general election.

Of course we didn't lose our sense of humour over the incident. Angie revised the list of possible prizes in the Labour Raffle. It now included 'a bicycle without a saddle' and 'a ride in a state car'!

Who fears to speak of '98?

As part of the Euro Campaign preparations I travelled to Newmarket in Co. Cork to team up with Jim Kemmy. Local Senator Bill Cashin had a function he wanted us to attend. Jim arrived resplendent in an anti-hare-coursing sweater (it had a hare as its badge). We attended the rather pleasant social function, made our speeches, and met the crowd. That night, the local organisation directed me to the accommodation they had very obligingly booked. It was a refurbished two-storey house at the end of a dark tree-lined avenue. I was terrified even before I got to the house, but luckily Bill Cashin spotted me on the road and drove me to my door. Inside, even on this warm autumn night (26 September 1993) I felt a chill go right through me as I entered the empty house. There was no way of locking the door, so I put some furniture against it and tried to sleep with the light on while I spent the night in terror. Exhausted in the morning I drove back to Dublin much worse for the wear.

Next day I told Bill Cashin of my ordeal. 'I'm not surprised,' he replied knowingly, 'there were up to a hundred local men hanged in the yard in front of that door after the 1798 Rebellion.' Thank God I didn't know beforehand!

Bernie for Brussels, Orla for the Balkans

In late 1993 the job of member of the Court of Auditors in Luxembourg came up. Its filling had not been included in any of the negotiations for Government, but Barry Desmond fought hard for the position. He was Labour's sole MEP, having been elected in 1989 for the Dublin Constituency. MEPs have replacement lists so that in the case of their death or resignation no by-election is necessary and the person next on the list can take over. Barry was given the job and it seems as if there was little or no opposition within Fianna Fáil to his appointment. The problems arose when it came to filling Barry's position as MEP. The next person on the list was Joan Burton, but Joan was now a high performing and high profile Minister of State and loving every minute of it. A more selfish person might have given it up for the comfort and money of the Brussels gravy train but not Joan. She was committed to her role in Government and she even gave me a document forgoing her rights in this regard.

The next replacement candidate was our Councillor for the Malahide local electoral area on Dublin County Council, Bernie Malone. A solicitor by profession, Bernie, and her barrister husband Frank, made a formidable political team. She was first elected to the Dublin County Council in 1979. Very famous in her own area as the enemy of greedy developers, she also contested the 1981, November 1982 and 1987 general elections. She had a reputation for having an award-winning temper, prone to occasional outbursts of tears and screeches; she had once thrown a gin and tonic at my predecessor Colm O'Briain – but other than that she was great fun. I had many enjoyable interludes with herself and Frank. When I telephoned her with the news of Barry's new job and her own consequent elevation she was on holidays in Barbados. Her friends were rather a strange bunch including Pat O'Malley, wife of the former PD Leader, Mary Harney, the PD Leader, and Renagh Holohan, the *Irish Times* columnist – not much chance for Frank to get a word in edgeways with that lot.

I suppose looking back on it now I can understand the aversion that Dick Spring, Fergus Finlay, and Brendan Howlin took to her. Big, bubbly, brash, outgoing and gregarious, Bernie was the diametrically opposite to their cold style. I was prepared to let her off and so was Ruairi Quinn. She would have a big problem retaining the seat but we were then the party of 33 seats and we held a Dáil seat in every Dublin constituency and two in Dublin North-East and Dublin South-West. Surely we should be able to get one MEP returned in Dublin.

Orla arrives

A strategy group had been meeting in Iveagh House and in the Tánaiste's Office in Government Buildings. Many names were discussed in the context of running for the European Parliament, including Joe Duffy of RTE. It was at one of these meetings that the name of Orla Guerin was first broached to us as a possible European Parliament candidate for Dublin, and I think it's fair to say that initially we were mightily unimpressed. There was one of those embarrassing silences after Dick Spring had mentioned her name. Looking at Fergus, I reckoned that she had already been asked. She was a journalist on *Morning Ireland*, an early morning RTE radio current affairs programme. She had also done some frontline reporting from the war in Bosnia. She seemed as a presenter to be too distant and humourless for the baby-kissing *bonhomie* that is part of Irish politics. I suppose my scepticism must have shown through as I was invited over to the Tánaiste's Office to meet her. I fell for her immediately. She entered the room wearing cream jodhpurs, her long brown hair falling down to her shoulders. Straight away she spoke with authority and confidence on matters relating to the party and the European Parliament. I spoke to her of the difficulties of running for the first time with an incumbent candidate who would have the advantages that come with having all the resources of an MEP. It did not cross my mind at the time that any attempt to run Orla Guerin on her own would take place.

I invited her to head office; I wanted to see how she would get on with the staff as a prelude to her mixing with the greater party membership. After this meeting, in the anteroom, which was Sally Clarke's office, I said to Dick Spring: 'If this goes wrong you will be very much damaged.' He looked at me sharply but did not reply. Of course, little advance thought had been given to this scenario. Bernie Malone was hardly going to accept it meekly without a fight. Orla wasn't even a member of the party and I had to take her into my own branch, where the members gave her a warm reception. All the Dublin TDs were taken into Dick Spring's office and briefed. It seemed that they would all support the new candidate, but I knew that Bernie Malone's own TD, Sean Ryan, was hardly going to support an imposition.

The close of nominations for the selection of Labour's candidates was on Thursday 10 January 1994 and, amazingly, on that very day I got a phone call from Sally Clarke telling me to extend the date. I told her that I couldn't; my powers as General Secretary just didn't extend that far. All such deadlines are decided by the Executive Committee or General Council. She told me that I had to and that was that. This was quickly turning into a nightmare. First Barry Desmond was given a £145,000 per annum job without anyone thinking about who would replace him, and then when his successor emerges, she is rejected in favour of someone who wasn't even recruited into the party and who has now obviously pulled out. To make matters worse, Cllr Mary Freehill was banging on the front door, which I'd had the foresight to lock, and now shouting in through the letterbox demanding a list of the validly nominated candidates. There was nothing for it except to sit down and write a letter to the branches. I informed them that head office was encountering difficulties with its postal delivery service and I had to regretfully extend the closing date for the nominations to the Dublin Euro constituency Selection Convention and was sorry for the inconvenience. I then went home wondering what could go wrong next.

The entire issue now took on enormous significance inside the party and gained huge publicity. Friendships were interrupted and branches split. All women over 40 seemed to join en masse with Bernie while Labour Youth adopted Orla. It really was the 'Bernie and Orla Show'. Those against Dick Spring now had a way to get at him and rallied behind Bernie. Kathleen O'Meara, Labour's former Press Officer left her job in RTE and set up an office for Orla Guerin. Henry Haughton got leave from CIE and went to work for Bernie. Of my own personal friends, most followed Dick Spring's lead, but many didn't. Vicky Somers, always an independent thinker, joined up with Bernie, as did the family of Dermot Lacey, the Youth Officer, Emer Malone of Dublin Central, and Cllr Mary Freehill. Even my own sacred space in the Long Hall was not unaffected; a drinking acquaintance in there just walked away from me muttering about Labour 'Doing in Bernie', and Willie the barman, a Fine Gael supporter, told me he was going to vote for her.

Moosajee Bhamjee TD (Clare) wishes Bernie Malone well on her 1994 European Parliament campaign.

The Selection Convention was held in the Riverside Centre on Sir John Rogerson's Quay in Dublin. It was a modern purpose-built centre we used frequently in those years. The day before, the General Council had met and exercised its powers to decide on the number of candidates to be chosen: now that number was to be one, in spite of the impression given to me and to the Dublin TDs. It was a bitter affair and ill-boded the campaign. Ann Connolly (Dublin South-East) asked where the party was going, was it just about winning seats? Bernie Malone had been a party member for 27 years and a public representative for 20, did that count for anything? John McAlinden (Dublin South-Central) criticised the morality of the affair and the opposition to it inside the party and in the press. Dick Spring replied and spoke eloquently. He said that he was central to this debate – he could have stood back and taken the easy option. But we had problems in Dublin and he would not put anyone forward unless he knew what they stood for. He maintained that the meeting knew well that the opinion polls indicated two candidates were a bad idea. The meeting voted 26 to 6 in favour of a one-candidate strategy.

The Convention was held on Thursday 24 February. I had contacted all the constituencies, the ministers, many branch secretaries and as many members as I could in an effort to drum up support for Orla. On the Tuesday evening, I calculated her support level to be about 100 delegates, on Wednesday I had it down to 98, and on Thursday it was down to about 96. It was slipping all the time, but I still thought she would pull through. The tension dripped down the walls of the Conference Centre. Michael D Higgins chaired the Convention and hated every minute of it, but he was the most popular Minister with the Dublin members and so was given the role. Maurice O'Connell, great-great-grandnephew of Daniel O'Connell, 'The Liberator', also sought the nomination and set the tone when, in a jibe against Orla Guerin's work as a Foreign Correspondent, said, 'I didn't learn my politics in Sarajevo', and the crowd jeered wildly. I organised the top table seating and sat between Bernie and Michael D. Bernie Malone's own speech was well-written by our man in Brussels, who also happened to be her brother-in-law, Enda McKay. This work landed him in deep trouble with the Sally Empire for many years to come.

Orla too had a great speech, but it was all in vain. The delegates had already made up their minds. Just before the result was announced, Frank Malone came up to the top table and said to Bernie, 'Congratulations you're the MEP for the next ten years.' Then Ross Connolly, grandson of James, and Labour's eternal Returning Officer came to the podium and announced the result. Bernie Malone had been selected by a margin of one vote. The result caused a sensation and the Hall erupted with cheers. Poor Orla, my heart went out to her at that moment, but she carried it well. I gave the delighted

Bernie a peck on the cheek – what a woman, what a victory! Dick and his empire went off to Iveagh House for a few drinks to drown their sorrows.

Orla went off to Wicklow to recuperate and I couldn't talk to her. I did leave a message for her: 'So sorry Orla, hope you can get over this.' It later transpired that none of the people who had invited her to run had bothered to telephone her to offer her a few kind words in those days after the Convention. A week later she was added on as a candidate but credibility had been shattered. We needed some way out of this mess and I thought I could provide it with an opinion poll. I commissioned one from John Colgan, who had provided the one in 1988 indicating a Labour win in the following year's Euro election. This time it showed quite clearly that Bernie Malone would beat Orla Guerin for the single Labour seat that would be available. Fergus dismissed it out of hand. 'The sample is too small', he said and Dick just looked on impassively as he let his last chance to get out of the self-imposed mess slip away.

Ruairi Quinn was to be Dublin Director of Elections, and at an Election Committee Meeting Fergus said that I should be National Director. It was to be a complete farce, with Bernie Malone metaphorically riding around the city in her chariot, like some Irish Boadicea with the heads of Dick Spring and Orla Guerin hanging from her belt while the populace cheered wildly. She even got an outing on the *Late Late Show* to put her case before the entire nation on TV. I had warned that Bernie Malone and Orla Guerin should never appear together with Dick Spring. Even that was screwed up when they all went to a photo opportunity with Dick Spring in Crumlin where the TV cameras obliged by filming Bernie staging a walkout, the choreography of which would have made a Hollywood director proud and it was obligingly carried on the *Nine O'Clock News*.

The count was in the RDS and no minister was there to witness the final moments. Many good and decent members had, for reasons of loyalty, supported Orla. Now these members felt abandoned as they waited without any ministerial company for the elimination of Orla Guerin and the election of Bernie Malone. I stayed with them till the bitter end and went drinking with them in the Horseshow House. It was an exhausting and draining experience but I wasn't going to desert them now. Bernie had her victory party in the Mansion House on the same night, but I was too tired to attend.

I've met Orla Guerin on a few occasions since. She later became Balkans Correspondent for the BBC and was based in Rome. In 1999, she had to flee Kosovo during the war there after death threats from the Serbs. She would have made a great MEP, but I wouldn't take from Bernie Malone's victory.

She proved to be a formidable campaigner and a great street fighter and went on to become a conscientious, hard-working, and respected MEP as well as the only Labour MEP ever to serve a full term in the European Parliament.

Pa Lowe makes his exit

That great old Meath Labour warrior Cllr Pa Lowe passed away in March 1994. His funeral was in the lovely little church in Longwood. As happened so frequently, I couldn't get a Government minister to attend. Emmet Stagg, ever obliging and I suppose anxious to rehabilitate himself, agreed to attend. This was an irony considering the importance of Pa's refusal to support Emmet in his battles against Dick Spring. The funeral was on Saturday 26 March 1994, and when I reached the church I saw the local TD, Brian Fitzgerald, and the other Meath councillors and constituency officers waiting outside to welcome the visiting minister. 'I couldn't get a minister,' I told him, 'but Emmet will be along.' 'Tell them thanks for insulting me', said Brian as he turned on his heels and walked into the church. 'If anybody in this party is talking to anybody else after this Government, it'll be a miracle', I thought to myself as I went off to pray for Pa Lowe's repose.

The June elections in 1994

One would be forgiven for thinking that the only election that took place in June 1994 was the Dublin Euro Bernie vs Orla clash, so full of it was the media and so much was it the general public's favourite political topic. But this was far from the case. Without even taking into account the Cork by-elections of later on that year, it was a time of European elections in the whole country, by-elections in Dublin South-Central and Mayo West and elections to Borough Councils, Town Commissions and to Udarás na Gaeltachta. The Euro results were quite shocking for Labour with the party returning only Bernie Malone in Dublin. Jim Kemmy was very badly beaten in Munster and in Leinster an increased vote failed to return either Michael Bell, who had come so close in 1989, or Séamus Pattison, his running mate. In Connacht-Ulster, Anne Gallagher put in a very creditable performance getting 8.5 per cent of the vote, higher than we ever got there before.

Michael Bell put the blame fairly and squarely on the in-fighting of the Dublin campaign. In a great confusion of the gender of the candidates he accused them of fighting like 'tom-cats' and driving votes away from the party. It was hardly as simple as that. The relatively high vote of Anne Gallagher and the failure of the older though more experienced TDs showed discernment in the electorate for a different type of politician than that which they chose to represent them in the Dáil. The victory of Greens in Leinster and in Dublin showed a desire by the electorate for a more radical and international view of European politics than we presented to them. There were by-elections in Dublin and Mayo on the same day as the European Parliament elections. In both cases, opposition parties carried the day.

In the local elections we put up quite a good show, mainly due to the branch structure, which is ideally suited to fighting these most localised of elections, where the quota is often less than 100 votes. We made modest but real gains in these elections, winning seven extra Borough and Urban District Council Seats and three new Town Commission seats. On Udarás na Gaeltachta we failed to win any seats. We just had to live with the results; as usual we were very bad at analysis, as we tended to avoid a post-mortem when we did badly. In the case of a victory, as in 1992, one was almost killed in the rush by those seeking credit. When we were beaten, there was great anxiety to move to 'any other business', lest the blame be allocated.

The issue of the advisers

We were now a year and a half in power and one of the issues of most irritation to the PLP was the issue of ministerial advisers. It was a difficult one for Labour as we were always in favour of ministers taking outside advice with them when they assumed office. This had happened in the 1973–77 Coalition Government and it was perceived to be successful. What was happening now though bore no resemblance to the previous arrangement. The numbers employed and the influence wielded had multiplied out of all proportion. Each minister was entitled to a programme manager – who was a kind of super adviser – and an ordinary adviser. In addition, each junior minister had an ordinary adviser. They were understandably resented by the backbenchers, who felt that they were an extra layer of bureaucracy between them and the ministers, as indeed they had to be to justify their own existence. Derek McDowell, the Dublin North-Central TD, told me that he didn't speak much anymore at his own constituency council meetings. This was because Gregg Sparks, a Spring adviser, was a member of the constituency and knew more about what was happening than the TD. This situation was very wrong. It challenged the primacy of elected representatives and undermined their role no matter how good and committed the advisers were, and some were very good indeed.

A new head office

It had always been my ambition to move head office back to near Dáil Éireann, where political life in Ireland is centred. One of my predecessors, Brendan Halligan, had moved to its present Gardiner Place location in 1974, where it was half a mile from Leinster House. Dick Spring said that when he had attended his first AC Meeting in 1981, members had been talking about moving and he wished it would be just done. I took him at his word. Selling 16 Gardiner Place in 1993/94 was the problem. Although our building was in good condition, it was a Georgian house not designed for modern office accommodation and this was in the time before the property boom. Our Financial Secretary, Aidan McNamara, found suitable new premises at 17 Ely Place, which was quite convenient to Leinster House.

The opening of Labour's new head office in 1994.
(L-R) Jim Kemmy TD, Marion Boushell, Dick Spring TD and Ray Kavanagh.

The house was very early Georgian of the 'Dutch Billy' style and though much smaller than the one in Gardiner Place, was exactly suitable for our needs. The decorative condition was better and because it was smaller it would be easier to maintain. The fact was that we could not buy it unless we got a buyer for our existing premises and I managed that with a stroke of luck. When the derelict building next door was sold, the developer started to convert it into apartments. Soon the builders were hammering and belting away. It was far too much for our delicate two-hundred-year-old building and soon huge chunks of plaster came crashing down in the stairwell. If any staff member had been around, they would have been history. Every cloud has a silver lining though, and the catastrophe was an opening for me to the developer, who soon offered to buy our building. I had to hide my enthusiasm from him. On 12 May the staff moved into Ely Place. I was over in Westport selecting local election candidates and came back the next day to a brand new head office.

Our official opening was on Wednesday 27 July 1994. It was a gloriously warm summer night and we held the reception in the Gallagher RHA Gallery that was just up the street and run at that time by the convivial Ciaran McGonigal. Gallons of wine were consumed and the comrades were in top form, the celebrations spilling out onto the street. Dick Spring performed the cutting of the tape ceremony and Jim Kemmy, as Chair of the Party, was there too, and the infectious good humour even affected these two. It was a lull between the crises of the 1993–94 Government. It was about this time that Feargal O'Boyle, a Labour Youth hopeful from Dublin South, asked me when was the time in the Labour Party that we would look back on as the best of times and I told him that the time was now.

CHAPTER 14

THE FALL OF THE HOUSE
OF CARDS

THE FIANNA Fáil–Labour Coalition that had taken power in January 1993 with the largest majority of any government in the history of the state was now under the severest of strains. It was tested in the final months of 1994 and found to be flawed and brittle. The Government that had commanded the votes of 100 TDs from its two constituent parties, as well as those of two independents, fell apart like a house of cards in November 1994. Its demise caused almost as much shock as its formation had done 22 months earlier. There had been some great moments, especially in the aftermath of the Downing Street Declaration in December 1993, but essentially the relationship had never been relaxed. It is fair to say that the Government was crisis driven and around the corner from every scandal lurked another. The final scandal during the lifetime of that Government, concerning the paedophile priest, Brendan Smyth, was the most lurid of all – but first there was the Beef Tribunal Report.

The Beef Tribunal, the first of the Tribunals of the nineties, was established in May 1991 following an ITV *World in Action* programme to investigate what many believed to be major fraud in the beef processing industry and it reported its findings on 29 July 1994. In its early life, it had been the cause of the break-up of the Fianna Fáil–PD Coalition with Taoiseach Albert Reynolds accusing his Coalition partner Des O'Malley of misleading the Tribunal. Now at the end of its life it came close to ending the next government with Dick Spring now playing the Coalition partner's role. The Report was to be a huge document of 900 pages and its reception had been flagged by Labour well in advance as a make-or-break event for the Coalition. Fergus Finlay had indicated this quite clearly to Emily

O'Reilly, a journalist at the *Sunday Business Post*. The scene set was to depend on the level of blame attributed to the Taoiseach Albert Reynolds and it was widely expected that the Report would be an indictment of many concerned with the beef industry.

The final issuing of the Report had hung over Labour like a cloud and had been mentioned by the PLP during the negotiations a year and a half earlier. Now that time, which seemed so far away then, had arrived. The problem was that if the Report, as expected, laid a lot of blame on Albert Reynolds during his period as the Minister for Industry and Commerce (1987–89) then Labour would be quite understandably asked what action it intended to take. If no blame was laid on Albert Reynolds, then it meant that a lot of Labour accusations were untrue and had caused the waste of enormous amounts of public money and time. A blaming Report would, I believe, have ended the Government there and then: the PLP would have met the following week and endorsed a move by Dick Spring to take us out. It was as good an exit scenario as any, especially for those who never wanted the Government to come into being in the first place. It wasn't to be, however; the Report turned out to be a drink of water, putting blame on nobody in high places and, Fianna Fáil claimed, exonerating the Taoiseach Albert Reynolds. However, strange events took place over in Government Buildings that night (Friday 29 July 1994) with stories of Albert Reynolds and his advisers hiding behind locked doors, of secret passwords and press briefings abounding (and being denied). Whatever happened, a general election didn't, and come August, everyone cleared off for the holidays. Those who wanted an end to the existing Government though, didn't have long to wait for another chance.

'We was waitin' for you'
The Cork by-elections of November 1994

One of the many surprise appointments to office in January 1993 was that of Gerry O'Sullivan of Cork North-Central, who had been first elected to the Dáil in 1989. It was expected that Toddy O'Sullivan, the more senior TD from Cork, would receive the promotion. A big, generous, outgoing man with a great sense of humour, he was appointed Minister of State at the Department of the Marine and very much enjoyed his brief. It was a great shock then when I met him late in 1993 and he told me of the medical tests that he had been undertaking. When he made his last visit to head office in the summer, this giant of a man had shrunk in size so much that at first I did not recognise him. The tests had revealed cancer. He died on 5 August 1994.

He was very deeply and genuinely mourned and had no enemies – very unusual for a politician.

After the summer recess, the by-election to replace Gerry was scheduled for 10 November 1994. Pat Magner was to be the Director of Elections in Cork North-Central and, mainly under his guidance, Lisa O'Sullivan, Gerry's daughter, was chosen as the candidate. It was an unfortunate choice; Lisa dreaded campaigning and was so shy that she needed encouragement even to go on a small canvass. I always remember her at the counter of the bar in the Imperial Hotel, the location of Pat's headquarters, saying to me as she gulped down a black coffee and sucked on a cigarette, 'I just hate this'. She was being a dutiful and loving daughter in contesting her father's seat. I thought it was a shame.

The Cork North-Central by-election coincided with a by-election in Cork South-Central to fill the vacancy created by the resignation from the Dáil of Pat Cox, MEP. Pat Cox was originally elected as a Progressive Democrat TD but had resigned from that party shortly after Mary Harney was elected leader in 1993. The party chose Cllr Joe O'Flynn who had been on the Corporation since 1991. Though Joe was popular and hard-working, the vacancy was for a PD seat and Labour had fewer aspirations towards winning than we had in Cork North-Central.

The election was a nightmare, with a hostile electorate baying for Labour's blood. Dick Spring worked hard and even brought over his troops from Kerry. I noticed a change in him from the more gung-ho earlier days of the coalitions; he was quieter and more thoughtful. Perhaps he was preoccupied with the internal coalition difficulties. One of the issues that was to dominate these by-elections was that of equality payments for women on social welfare. This amounted to about £400 million that would have to be taken from other areas of expenditure. A decision against Ireland due to non-payment had been taken in Brussels as far back as 1986 but nothing had been done. Substantial payments were due to many women. The issue was very cleverly and justifiably highlighted by Kathleen Lynch, the Democratic Left candidate, who eventually won Gerry's seat.

Canvassing in Knocknaheaney, a working-class suburb, I knocked on a door that was answered by a woman in her thirties. 'Who are you from?' she demanded. I knew I was in trouble straight away and replied 'Labour'. She folded her arms and called her friend. Then she eyeballed me and said, 'We was waitin' for you'. Many minutes later I stumbled away having had an earful of equality payments, Labour ministers' use of the Government jet and of course Dick Spring's stay in the Waldorf Astoria Hotel in New York, which was always good for a bit of abuse. During a visit to the United Nations in that city he had failed to stay in the Irish-owned Fitzpatrick Hotel. Having been an item on the popular afternoon radio show hosted by Marian Finnucane, the story became a symbol of Labour's extravagance in Government. What the young woman said was all negative, hostile, unfocused stuff, but it was based on a feeling that we had let them down.

The count took place on Friday 11 November in the Neptune Centre, a large sports complex on Cork's northside. It was to prove to be a watershed for Labour in more ways than one. In Cork North-Central, Kathleen Lynch's was the second by-election win for Democratic Left in five months. It was another indicator of the wisdom of those who had tried to take that party into government back in late 1992. Labour got 10.7 per cent of the vote in a former stronghold for the party. In Cork South-Central the result was worse, with the party coming in with 6.6 per cent of the vote. Hugh Coveney of Fine Gael won the seat.

As soon as I had tallies, I telephoned Sally Clarke with the figures. 'I hope you know that things aren't going very well here either', she told me and undertook to get the figures to Dick Spring, who was at the fateful Cabinet meeting. I just couldn't believe that Fianna Fáil or Albert Reynolds and his advisers would use this day to ram the appointment of Harry Whelehan as President of the High Court down the throats of the Labour Party. It showed a total lack of understanding, not only of the Labour Party, but also of how coalition government works. I suppose they thought that the party would be too demoralised to object to the appointment. This is not how Labour works; the party has had a litany of defeats since its foundation and one more only strengthens the party's resolve. Pulling 'a stroke' on the day of the Cork counts was guaranteed to blow up in Fianna Fáil's face. And blow up it did; Dick Spring refused to accept the appointment and led his ministers out of Government that very day. Sally had told me that he would ring me later on in the day, which he did at around 5.00 p.m. 'Is that the Tánaiste?' I jokingly asked. 'It is, but it mightn't be for much longer.' He asked me what I thought we should do. After three weeks canvassing in Cork South-Central and with the hostile reception we received on the doorsteps uppermost in my mind I told him that at all costs we must avoid a general election. With the benefit of hindsight, especially when the facts relating to the Fr Brendan Smyth case are taken into account, I realise that I was completely wrong, only a general election would have cleared the air.

Fr Brendan Smyth was a notorious paedophile resident in Co. Cavan in a house of his Religious Order, the Norbertines. On 30 April 1993 the RUC had delivered no fewer than nine extradition warrants to the office of Attorney General, Harry Whelehan, for crimes committed in their jurisdiction. That nothing was done about these warrants was a major scandal and the fact that the crimes were against children outraged everyone. The only reason Brendan Smyth eventually served time was that he gave himself up to the RUC. When all this came to light, even Fianna Fáil people couldn't understand why Albert Reynolds had persisted in his plan to promote Harry Whelehan. I now think that the electorate would have understood Labour's reluctance to continue on in this impossible arrangement and allowed us a mandate that would have lasted until 1999. Fianna Fáil had a lot of internal sorting out to do concerning its baggage from the Haughey years, its leadership, and its ethical space. Ironically, events were to allow it to start some of this work in the next two years. I don't deny for one minute that there were many in Labour waiting for this opportunity to pull out of coalition with Fianna Fáil, but even if that had not been the case, the behaviour of Albert Reynolds and his ministers on that day was outrageous.

That night I stayed with the troops and we enjoyed a few drinks together. It was a confused, sorry little gathering; yet again in a difficult time the troops were deserted by those who purported to lead them. I don't think anyone realised that the Government was on the point of collapse, though we understood only too well the bind Labour was in. That night we just didn't see any way out. The next day I headed back to Dublin to face an emergency meeting of the PLP. It was called for the following day, Sunday, at midday in Jury's Hotel in Dublin's Ballsbridge. On the way in I met Brian Farrell, the RTE broadcaster and the doyen of political reporting in Ireland. I greeted him with '*Dies irae Dies ille*'; the name of the pre-Vatican II hymn meaning 'Day of judgement, day of wrath'. To my surprise he stared back blankly at me. If the reporters outside didn't know what I meant, the parliamentarians inside sure as hell did!

Partners become gobshites

There followed the most unbelievable political meeting I ever attended. The anger of the TDs, senators and our one MEP (Bernie Malone), who arrived in late from abroad for the meeting, was tangible. Backbencher after backbencher arose to say that even if a general election meant losing their seat then so be it. They supported the course being pursued by the party leader. Their outrage was particularly heightened because of the Fr Brendan Smyth affair and the fact that his warrants had not been processed. It was also a golden opportunity for the opponents of the Coalition. The members echoed Dick Spring's opening remarks when he said that electoral considerations should not guide us now, but rather what was right for the country. Senator Anne Gallagher spoke most passionately and with her big eyes glaring she denounced Albert Reynolds and his ministers: 'Jesus Christ,' she intoned. 'we can't let gobshites like that continue running the country as they have done for the last 70 years.' She was referring to an interview in which Chief Whip Noel Dempsey referred to Albert Reynolds as 'an honourable man', which incensed many. In a great put-down, Jim Kemmy said that he really admired TDs like Pat Upton and John Mulvihill who could have said to Dick Spring 'I told you so' but didn't.

The situation in Northern Ireland, and in particular the IRA cease-fire of 31 August and the Loyalist cease-fire of 13 October, was cited as a reason for continuing with Fianna Fáil. None mentioned Albert Reynolds, though he was more important than his party in this process. The meeting seemed unconvinced that the retention or removal of the present Government would make much difference to the peace processes now that it had been started. Only Dr Moosajee Bhamjee of Clare expressed his clear preference for continuing on with Fianna Fáil. This view was shared, though not expressed, by the senior ministers, particularly Ruairi Quinn and Brendan Howlin.

Many believed that the die was cast and that a general election was inevitable. However, a tactical campaign was now taking shape, centred on Dick Spring's call on the Taoiseach to explain himself on Tuesday when he addressed the Dáil. This put the ball in Fianna Fáil's court and left the onus on them to respond: this response could be evaluated and then accepted or rejected. It demanded absolute confidence in Dick Spring and his judgement with nobody stepping out of line before the response was heard, especially with regard to media comments or interviews. Fianna Fáil, and Albert Reynolds in particular, must be pressurised into responding and explaining again and again – the focus had to be kept on them. They would be hounded by the media into defending the indefensible. The issue was now much more than the appointment of Harry Whelehan to the Presidency of the High Court, it was now about their handling of the Fr Brendan Smyth extradition warrants. 'Let them sweat blood', demanded Michael D Higgins.

It was all fine except for the endgame. This was spotted by a few and dominated the end of the meeting. Brendan Howlin proposed and Ruairi Quinn came in strongly behind a process that would see the Taoiseach apologise in the Dáil on Tuesday and then outline a method for 'rebuilding trust'. John Mulvihill nearly exploded, 'Am I getting this right,' he asked, 'if Albert Reynolds apologises on Tuesday we go back into Government with him on Wednesday?' Here was the crux of the problem: what response could possibly satisfy? It was decided not to have a special PLP meeting to evaluate Albert Reynolds's response; this was to be left up to Dick Spring. This was an enormous and dangerous responsibility, leaving the fate of the Government in his hands and taking all responsibility away from the elected parliamentarians. It moved this crucial decision to the offices of Dick Spring and to those with direct access to him. This gave his ministerial colleagues who favoured a return to Fianna Fáil-led Government a big advantage. But Dick Spring now had little option with regard to Albert Reynolds's fate; he could hardly be absolved now. The longer Labour stayed out of Government with Fianna Fáil the more Albert Reynolds was doomed to the backbenches. Róisín Shortall asked what would happen if Albert Reynolds did give an apology on Tuesday; were we laying ourselves open to being trapped into returning? She was also the first to mention her favoured option: the idea of bringing together an alternative Government without Fianna Fáil and without a general election.

There was no doubt in Liam Kavanagh or in Séamus Pattison's mind that the experiment with Fianna Fáil was over and had failed. Now we would have a slimmer party but it would have more integrity. Jim Kemmy yet again won the prize for bluntness; he felt that Albert Reynolds was cornered and would give any guarantee he was asked. Sean Duignan, the Government Press Secretary was a skilful public relations man and Jim warned, 'Don't blow this one'. But Dick Spring seemed strangely detached, as if an apology would suffice and said that he saw little hope of an alternative Government. Thus the meeting ended and it was all to play for between those who wanted a return to a Fianna Fáil-led Government and those who wanted other options explored, most notably that put forward by Róisín Shortall – the construction of an alternative Government without an election. This was the so-called 'Rainbow option'.

Because of the uncertainty, Dick Spring was to lay himself open to all sorts of pressures from those around him. Behind the scenes, certain Labour and Fianna Fáil Ministers were talking to one another and making deals. It is now public knowledge that these included Ruairi Quinn, Brendan Howlin, Charlie McCreevy and Noel Dempsey. Pat Magner and Máire Geoghegan-Quinn were also involved. The culture of Fianna Fáil was creeping into Labour. It was dynamite for a party like Labour that finds this type of conspiracy politics to be anathema. If it had succeeded it would have split the parliamentary and the membership right down the middle, as it was, it left a residue of bitterness.

On Tuesday 15 November 1994 the Taoiseach Albert Reynolds addressed the Dáil on the Fr Brendan Smyth Affair, but his real aim was to get Labour back into Government. The speech did nothing to allay the sense of outrage felt by the general public and Labour activists. I watched it on the monitor in Declan Bree's office in Leinster House with Diarmuid de Paor of RTE. It seemed from the speech that he regretted what had happened and that it had been a really good Government. When it ended we were amazed. 'Was that it?' Albert obviously had no idea as to the extent of the offence he had caused. At this rate we were heading for a general election by default.

Dick Spring had once offered me this advice: 'You can say what you like, but don't put it in writing.' He was now going to breach this golden rule, with almost catastrophic consequences. He was due to address the Dáil on Wednesday afternoon, but on that very morning Senator Pat Magner handed him a piece of paper and asked him to sign it. It was a solemn undertaking that he would bring Labour back into Government not only with Fianna Fáil, but also under the leadership of Albert Reynolds! This paper was the fruit of the whole night's work. It read:

> On the basis of the statement prepared by me being incorporated in the Taoiseach's statement, I will lead my ministerial colleagues back into Government, to complete the Programme for Government.

This paper was now signed by Dick Spring, dated 16.11.94 and timed 10.22 a.m.

The beheading of a Taoiseach

Albert Reynolds was to address the Dáil and basically denounce everything he had done since the previous Thursday. It was to be a major humiliation, but then Fianna Fáil, as we knew, would do anything to hold onto power. This was the type of trap to which Jim Kemmy and Róisín Shortall had referred at Sunday's PLP meeting. Almost as soon as Dick Spring had signed the paper he regretted it and it took all the ingenuity of Fergus Finlay, who had not been present when the signing took place, to get him off the hook.

Some new information had come to light. It seems that the new Attorney General, Eoghan Fitzsimons, had another case in his office: the Duggan case, in which an extradition warrant similar to Fr Brendan Smyth's had been executed. This meant that there was no justification whatsoever on grounds of lack of precedent for the Smyth warrants to have remained untouched for all its time in the office of the Attorney General.

Within one hour of Dick Spring signing the agreement to go back into Government, the scene changed dramatically. Dick Spring was contacted by an unknown source and advised to check out when the Attorney General first informed Albert Reynolds about the Duggan case. Spring rang the Attorney General and requested a specific answer to that question. The reply from the Attorney General was to confrim that he had told Reynolds on Monday, i.e. two days earlier.

Thus, Albert Reynolds had this information on the Monday and had not informed the Dáil. An animated Dick Spring led Mervyn Taylor, Ruairi Quinn, and Brendan Howlin straight into the Taoiseach's office. They refused to sit and stood around him intimidatingly, Dick Spring informing him that the deal was off. Ruairi Quinn announced that they had come for a head, Albert or Harry's, and it didn't look as if they would get Harry's. Albert Reynolds was shattered and in spite of his pleadings the Labour ministers just turned on their heels and left. It was all over in less than two minutes. This was the political execution of Albert Reynolds, Taoiseach since 1992, and many times a minister since his first election in 1977. It was as swift and decisive as if it had been done by guillotine.

A rumour that Michael Bell was the person who contacted Dick Spring and advised him to contact the Attorney General has been denied to me by Bell. Dick Spring never revealed the identity of his informant.

In the afternoon Dick Spring addressed the Dáil on the whole matter. It was his finest hour and the speech, his best ever, was delivered in a hushed house and covered not only by the national media, but also by the world's press. Dick Spring outlined the sorry course of events and Labour's response to them.

> What the Labour Party wants is an accounting, a true and fair accounting, and nothing more than that. We were hoping yesterday to hear something that would convince us that it was right to prevent the Attorney General from explaining his actions before publicly promoting him. We were hoping to secure some kind of convincing explanation that the Attorney General's apparent attitude, that everything about this case was handled reasonably, could be reconciled with the actual circumstances of the case, or else an acceptance that the Attorney General's account was plainly wrong and grossly insensitive. We were hoping to hear some sort of admission that a serious error had been made in promoting the Attorney General to a place where

he is immune from questioning despite the strongly held
convictions of more that a third of the Government, and that the
people had been let down by a reckless and impetuous act. We
heard none of those things.

He went on:

In the course of his speech, the Taoiseach correctly refused to
excuse the failure of the Office of the Attorney General for its
handling of the Fr Brendan Smyth case. Unfortunately, the
Attorney General, in his presentation to Government, did seek
to excuse that failure. In effect, he endorsed the handling of the
case on entirely spurious and offensive grounds.

Finishing off he set off the time-bomb that had been ticking since the
previous Friday when it had been switched on by Albert Reynolds's
proposal to promote Harry Whelehan to the Presidency of the High Court.

For the reasons I have outlined it will be obvious to the House
that neither I nor any of my colleagues can vote confidence in
the Government at the conclusion of this debate. All my Labour
colleagues in Cabinet and all Ministers of State who are
members of the Labour Party will resign from their offices
before the vote is taken. The House is entitled to nothing less
from us.

Changing horses in midstream

On Thursday, Albert Reynolds resigned as Taoiseach and Fianna Fáil
dropped him like a hot potato. Charlie McCreevy, the Minister for Finance,
was philosophical about it. 'Poor Albert,' he said, 'was hanged for the
wrong crime.' I had seen Máire Geoghegan-Quinn that morning on her way
to work. Strapped into the front seat of her state car she was dressed
immaculately. But her face, locked in a grimace that could turn milk sour,
told it all.

Bertie Ahern, the acceptable face of Fianna Fáil, moved in to replace
Albert as leader and it looked for a while as if Labour would accept this and
let bygones be bygones. The same old tactic of agreeing to everything
Labour could possibly want in the policy area was set in place again and a
return to Government with Fianna Fáil was enthusiastically endorsed by
Ruairi Quinn and Brendan Howlin. But the logic emanating from the case
of Albert Reynolds now had to be pursued. After all, if Fianna Fáil were so
dreadful under Albert Reynolds, could they be radically different under
Bertie Ahern? And yet Bertie Ahern was so different, it was impossible to
dislike him; he was friendly, personable, and sensitive to Labour's agenda.
He was a trade union supporter and had opposed the tax amnesty. Could he

really be in Fianna Fail, much less its leader? Joan Burton, the Dublin West TD who lived in his Dublin Central constituency, briefed the PLP on the subject, while Dick Spring rolled his eyes to heaven. 'Nobody is safe from Bertie Ahern in Dublin Central.' she explained. 'You could be in your house at 9.30 p.m. on a Saturday night and a knock would come to the door and there he'd be. "Is everything alright Missus?" he'd ask, "I'm Bertie Ahern and I'm just calling around to say hello!"' If opportunism was the name of the game, Labour should have left Albert Reynolds where he was. Now we would have a Fianna Fáil leader who could fight us for the Dublin's PAYE workers' vote.

In spite of all that had transpired there was a rearguard action to get us back in with Fianna Fáil, but it was doomed from the start. The time for that had passed. We held consultative meetings all around the country and I marshalled in the troops. They were universally proud of the heights to which Dick Spring had taken the party. In the Riverside Centre, 500 Dublin members assembled just eight months after the bloody European Selection Convention that had been held in the same room. This time they heard Dick Spring ask them for their opinion on the crisis. He then announced that the party would turn down the increases in ministerial pay that had been decided so insensitively just before the Cork by-elections. As the audience cheered, I looked at the shocked faces of Ruairi Quinn and Michael D Higgins; he hadn't consulted them before he turned down their pay rises. This man was living dangerously!

Change partners and dance

The Irish Times again resumed its pivotal role in Labour's affairs. On Monday 5 December 1994 Geraldine Kennedy announced that she has been informed that Fianna Fáil ministers knew about the Duggan Case on Monday so they were just as guilty as Albert. *The Irish Times* expressed 'incredulity' that Dick Spring would now go back in with Fianna Fáil. He acted right on cue, much to the disgust of ministers Howlin and Quinn, and negotiations with Fianna Fáil were terminated.

I had loyally supported the arrangement decided upon by our Delegate Conference, but from my point of view it could not have lasted another year after the humiliation of the Cork by-elections. It would have taken a very brave party leader indeed to come to a meeting of the PLP and announce a return to Government with Fianna Fáil. We had already lost one of our Research Officers, David Grafton, who resigned in protest at what he saw as our preparation to return to Government with Fianna Fáil. A new government with Fianna Fáil would have led to mass resignation within Labour.

Frantic negotiations were now begun with Fine Gael and Democratic Left – they couldn't believe their luck! But the numbers now added up to a slim Dáil majority and all talk of a rotating Taoiseach or the rivalry between Democratic Left and ourselves was dropped. However, from the start there was to be no doubt about who would call the shots: it was to be Dick Spring. The virtual beheading of Albert Reynolds and ending of the previous administration left that clear. In future, all major moves would be made with the agreement of the Labour leader or not at all. The only difficulty to arise in the negotiations was the allocation of ministerial seats. We were to keep all our positions, and if Democratic Left were to have two full Cabinet seats then Fine Gael, the largest party in the Coalition, would be in a minority. So it was decided that one of the junior ministers would sit in the Cabinet but not vote. This was to be Pat Rabbitte, who was to become the so-called 'Super-Junior Minister'; he was Minister of State at the Department of Enterprise and Employment.

(L-R) Michael D Higgins, Minister for Arts, Culture and the Gaeltacht; Willie Penrose TD; Ruairi Quinn, Minister for Enterprise and Employment; Senator Jim Townsend; and Ray Kavanagh at the Leinster Euro Convention, Newbridge in 1994.

CHAPTER 15

THE MORE THINGS CHANGE, THE MORE THEY STAY THE SAME

THE NEW Government came into power on Thursday 15 December 1994 and John Bruton, the Fine Gael leader, much to his own surprise, became the new Taoiseach. It was a far cry from the acrimony between himself and Dick Spring of just two years previously. So Labour kept its six seats at the Cabinet table. One of the eight Fine Gael ministers was to be the North Tipperary Deputy Michael Lowry, who formed a good relationship with Dick Spring. Dick predicted that Lowry would become the next leader of Fine Gael.

The same persons were appointed as Labour ministers but many changed responsibilities. The most dramatic of all was Ruairi Quinn's assumption into the Department of Finance. Fergus Finlay thought that this might lessen Ruairi's disappointment at being out of Government with Fianna Fáil. It didn't, even though the Finance Minister is the most senior Cabinet member after the Taoiseach. It was surprising since his previous ministry, that of Enterprise and Employment, though competently handled, was hardly the success of the period. May Day did become a public holiday under has aegis, though the Irish Congress of Trade Unions (ICTU) claimed most credit for this, and he also introduced the Credit Control Act. But it wasn't these that he hankered after; rather it was being midwife to the Labour–Fianna Fáil Coalition – he didn't get a whole pile of sympathy for his predicament.

Brendan Howlin was in an entirely different situation. As Minister for Health he had been a high profile, high achiever. He had dramatically cut hospital waiting lists, allocated vast sums to the area of mental disability, and led an anti-Aids Campaign. Under the new Government, he was to be Minister for the Environment; a high spending, high profile Department that is traditionally of great interest to Labour due to its involvement in local government and house building in particular. Oddly, Brendan Howlin did not shine here and it appeared to the PLP that most of his initiatives, like the abolition of the dreaded water charges and the state funding of political parties, had to be dragged out of him. The Dublin Councillors became particularly hostile to him, believing him to be a fundamentally anti-Dublin minister. This perception was to have dire consequences for him when he sought the leadership of the party just three years later. As for the high profile usually associated with his Department, he simply seemed to disappear without trace.

Dick Spring, Niamh Bhreathnach, Michael D Higgins, and Mervyn Taylor maintained their Departments: Foreign Affairs; Education; Arts, Culture and the Gaeltacht; and Equality and Law Reform respectively. As for the Ministers of State, though the numbers remained the same, the jobs changed – except for Eithne Fitzgerald, who remained attached to the Department of Finance and the Office of the Tánaiste. Brian O'Shea moved from the Department of Agriculture to the Department of Health, thus becoming Labour's standard-bearer there. It was the first time since 1948 that Labour was in Government without taking the Department of Health. If Brian O'Shea had been the Minister perhaps the tragic mishandling of the cases of the haemophiliacs infected with contaminated blood products, which continued through this period, would not have taken place. Joan Burton moved out of the Department of Social Welfare and into Foreign Affairs and Justice. Most inexplicable of all, Emmet Stagg, who as Minister for Housing had arguably been the most successful of all the junior ministers, was moved out of the Department of the Environment and into the Department of Transport, Energy and Communications. Here he was immediately at loggerheads with the Minister, none other than Michael Lowry. So Labour was seriously shortchanged in the allocation of the junior ministries, though I have never heard it argued that the choices were anything other than our own.

The new Government was to be called 'The Government of Renewal'. Many in Labour thought that since we had it right at last, perhaps we could now move on and wipe the scandals and the bitterness of the previous few years from memory. It didn't happen that way and it seemed as if the electorate still wanted to let Labour know what it felt about its decision to go with Fianna Fáil in early 1993. Trying to get rid of this threat of retribution was to be the subconscious and sometimes the conscious background to much of Labour's actions in the next two and a half years.

Meeting with Sinn Féin

The Peace Process continued in spite of the prophets of doom. Dick Spring as Minister for Foreign Affairs continued to play a key role. With Fianna Fáil being nationalist, Spring was a more reasonable choice of partner for the moderate Unionist. Now with Fine Gael, which seemed more sympathetic to the Unionist position, he appeared to be in the Republican corner. It was therefore our turn to meet a delegation from Sinn Féin led by Gerry Adams. I hadn't met him before and was surprised to find him so charming and pleasant. He had a very impressive grasp of how relations had been between Sinn Féin and Labour for the previous 89 years (almost non-existent!). The main problem, he indicated, was the refusal of the British Government to move any further after the Downing Street Declaration: ministers would not deal directly with Sinn Féin, which was a party of 12 per cent in Northern Ireland; there had been no progress on the release of Republican prisoners, which Sinn Fein needed to appeal 'to the wider Republican family'; and there had been no move on police reforms. The IRA would laugh him out of it if he went to them and asked them to decommission their weapons on the basis of what had been achieved so far. As for decommissioning of weapons, perhaps we should ask Proinsias about his experience, he jokingly suggested. Proinsias De Rossa's party, Democratic Left, was descended from Official Sinn Féin, whose armed wing, the Official IRA, never decommissioned. It was a very creditable performance and certainly broke the ice as far as the parliamentarians present were concerned. Dick Spring promised to bring their concerns to the attention of John Major, the British Prime Minister. The Sinn Féin delegation included Christy Burke, the Dublin City Councillor; Pat Doherty, the Sinn Féin Vice-President; Lucillita Bhreathnach, their General Secretary; Rita O'Hare, their Press Officer (who very famously was supposed to have smuggled gelignite into Long Kesh Concentration Camp 'on her person'); and Joe Malone. On Labour's side we had Ruairi Quinn, the deputy leader and Minister for Finance; Michael Bell, the PLP Chairperson; Derek McDowell TD; Brian Fitzgerald TD; Sean Kenny TD; Senators Anne Gallagher and Sean Maloney; Dick Spring and myself. At one stroke the meeting dissolved any suspicion on our side about Gerry Adams' commitment to peaceful means in Northern Ireland.

In the following year, 1996, we were to repeat the exercise and good relations continued. By then, Sinn Féin's embrace of the electoral process was accepted by all bar the most die-hard.

Bonnie Prince Charlie II

Diametrically opposed to the meeting with Sinn Féin was the garden party in the British Embassy during Prince Charles's visit of 1995. Each year I got an invitation to Queen Elizabeth's Birthday Celebrations at the British Ambassador's residence. It was a beautiful Victorian mansion in Sandyford called 'Glencairn' that has since been sold for more modest quarters in Rathfarnham. In 1995 the invitation arrived as per usual. I have to admit that I didn't always attend as many of these embassy parties were boring as hell. This year I knew it would be different as both Angie and Marion smiled when asking whom I was taking to the Ambassador's Residence. Prince Charles would be there so I had no choice really, when these two women decided they were going to meet Prince Charles then nothing would stop them. So, accompanied by Marion and Angie I drove out to 'Glencairn' on Wednesday 31 May. I felt like the coachman driving two Cinderellas to the ball.

It would be quite interesting I thought: I'd meet the type of person that would have been hanging around the vice-regal lodge during the British occupation. The place was packed; this was obviously a premium event. Henry Mountcharles and his lovely wife Iona were there. Matt Russell, just out of the Attorney General's Office having been a key person during the Brendan Smyth Affair and recently settling with the Government, was surrounded by admirers. The place was full of Fine Gaelers. Ivan Doherty, their General Secretary, agreed with me when I said that Fine Gael was really a Commonwealth party (and *I* was only joking!) Hugh Gillanders, their former Youth Officer was also there. The Prince came round and shook hands with everyone and seemed relaxed and to be enjoying himself. He wore a shirt with blue stripes, the collar was slightly, but very visibly, frayed – I liked him for that, it takes a certain lack of vanity for someone so rich and surrounded by so many flunkeys to insist on wearing a favourite and comfortable shirt for one more time. He was friendly and outgoing; nevertheless, I was delighted to get out and into the Long Hall for a few drinks with the commoners.

National conference in Limerick 1995

The year 1995 was full of promise for the Labour Party. There were still more than two years left before a general election had to be called. The new Coalition arrangement would remove some of the odium that attached itself to the party during the previous administration and many policy initiatives were now coming to fruition. Among these were Niamh Bhreathnach's abolition of fees for third level education and her 'Breaking the cycle' initiative, which targeted extra resources at schools in deprived areas. On the issue of divorce, this would be the year to get it through – just ten years after the failure of the last referendum on the subject. The economy had picked up, we were to enter the first year of the so-called 'Celtic Tiger' and peace was to be lost and restored in Northern Ireland. President Bill Clinton was to visit Ireland and receive a John F Kennedy-style welcome. The year would end with the Michael Lowry scandal for Fine Gael and for once Labour would not be blamed. This was in contrast to scandals during the previous administration for which Labour was always given a large share of the responsibility. It took some doing for the party to come out of a year like this lower in the opinion polls than it went in – but that's what happened.

It started off positively enough: our National Conference was due and Jim Kemmy wanted it in Limerick to celebrate the anniversary of its charter. The venue was to be the impressive University of Limerick, where its magnificent Concert Hall was to be the main arena for our deliberations. The previous conference had been in Jury's Hotel in Waterford, where the cramped surroundings and the generally hostile air outside had led to frayed tempers and bad memories of an otherwise uneventful conference, especially considering that it was our first in Coalition with Fianna Fáil. Now in Limerick, the feeling was that we had at last got it right. From my point of view, there was much less handling of Conference necessary in Limerick than there had been in Waterford as the party was now displaying a satisfaction with events that was previously missing, even the PLP was becoming a bit happier. This was our middle conference between the 1992 and 1997 elections and I hoped to get the party back into a campaigning mode. Good media coverage would be necessary for this to happen. Here we were to hit the rocks at the start of our year of lost opportunities and, I suppose, of Dick Spring's slip from being a sure and steady captain of the Labour ship.

Relations between Dick Spring and Mary Robinson had never been great, even in those euphoric days around her becoming President. It was always very frustrating for me because they both stood for a new Ireland and had so much to contribute to each other's work. Mary Robinson's invisible contribution to Labour's 1992 election victory was enormous, as was Spring's visible contribution to her Presidential Election victory in 1990, and yet like naughty siblings, they could never get on. I chose to ignore the whole thing in the hope that the general public and the party members would never have to know. In any case, I don't think that a public bust-up was ever inevitable. People in politics who can't stand one another can work perfectly well together for years – even a working lifetime – without letting their personal antipathy interfere, as I myself can testify.

Anyway, in the week before our all-important National Conference in Limerick, Dick Spring hosted one of those lunches for Political Correspondents in the luxurious surroundings of Iveagh House. It was supposed to butter them up – as all these dinners are. Food and drink of the finest is consumed at the taxpayers expense and then there is a briefing for the journalists who head off and write a complimentary piece about their host. That's the theory at least. On this occasion, however, President Mary Robinson was just home from a state visit to Chile that like most of her events was high profile and widely reported and commented upon. She had briefly met the former dictator Augusto Pinochet, and had not given enough time to the Irish community in Santiago, or so they said. It was all taken with a grain of salt by the public who knew that Mary Robinson was the best ambassador they had ever had. She had also raised some questions about the progress of political events in Northern Ireland. It was widely believed that many in the Department of Foreign Affairs were out to get her since she had formally acknowledged Gerry Adams by shaking hands with him on a visit to Belfast. This, it was alleged, involved her in a political role.

I was not at this lunch, but was told that when in a relaxed mood after the dinner, Dick Spring let his fairly strong feelings about the President's unwillingness to be a token office-holder slip. It was too good a story to let lie and it dominated the headlines for a week without the Minister actually being named. Enter the indomitable Bride Rosney, Mary Robinson's Adviser, who got hold of the story. Bride was rearing for a row and challenged the anonymous minister who had criticised her President to jump out and make his attacks in public. It was a disaster for the party. Everyone knew it was Dick Spring and of course neither himself nor Fergus Finlay could make any further comment. When our Conference took place on the following weekend, this was all the journalists wanted to know about. All the work that went into the Conference was wasted; it might as well never have happened. Attacking Mary Robinson in the nineties was to attack the icon of the age. It was not on.

By-election in Wicklow

The Independent TD for Wicklow, Johnny Fox, had died earlier in the year and the Wicklow Labour Party, which still hadn't come to terms with Liam Kavanagh's exclusion from Cabinet, was faced with finding a candidate. The person pushing himself most was Tim Collins, an Adviser to Brendan Howlin. He had formerly been Mary Harney's Adviser when she was in the

Department of the Environment during the Fianna Fáil–PD Coalition. He had been a leader of the junior hospital doctors during their strike in the eighties, but was now intent on making a name for himself in politics. He had sought a senate nomination in 1993 from amongst the four allocated to Labour as part of the Coalition agreement with Fianna Fáil. I suppose that the employment given him by Brendan Howlin was a substitute for this.

Labour's campaign started early. It began on Tuesday 6 June for a polling day of 29 June. I went to Wicklow almost every night and was delighted to find quite a warm welcome on the doorsteps. It was the direct opposite to the experience in Cork just eight months earlier. The results of the election were quite satisfying; Labour got 17 per cent of the vote, the highest we were to achieve at any by-election during this period. It seemed as if the electorate was giving us one last chance.

President Clinton drops in

As part of his support role for the Peace Process in Northern Ireland, and in pursuit of that all-important Irish vote, President Clinton paid a short visit to Ireland in late November–early December. He was accompanied by his wife, the redoubtable Hilary Rodham Clinton. On 1 December he addressed a huge public meeting in Dublin's College Green. The city centre streets of Dublin were closed to traffic for the day and for the first time in my lifetime the citizens felt that they owned the city as they walked the car-free streets. I had been a great admirer of President Clinton since his inauguration in 1992. He had stopped the dinosaur of American illiberalism, conservatism, and fundamentalism right in its tracks. Hilary's health policies, sadly defeated, were the nearest to a European welfare state model that had been tried in the States in a lifetime. He wasn't doing too well in the polls just at this time and we hoped that the success of the Northern Ireland Peace Process and his sponsorship of it would be of help. His Ambassador in Ireland, Jean Kennedy Smith, sister of the assassinated President, added to the Irish influence in the White House and ended the lamentable alliance between the American Government and those Whitehall diplomats and politicians who pursued a 'military' solution to the troubles in Northern Ireland.

Dublin's Camden Street has featured for many years now a great pub called Cassidy's, which is commodious, friendly, and well run. Some bright spark came up with the idea of taking President Clinton there. Why not, it would make a difference to the usual monumental places to which he would be taken. It was also an opportunity for those who wouldn't be invited to anything else to get close to him. I was invited and, with the rest of the group (who included the staff of head office) we assembled at Iveagh

House. There we were marshalled by Sally Clarke and given our 'best behaviour' briefs. She then frogmarched us up Harcourt Street behind her. It was like Mother Goose and her goslings! When we arrived at Cassidy's the door was guarded by burly secret service agents who were reluctant to allow us to enter in spite of Sally's accreditation – but they would not stop Sally. Inside there was a strange almost eerie atmosphere created by the strict rules never before enforced in an Irish pub: no smoking and no drinking. Hilary was very anti-smoking and the cigarettes must remain unlit until she departed. If the Clintons thought that this was anything like the noisy, smoke-laden, booze-smelling Irish pub, then they were much misled. Soon Hilary arrived, shook hands and left, this was a bit of an anti-climax, she seemed terribly shy and ill at ease. The President was a different matter however. He gripped everyone's hand as if gripping that of a long-lost friend and smiled that big American toothy smile of his. Dick Spring took him through the crowd introducing him as he went, then he came into the back bar where he had a pint. At least a pint was served to him, when he departed I saw most of it left behind.

Senator Donie Cassidy, the Westmeath promoter, impresario, and hotel and waxworks owner, decided that his family name, which he shared with the President's mother, gave him a special entrée into the President's party. So he asked Dick Spring for a lift in the state car, obviously including an invitation down to the pub. I don't think Donie was well versed in the Tánaiste's reputation for hospitality – he didn't make it.

That night the state dinner for the Clintons was held in Dublin Castle. It was the social event of the year and caused more tears that Cinderella's Ball. About 1000 guests can be invited to St Patrick's Hall where these functions usually take place. Fergus Finlay was good enough to ask Marion Boushell and myself along. The junior ministers were not asked and neither were most of the parliamentarians, so there was great annoyance value in waving the invitation around.

The dinner itself wasn't as glamorous as one would have expected, but I suppose that it's just being present at these affairs that counts. It's like the religious definition of heaven as 'being in the presence of the almighty'. We sat at a table with White House staffers, some of whom were the now infamous 'interns' – but it was before Monica Lewinsky's time. They were young, eager and talked to us about the logistics of a US President's travel arrangements; he takes the contents of two jumbo jets, including whatever cars he will require while abroad. It sounds very much to me like the medieval progresses of the Holy Roman Emperors and probably the only example left on earth of such arrangements centred on one person.

'The right to re-marry'

The autumn and early winter of 1995 were dominated by 'the right to re-marry' referendum campaign. Very early on we decided to drop the 'divorce' tag, as it was too negative and restricting. Most of us had been involved in the 1986 Campaign and were anxious that the lessons of that time would be put into practice. Mervyn Taylor, as Minister for Equality and Law Reform, took overall responsibility for the proposal and piloting it through. He adopted the most modest and moderate form possible, setting himself firmly against any easy divorce solution. His proposals allowed for divorce only when the couple had been living apart for at least four years and adequate provision had been made for the children. As things turned out, his judgement was to prove spot on. He travelled all around the country at the suggestion of Richard Humphries, his Adviser, and gave interviews to many local radio stations, which were now proving to be a most influential medium in Ireland.

On the political front, Niamh Bhreathnach was appointed National Director of Elections. She was not experienced as a national campaigner and her appointment caused much negative comment inside the party. I think that the fact that she was happily married was a strong influencing factor; decision-making was becoming increasingly eccentric over in the Sally Empire. Niamh set about getting the party moving and she had an uphill job in this as people had settled into a kind of torpor on the issue, believing that in nineties Ireland it would go through easily enough. It was just the type of attitude that the anti-divorce lobby, fronted by retired judge Rory O'Hanlon, required. Immediately they set about terrifying the populace about the high cost in financial terms of the proposals and the breakdown in families it would cause. Niamh Bhreathnach, when questioned about the cost of a divorce on the morning radio programme *Morning Ireland*, seemed to avoid the question. Although Fianna Fáil did not oppose the referendum, they wouldn't, I felt, lose any sleep if it were defeated; its grass-roots were now talking about divorce being only for the rich. The anti-divorce lobby launched a huge billboard and poster campaign. These included posters predicting widespread breakdown in families with such slogans as 'Hello Divorce, Bye Bye Daddy' and 'Divorce hurts'.

At this stage the campaign was in real trouble. I went to see Dick Spring to tell him of the gravity of the situation. I wanted to be careful not to undermine Niamh Bhreathnach but I was seriously worried. It was 16 October and at this stage I could see the referendum being lost with dire consequences for liberal Ireland; the fundamentalists would be on the move again and all our new-found liberties of the nineties would be under attack. It was well known that they would demand an abortion referendum if they won this one.

Polling day was Friday 24 November so there wasn't much time left. We had changed the day of poll to a Friday to encourage students to vote in the hope that most of them would be in favour of the proposals. A more inclusive national campaign than the Labour one was now taking shape. It was called 'The Right to Re-Marry Campaign' and it contained some hard hitters. A young barrister from Meath called Peter Ward took part in television debates and was a great hit, especially with women. I booked the new Civic Offices for the group who held a family day there. Celebrities like U2's Bono supported it.

On the Labour side we organised regional meetings. Dick Spring agreed to address the ones that I set up for him in Cork, Kilkenny, Limerick, and Dublin – Dick was never shy when it came to work. They weren't very well attended but they mobilised the support of the key party activists. In Kilkenny, I heard Séamus Pattison make the best speech of the campaign: he spoke as a committed Catholic and called for the extension of Christian tolerance to those in our society who had family troubles and to create a legal framework that would allow people to seek happiness in their own personal lives. It was low-key, quiet, and sincere. Dick Spring spoke everywhere of the modest nature of the proposals and said repeatedly that a year after these proposals were agreed people wouldn't even remember them.

On Wednesday 22 November the PLP met. I told them that they would be back on the following Wednesday hurling recriminations at one another unless they treated the referendum with the utmost of urgency. It would be lost unless they pulled out every vote on Friday. Declan Bree, who was always a great support, demanded that I name names so that those who were not pulling their weight would be exposed. He was one of the few who ran a great campaign in his constituency.

The count was on Saturday 24 November and my worries proved justified. The referendum was carried by only the slimmest of margins. On a 62 per cent poll, just 50.3 per cent voted in favour, while 49.7 per cent had voted against the proposal. It was a close shave. We had a Victory Party that night in The Riverside Centre and the comrades imbibed to celebrate their victory. It was a considerable achievement considering the strength of the forces waged against it and it would never have happened but for the Labour Party and the 1992 election result. Sadly though, it was to be the last great achievement of that liberalising era in Irish history.

Money is the root of all evil

The European elections had been a major financial drain on the party. No significant funding comes in for them; people just don't get as passionate about them as they do about national elections. Matters were made much worse by the bitter rivalry between the candidates in Dublin. Those contributing were more likely to contribute to the individual candidates rather than to the party. The party spent £155,000 on the campaign and this was outside what the individual candidates spent. The large number of by-elections was also causing a financial haemorrhage, the outing in Wicklow alone costing over £27,000. This was an extravagant amount and though this cost was reined in subsequently, it never came in at less than £10,000. Head office, on the other hand, was run on a shoestring and salaries though adequate were not high.

As part of our 'Programme for Government' with both Fianna Fáil and Fine Gael, we had included a provision for state funding of political parties. This is the only method to avoid the undue influence of rich donors. The problem always lay with donations to individuals, not with donations to parties. Money received by parties is properly recorded and in some cases published. Money donated to individuals can be spent on campaigns but sometimes it is not. In any case, it leaves the individual very much beholden to the donor and this is very wrong and dangerous in a democracy. The new proposals were to limit expenditure and to make public contributions over a certain amount. I went round all the ministers in 1993 to urge them to progress the state funding issue and though they all reassured me of the imminence of these proposals, I was doubtful. These proposals were bound to be controversial and things weren't going too well just then – anyway, Michael Smith of Fianna Fáil was Minister for the Environment and he could always be blamed for the hold up. Nothing happened as 1993 passed, and then 1994.

Now in 1995 we had a Labour Minister in Brendan Howlin and still there was no sign of a penny coming. Nor could I see any desire from the Department to move on this important piece of legislation; it was most disappointing. I approached Dick Spring with a view to asking him to do a business appeal. This would entail his sending a letter to the business community, which was common practice during a general election. It is unusual to send one outside of election time but this was an emergency. He refused my request on the basis of the impropriety of a party in Government appealing for funds while it was preparing legislation to restrict such funding. I though this was an honourable and reasonable refusal and proceeded to make do as best as I could with existing funds and to borrow again. I had already taken out a £90,000 loan from the Bank of Ireland in 1994 to cover part of the European Parliament election costs. Now I would have to borrow again, some extraordinary juggling was called for. I would use the money to tide the party over until the state funding eventually arrived. I was beginning to feel like Billy Bunter who waited through 47 volumes in the hope of the arrival of the postal order that never came. It was now April 1995.

To make matters worse, Bernie Malone was having an attack of the same Euro tightness disease as had afflicted Barry Desmond when he became an MEP. She refused to pay her party subs for which she had signed up at her Selection Convention. It took an entire campaign inside the party's Committees and the intervention of Jim Kemmy to get her to change her mind.

In July I was summoned over to Gregg Sparks office to give a low-down on the party's finances to himself, Fergus Finlay, and Sally Clarke. Being very open about the difficulties of the financial management of the party I welcomed their interest. Afterwards, I was informed that an accountant, Brendan Foster, a friend and former colleague of Gregg Sparks in his accountancy firm, would do a report on the finances of head office – this I was happy about too. Brendan Foster turned out to be a very decent guy. In the end, he reported that head office's finances were well, if informally handled, and that the General Secretary should have more and not less control over them. I don't think this was quite the conclusion desired over in the Empire, well done Brendan Foster! When the Report was ready I met Dick to discuss it and it was then that he dropped the bombshell. He had decided to do a business appeal after all, but would not hand over the money to head office – he would administer it himself through people in his office. There was nothing I could do really but I did feel very let down. I recognised this as part of the turf wars that happen in every organisation and I knew that 'what can't be cured must be endured'. But it was also very dangerous to the reputations of those involved. Though they were all honest people they were not the Labour Party for whom the money was intended, nor were they its head office where people expected and received scrupulous accounting and reporting. When aspects of this affair were published in newspapers many years later, it did these people no credit at all. It emerged that this account had been used to pay bills outstanding from Orla Guerin's Euro campaign and that the Kerry Group had paid bills amounting to £25,000. These were the famous 'pick up payments'. If left in the hands of head office, things would have been handled differenlty by Marion Boushell or myself.

Other amounts received by Dick Spring from this appeal included £50,000 from Smurfits, £39,000 from the Bank of Ireland and £36,000 from the Allied Irish Banks. In total, £240,000 was collected. All this was very unsettling, but worse was to follow.

The McKenna Judgement

As the year went by we expected an electoral and political boost from our reverting to a Coalition with Fine Gael and Democratic Left. The Wicklow by-election had proven that this was possible though the divorce referendum showed a pitiable lack of fight in the party. However, it was the party's attitude to the McKenna Judgement that demonstrated most the rot that had set in. Since the Single European Act referendum in the late eighties, the Government had spent taxpayers' money promoting its side of various referenda. The other side had no access to such funds. This was clearly undemocratic and blatantly unfair and Labour had always opposed it. It was very much in line with what I would have considered to be a Fianna Fáil view of politics; a system devoid of policy or debate and based primarily on personality. It would be politics by PR firm.

Now that we were in Government it appeared that we were prepared to do an about-turn on the subject and it seemed that Quinn McDonald Pattison, a leading Public Relations company, was to be given the Government contract to 'explain' the terms of the Government proposal in the divorce referendum to the public. Of course, it would have suited lazy Government ministers who wouldn't even have to bother campaigning – the PR firm would do that and be paid for it by the Exchequer! Patricia McKenna, the Green Party MEP for Dublin, challenged this carry-on in the courts and won. Her case is called the McKenna Judgement and forbids the use of public funds to promote the Government side only in a referendum. It stands as a landmark for democracy and fair play and sadly it had to be foisted on the Rainbow Government. To make matters worse, the head of the company to which the contract was to be awarded was Conor Quinn, brother of Ruairi. Talk about insensitivity to public concerns about jobs for relatives!

One of the reasons the new Government was so enthusiastically supported in the initial stages was that we expected a radical change in behaviour to the previous administration. Now it was becoming increasingly clear that all that had occurred was a change in dancing partners. Would a reshuffle help? Many thought so; the ministers had become complacent, predictable, and a law unto themselves. The McKenna Judgement and their failure to campaign in the divorce referendum were key examples – but there were others. Even in late 1995 it could have all been turned around. If not, we were to be damaged electorally, possibly in a drastic fashion – we were less than two years at most from a general election. With the agreement of six TDs I was to go to see Dick Spring and put this to him and I expected him to be amenable to some sort of change; he too was aware of the increasing inertia of the Labour side of the Government. It was December 1995 and difficult to get in to see him. My appointment was later that month, which would be the day of the last Cabinet meeting of the year and his last day of the year in Dublin. The appointment was for 4.30 in the afternoon.

When I arrived at his offices in Government Buildings, Sally told me that as it was the last Cabinet meeting of the year, they were having champagne and so he would be late. I suppose I should have left at that stage and rescheduled the meeting but I remained on. When he arrived I was standing in the outer office where Sally was based. 'You're not getting any of the money', he said. I didn't say anything. 'Michael Smurfit gave us £50,000', he continued. 'Why did Michael Smurfit give the Labour Party £50,000?' I asked. 'He must like what we're doing', Dick Spring replied. The reply hit me like a hammer blow. I have nothing against Michael Smurfit, in fact I have never met him and I presume he is a decent fellow; but I was the General Secretary of the Labour Party and to me the scruffiest, most cantankerous member of the Labour Party was worth more than a hundred Michael Smurfits even if each one was brandishing a cheque for £50,000. I had believed the leader of the Labour Party shared my view. I turned and left the office.

From then until his resignation 23 months later, I only spoke in a friendly way to Dick Spring once and that was on the morning after his mother's death. That day I did what I had never done before in almost ten years as Labour's General Secretary: after considering the situation about the reshuffle over a coffee in the Dáil Bar, I telephoned a few TDs and told them that the proposal had not been received well and I went straight home. I didn't return to my office until the next day. Oddly enough the next day they told me in the office that Dick Spring had been looking for me on the previous evening. I never found out why.

CHAPTER 16

AT THE END OF THE RAINBOW

THE ECONOMY was now moving into boom and Ruairi Quinn was the first Finance Minister in living memory who could announce a budget surplus, which he did in his 1996 Budget. Labour had previously been in power during recessions even going back as far as the Suez Crisis of the mid-fifties. Now for the first time ever it was in power with money to spend. It would take talent to screw this one up.

By-election blues

There were two by-elections in 1996 and both took place on 2 April. Neither boded well for the Government, yet this was the period when much of the groundwork we had done for the previous three came to fruition. Though the Government itself had the support of the electorate in the opinion polls, as a political party, Labour didn't. It was now obvious that we had not shaken off the blame for keeping Fianna Fáil in power after the 1992 general election.

Cllr Michael O'Donovan, a West Cork man who had taken over Joan Burton's council seat when she became a Minister, fought the Dublin West by-election for us. The by-election was caused by the sad death of Brian Lenihan, the universally popular former Tánaiste. As Joan Burton aptly put it: 'The last thing we wanted was a by-election in an urban area.' Service charges were still hanging around our neck like a millstone and they were being exploited ruthlessly by Joe Higgins, our former militant comrade who was now based in Dublin West. The party had introduced a Residential Property Tax which had severely damaged the Dublin vote as houses were more expensive there and thus more likely to be in that category. Gay Byrne, the popular host of the RTE radio morning talk show was a particular critic of the tax and he had an enormous following – we were just going to get a hammering in Dublin West. But we fought on, had a good candidate and fought a competent campaign under Conall McDevitt (later to be SDLP Press Officer) who acted as Director of Elections. Polling day was 2 April and the party members held their breath when it appeared that Joe Higgins might win. I was in the RTE mobile studio in Donegal at the time and was prepared to welcome his election as a left-winger. Not so at the count, the Labour activists cheered wildly when Brian Lenihan Jnr won the seat. It's a pity Joe didn't win; Joan Burton might have won it back from him at the general election as by-election victors often find it difficult to hold onto their seats at the following election.

If the mood in Dublin West had always been realistically pessimistic, then the mood in Donegal North-East had always been upbeat. The veteran TD and former Fianna Fáil Minister Neil Blaney had finally 'shuffled off his mortal coil' at 71 years. He was still a sitting member of Dáil Éireann though now an Independent Deputy. He had lived in Dublin for many years and his local 'eyes and ears' was his brother Harry, who now became the candidate of the independent Fianna Fáil faction that Neil represented. Harry belonged to that gruff rural tradition which occasionally throws up representatives and causes electoral upset. Very republican but also anti-urban, he refused to travel to Dublin to film a party political broadcast with the national broadcaster telling them that 'no-one around here watches RTE anyway'.

Labour had one of its star performers in Senator Sean Maloney, a charismatic psychiatric nurse from Letterkenny. Niamh Bhreathnach told me that the women from her Department loved it when Sean Maloney telephoned. A very professional campaign was run under the direction of Larry Masterson. Marian Gaffney, Sean's Secretary in the Senate moved up to Letterkenny and took over the Secretariat of the campaign, making an enormous contribution. Marian worked sometimes 18 hours a day, and once I had to ask her to leave the office and go and rest when I found her there at 12.05 a.m.

Sean Maloney got 13 per cent, increasing his vote from the 1992 general election. Cecilia Keaveney of Fianna Fáil won the seat, narrowly beating off the Harry Blaney challenge. This was also the first election in which Sinn Féin reaped the political benefit of their participation in the Peace Process with Pat Doherty, their Vice-President, garnering a very creditable 8 per cent.

Dressing for dinner

I was given an invite to the State dinner for the President of Zambia. I was not informed of the dress code but assumed that it was formal eveningwear as a head of state was the guest of honour. So I decked myself out in my monkey suit and my partner, Marian Gaffney, was in her evening gear too. Just as we entered Dublin Castle I saw that none of the men were dressed similarly. I was mortified for myself and for Marian though it's not so bad for a woman as ladies' evening wear does not stand out so much. I met Bride Rosney on Battleaxe Landing and she confirmed my fears. 'Its never black tie for African Presidents', she informed me. 'I'll kill the first person who thinks I'm a waiter', I told her.

At dinner we shared a table with the visiting President's Head of Security. An enormous burly fellow he sat beside Marian and confided in her that his favourite singer of all time was Daniel O'Donnell. After dinner I went to the toilet and passed Bride Rosney's table, where she sat with Peter. On my way back she was waiting and shouted, 'Waiter, more wine please!'

Crime on the streets

Time and again Róisín Shortall, Tommy Broughan, and Joe Costello raised the issue of the rampant gangsterism based on the trade in heavy drugs in Dublin – mainly heroin. They graphically outlined the desolation this caused in mainly poor communities. This topic particularly demonstrated the polarisation in the PLP between city and country, ministers and backbenchers and new hungry TDs and those who had been around for years. At times when Roisín spoke on the subject, outlining the terror tactics of the drug barons and their henchmen, she was outlining a city of horror. She spoke of community activists having their houses wrecked and their children threatened in order to stop their parents' activities as any improvement in the community would damage the control the drug barons had over it. And yet she maintained that if the drug problem were removed from Dublin, it would become one of the most crime-free cities on Europe. She was largely ignored by the ministers and frequently indicated her intention of withdrawing from the PLP meetings entirely. She wrote a policy document for the party, 'The Drugs Menace and Organised Crime', which was sadly ignored.

I was having lunch with Jim Kemmy and John Mulvihill in the Dáil Restaurant on 26 June 1996 when Liam Kavanagh walked in and told us that the journalist Veronica Guerin had been murdered on the Naas dual carriageway. Now at long last we got some action and the Government stepped in decisively with criminal assets legislation, bail reform, a drug trafficking bill as well as the recruitment of extra Gardaí and support and forensic staff. All the measures were long overdue and had an almost immediate effect – but what if Veronica Guerin had not been murdered?

Would Róisín Shortall and her urban colleagues still be shouting like voices in the wilderness? Many thousands of people, predominantly young men, had become addicted to heroin in the previous 20 years and many hundreds had died from related illnesses, especially Aids. During this period the drug barons had operated without any fear of the law, they were described as 'The Untouchables'. This was also the period of enormous corruption in politics and business as exposed by the Tribunals of the nineties and beyond. It has never been investigated if there was a connection between the two.

The Connolly memorial

Beresford Place opposite Liberty Hall was inappropriately named after the great Victorian Conservative and anti-Catholic champion, the Marquis of Beresford. In 1996 it was re-named Connolly Place and a magnificent memorial to the great Labour leader (created by Eamonn O'Doherty) was unveiled there on 12 May, which was exactly 80 years to the day since his execution in Kilmainham Jail. It was unveiled by the President of Ireland, Mary Robinson, who made a highly-charged and learned speech on the occasion. Her knowledge of his works and her allusions to his campaigning and to other socialists of his era riveted the trade unionist and Labour crowd. In particular, her reference to that wonderful Irish–American, Mary Gurly Flynn, and to Connolly's publications in Yiddish, showed the depth of her knowledge and commitment to her subject. But it was her reference to the Spanish Civil War as 'The Anti-Fascist War' that really got the crowd going. This reference is of course a clear indication of whose side one is on and to have the President of Ireland express such views was a great experience we knew would probably never be repeated in our lifetimes.

In the following year (on 12 March 1997) she indicated that she would not be seeking a second term as President. If she had stayed on, she would undoubtedly have been re-elected, probably without a contest, and Dick Spring would not have resigned as leader of the Labour Party. Such are the imponderables of politics. I was very sorry to see her go. To me she represented both in style and substance the type of Ireland in which I wanted to live.

The political director

With the by-elections out of the way it was time to start planning for the general election. The Sally Empire took an initiative and I was summoned over to Dick Spring's Office to have it outlined. Fergus Finlay was to move into head office to get us ready for the election. He was to have his own budget of £120,000 from the money collected by Dick Spring, which now amounted to almost £240,000. A Strategy Committee would also be established and chaired by Brendan Howlin. There were to be regional conferences in Dublin, Leinster, Connacht-Ulster, and Cork. There was also to be a programme of work for the ministers and a consultative process for the PLP (Nobody ever really found out what these last two meant.) I supported these initiatives though the lack of finance for head office still rankled while Fergus was to have almost unlimited resources. Fergus was quite apologetic about the proposals as he probably thought that I would resent his move to head office, but I did not at all. The more resources aimed at the general election the better; if he did his work well then the party benefited and if he didn't then he would take responsibility. It was as simple as that, anyway, I had no intention of discontinuing my own preparatory work for the election. Frank Malone (husband of Bernie) telephoned me to sympathise; he was not a fan of Fergus whom he considered to be part of the problem rather than part of the solution. He told me that I could take an action for constructive dismissal, and then joked that I might get my hands on at least £100,000.

The plan was made public on 15 May 1996 and Fergus Finlay moved over to head office until he resigned just 18 months later. In fairness to him, he had no experience at this kind of work. The only campaign he had run before was Orla Guerin's ill-fated Euro campaign and that didn't exactly cover us with glory. Though initially welcomed by the PLP, the process didn't seem to make any positive difference. The ministers carried on as before, working hard but independently of each other and behind the curtain of their advisers. The party continued to have a bad press and the PLP remained a battleground between the ministers and the backbenchers. Brendan Howlin called his Committee together in the autumn but it didn't seem to have any purpose. At its first meeting he asked me how many seats we would win at the general election and when I replied, 'Based on the current opinion polls, at least 16', I was greeted by howls of derision.

Over the next year I organised the regional conferences, which were well attended by the members – even the Connacht-Ulster one which was held on a freezing Saturday (23 November 1996) in Galway. Dick Spring was in such bad form that day that he did not speak once from the time we sat on the platform in the Great Southern Hotel in Eyre Square until he left at 4.00 p.m. The party has always been weakest in Connacht.

The Cork Conference was held on 8 February 1997. It wasn't well attended boding ill for our results in that province. It was memorable for the

20-minute speech Brian O'Shea made in his allocated three-minute slot while the freezing delegates waited for lunch. Niamh Bhreathnach stated during her address: 'after this speech I will go amongst you and answer questions about my proposals', while Brendan Howlin tittered audibly on the platform at her messianic pretensions. Liam Hayes, the Director of Elections from Tipperary South called for Brendan Howlin to resign over the handling in the Department of Health of the Hepatitis C Scandal. Fortunately, the press had been so bored that they left early. The Cork Conference was the best indication yet as to the problems facing the party. We were in Munster, which is the traditional stronghold of Labour, and in 1996 we had nine TDs (including the party leader) and four senators in the province. And yet we found it difficult to fill Connolly Hall in the city and our deliberations turned out to be defeatist and dull. It didn't take a political genius to tell that we were heading for a drubbing in Munster.

The Leinster Conference was quite different, however, much more upbeat, lively, and positive. It was held in the Killeshin Hotel in Portlaoise. It too reflected the reality of the party in this province where Labour was to do much better in the general election than in Munster. The reason these Conferences are such good gauges of party strength is that they attract the most committed and active members and thus one can use them to judge the state of the organisation. The key people in the constituencies always turn up to these meetings. Leinster had them in abundance and they were in top fighting form. The Munster delegates were tired, old, and cross.

Final achievements

The twenty-seventh Dáil, spanning the period from January 1993 to June 1997, was to have two Governments with no election in between. Labour participated in both. The highlight of the party's achievements came in 1996 (it takes a while to draft, plan and produce legislative change). In that year Niamh Bhreathnach was able to abolish third level fees, a policy first advocated by James Connolly back in 1895. Her targeting of 25 urban and 25 rural schools for extra resources was a major anti-poverty measure. This was the 'Breaking the cycle' initiative. On Halloween Night of the same year Michael D Higgins opened Ireland's first all-Irish Language TV station 'Teilifís na Gaeilge'. It was a major achievement for the Irish language, bringing it into every home in Ireland. In December, Brendan Howlin abolished the dreaded water charges, which had been another significant policy platform. Eithne Fitzgerald brought in her Freedom of Information Act giving citizens access to their own files held in Government offices and much more. The year also saw Ireland host the EU Presidency and Dick

Spring and Ruairi Quinn played key roles in the work of the Presidency in terms of its main business of monetary union.

There were some disasters along the way, but these were more of style than of substance. Eithne Fitzgerald organised a fundraising lunch for business people 'where they could meet Finance Minister Ruairi Quinn'. This was privileged access for the price of a contribution to Labour, her critics argued, so Eithne dropped the whole scheme. Michael D Higgins got into similar hot water when the Chairperson of the Independent Radio and Television Commission, Niall Stokes, sent out an invitation for a fundraising race night for Michael D's Galway West constituency. Michael D, of whom he had been a long-time supporter, had appointed Niall to his position. More uproar followed and I went on radio on this one. Síle de Valera TD, Fianna Fáil's shadow Minister for Arts, Culture and the Gaeltacht had called for Michael D's resignation over this issue and Fergus asked me to go on the Sunday news programme *News at One*. I thought it best to attack, so I launched into an attack on Síle's grandfather, Eamon de Valera, who had engaged in fundraising in the United States in the twenties for the *Irish Press* newspaper. A member of the de Valera family complained to the Broadcasting Complaints Commission that RTE had responded inadequately when I had allegedly slandered old Dev! 'Ah,' I thought to myself, 'that hit the mark.' The complaint was dismissed. The interviewer was none other than Una Claffey, who in 2000 went to work for the Taoiseach Bertie Ahern. I bet Síle de Valera wasn't on that Interview Board.

The year was ending badly for the party. With no improvement in the opinion polls it seemed to me that there was little or no prospect of returning to Government. More damaging to the future of the party was the number of seats we would lose and the consequent destruction of morale. This would give rise to a new and dangerous type of animal according to Pat Upton; this would be 'the former TD'. Furthermore, Dick Spring and Ruairi Quinn had fallen out completely. The final breakdown in relations occurred over the Public Service Pay Talks. Ruairi had wanted a five-month pay pause and Dick Spring had intervened to reduce this to a three-month pause. However, the underlying cause of the break-up was the split with Fianna Fáil back in 1994, of that I have no doubt. There was also the question of the sale of the small state-owned Trustee Savings Bank (TSB) to the giant Australian-owned National Irish Bank (NIB). Ruairi was very enthusiastic about this, but when he brought this proposal to the PLP it was spoken against by his Cabinet colleague Mervyn Taylor. It was unclear as to why Ruairi was so committed to this venture other than that it made good business sense for the NIB and the state coffers would benefit from the sale.

Labour Party members are generally not in favour of the sale of state assets and the exchequer was replete with cash. The other members of the PLP now smelt blood and shot down the proposal out of hand. The sale was also opposed by Fergus Finlay. This and the pay talks led to a complete breach between Ruairi Quinn and Dick Spring. In a way, it didn't matter who was in the right and who was in the wrong; this dispute was a disaster for the party with leader and deputy leader sniping at one another and pulling in opposite directions.

Timing of the general election

As 1997 loomed the two major strategic problems facing the party were the timing of the general election and the electoral strategy to be pursued. On the subject of the former, Ruairi Quinn favoured leaving it until the winter so that he could introduce another budget. With the economy in boom this would be a 'good news' maybe even a 'giveaway' budget. The arguments for an earlier summer election were Labour-centred. We could campaign harder and get our vote out better in the summer. Fergus Finlay favoured this time. The whole affair, however, was to become just another aspect in the Spring/Quinn row. Not surprisingly, the election date chosen was that favoured by Fergus Finlay, and Ruairi was deprived of a chance to present another budget. It was to be a summer election and polling day was to be 6 June 1997 to dovetail with Labour's National Conference that would be held in Limerick University on 11–13 April.

The Limerick Conference 1997

The main business of the last Limerick Conference held under the leadership of Dick Spring was to be the question of the election strategy of Labour in the upcoming general election. It was a desperately fought strategic decision. Those favouring a return to a coalition with Fianna Fáil wanted an 'open door' policy, with Labour not outlining any decision on future partners until after the election. Most felt that this would be a clear indication to the electorate of a desire for a return to a Fianna Fáil–Labour alliance and that the electorate would punish such an approach severely. The other option was to rule out a coalition with Fianna Fáil and to go for support for the Rainbow Coalition with the current partners Fine Gael and Democratic Left, but not rule out other groups like the Greens. This option commanded majority support right across the party. The PLP and the membership supported it overwhelmingly and it had pockets of opposition only among the ministers and the trade unions. It was not a cure-all for our troubles and many of us appreciated this. The electorate was still anxious to avenge Labour's entry into coalition with Fianna Fáil in 1993. We would suffer as a result but this strategy would still give us a strong enough base to recover in the shortest possible time. If developed after the election it could lead Labour back to government in a reasonable timespan.

Marion Boushell and Ray Kavanagh on the stage at the 1997 National Conference.

The Conference itself was almost entirely dedicated to this question in a way unimaginable in the two other main parties in Ireland. On Saturday night Dick Spring outlined his strategy to the packed Concert Hall. Labour would on no condition consider re-entering Government with Fianna Fáil. It was what the Conference was waiting for and the delegates burst into applause. At last Labour was recovering its lost identity. Just as the platform party was leaving the stage after the speech, Róisín Shortall came over to me. 'That,' she said, 'was worth about four seats.' I was inclined to agree with her.

Jim Kemmy too made his final speech to a Labour Conference. He was to be dead within six months and must have been very ill at the time though none of us had the slightest inkling. The Chairperson addresses Conference on the Friday evening at the start of proceedings and he dedicated a major part of his speech to apologising to the women infected with Hepatitis C through the use of contaminated blood transfusions. He called it, 'The greatest health scandal in the history of the state' and he asked that the women be treated with dignity and generosity. He also called on delegates to remember the vision of the Labour Party, especially its fight against poverty and lack of opportunity. It was a speech of great sincerity and passion; a very fitting swan song for Labour's gentle giant.

The campaign grinds to a start

The Campaign Committee had been meeting for almost nine months now but was never more than a debating forum and sounding board. One of the debates we had was on tax cuts. I alone was vocal in demanding that Labour should be to the fore in demanding these. The PAYE worker had carried the state since the sixties while all other sectors had been passengers. Now it was time for recognition of this by means of generous tax breaks. My colleagues on the Committee looked at me as if I was an interloping PD. I also suggested that tax rates be reduced rather then tax bands on the grounds that the taxpayer needs to understand what he or she is getting. The party went on with its minimal relief proposals and marginalised itself in the subsequent debate on the issue during the campaign.

The Dáil was dissolved on Thursday 15 May 1997, but of course we had advance notice. Incredibly, Labour's Manifesto was not ready and it was not to be launched until the following Tuesday. Even then there were not enough copies to go round and it was not until the following Friday (just two weeks before polling day) that we got sufficient copies in head office to distribute even to those few who requested them. It didn't really matter anyway; it was not an inspiring document. It contained a commitment to reform the laws on libel. Dick Spring had not been briefed on this and, unfortunately, when introducing the Manifesto he denied its inclusion when questioned by a journalist. Fergus Finlay had to send him up a note asking him to correct himself – it was an embarrassing start. The campaign itself never really took off.

The Campaign Committee met each morning at 8.00 in head office and Fergus occasionally reported to it what he was doing and occasionally he didn't. It soon descended into being a complete talking shop. My friend Ann Connolly, who was a member by virtue of her membership of Labour's General Council, just couldn't understand what was going on, having heard stories from me of previous Election Committees. The function of this one soon became a review of the morning papers and then we would go to our respective offices and continue with our own work. Meanwhile the party lost the centre stage in the campaign. It was now a struggle between Fianna Fáil and Fine Gael, both parties doing well at the expense of Labour. In retaliation we lashed out at the PDs. Strategy went out the window. The PDs were in an arrangement with Fianna Fáil and a reduction in their vote meant that their residual vote transferred to their major partner. This is what happened in the two Cork City constituencies and in Laois-Offaly, enabling Fianna Fáil to win that crucial third seat in a five-seater. I spoke to Dick Spring twice during the campaign about the need for a major Labour initiative to wrest some publicity from the two major parties and boost our dangerously low levels of support. He told me that I didn't know what it was like 'on the ground'. I concentrated on supplying constituencies with their election requisites (posters, leaflets, abridged manifestos, stickers etc.) and to answering the hundred odd questionnaires with which we were swamped. It seemed as if there was nothing to do but batten down hatches and await the passing of the storm.

Ironically enough, in terms of props it was one of the best campaigns we had run: the organisation had been kept intact from the previous campaign and we never had more canvassers or material and the materials were never of such high quality. Posters were abundant and advertising hoardings were hired. Money was no object and almost £500,000 was donated to the campaign, an enormous and unprecedented amount by Labour standards. Much of it was spent on foolish peripherals that in my opinion only damaged our credibility as a party of modesty and restraint. A woman telephoned head office during the first week and asked me about Labour fundraising. I told her that we depended a lot on small donations from private well-wishers and members. This at least had previously been the case. 'What about the Labour aeroplane then, how can you afford that?' she asked triumphantly. I told her that there was no such thing and our conversation came to an end. Two days later I was out of the office for a sandwich when I looked up and there it was, an aeroplane flying over central Dublin with a banner trailing with the message 'Vote Labour'. The bill for this piece of nonsense was £15,000.

There were some highlights however. Labour committed itself to a new Children's Hospital for the northside of Dublin. There was also a proposal to plant a tree for every citizen in the state as a Millennium project; this idea, I believe, emanated from John Rogers. There was also the idea of a 'Social Guarantee' that would mean that all school leavers would have certain training rights. Other than these, the press campaign seemed to pass us by. There were outraged complaints from campaigners and candidates, all of whom demanded that Labour take the initiative. In the constituencies the fight was bitter and hand-to-hand and this was where I tried to assist, giving what little help I could to the beleaguered constituency campaigns. More that any campaign since the early eighties, the 1997 one was fought locally; the big picture had faded.

When the results finally came in they were shocking in their clinical garrotting of the PLP as the opinion polls had accurately predicted. The two MRBI polls commissioned by *The Irish Times* in May had given Labour 10 and 11 per cent. The election results came in at 10.4 per cent. There was no arguing with the figures, but the devastation to real lives was not so easy to accept. Of the 33 deputies elected in 1992, just 16 held onto their seats. One had died in the meantime (Gerry O'Sullivan) and three had decided not to contest again (Mervyn Taylor, John Ryan and Moosajee Bhamjee). A staggering 13 seats had been lost, including those of Minister for Education Niamh Bhreathnach and junior ministers Eithne Fitzgerald, Joan Burton, and Toddy O'Sullivan. Backbenchers who lost their seats were Declan Bree in Sligo-Leitrim, Joe Costello in Dublin Central, Brian Fitzgerald in Meath, Pat Gallagher in Laois-Offaly, Liam Kavanagh in Wicklow, Sean Kenny in Dublin North-East, John Mulvihill in Cork East, Sean Ryan in Dublin North and Eamon Walsh in Dublin South-West. Most had no profession to fall back on. We had won one new seat: in a stunning performance in the new South Kildare constituency Jack Wall had carved out a win for Labour in a difficult three-seater constituency.

A numbness hit the party that I had never experienced before. We had never ascended to such heights as we had in 1992, but now we had lost what amounted to a small political party – 13 seats. Going into the 1992 election we held 16 seats but it was not as simple as saying that we were back to where we had started. The electorate was hardly likely to reward us with a gain in the near future without our earning it in some extraordinary way. After all, they had given us our chance and in their opinion we had blown it. It would be a long hard road back, possibly encompassing two general elections. I was prepared to do it, it was the least I owed to my grand old party, but I had to put a limit to my time in the job. I was now 43 years old and had to think of life after Labour. I couldn't visualise myself continuing on after my fiftieth birthday and so I put that as the outer limit of my stay. By then, with consistent organisational and parliamentary work the party could be back in government. I put this to Dick Spring when I discussed the matter with him in July and he was dismissive of my analysis. He also refused to accept the veracity of Fergus Finlay's intention to leave his job in the near future as Fergus had confided in me earlier in the year. I suppose leaders must be allowed a certain space for denial after a defeat of that magnitude. Jim Kemmy had already warned me that Dick Spring would not follow the path I proposed. 'You won't find Dick Spring sitting around draughty halls in rural Ireland with you after all the trappings of office', he had warned.

Defeat is an orphan

The new PLP met on Wednesday 11 June. It had now almost halved in size. It was a sad enough little bunch that met on that day, but first there had to be the ritual lashings. As would be expected the cat o' nine tails really came out with a vengeance. Dick Spring raised hackles at the start of the meeting when he asked why we hadn't seen a defeat of this magnitude coming. He also said that we must ask ourselves about regional variations, why the vote increased in Westmeath and collapsed next door in Meath.

The next hour of the meeting was taken up with discussing the forthcoming senate election. During this debate Jim Kemmy very graciously proposed that I be given the senate seat vacated by Jack Wall as he had been elected to the Dáil. It would be for a period of about two months and would give me access by right to the Dáil facilities. I was a bit embarrassed but very proud to have Jim do this and thankful that he was supported by Ruairi Quinn. I knew there wasn't any chance of Dick accepting this but it was a nice compliment.

As the debate dragged on it seemed that it was a ploy to avoid any substantive discussion on the election rout. But on this occasion the Dublin backbenchers were not to be fobbed off. Róisín Shortall spoke for them when she said that certain people had been dining out on the strength of the success we had enjoyed in 1992. The top table squirmed. No one, she said, would admit any mistakes were made and this was consistent with the treatment of backbenchers for the previous four years. The backbenchers were taking the flak on the streets for the mistakes of non-elected officials who were living in the lofty towers of Government Buildings, out of touch with the public and out of touch with the people. The imposition of the Residential Property Tax and the failure to abolish water charges until it was too late was an example of this. The election campaign had been seriously lacklustre with the same old faces trotted out again and again with nothing to say. She was now doubly depressed having heard the attitude of the leadership.

Pat Upton said that he felt sadness about what had happened to the party and bitterness about what had happened to himself. As for the idea that we had not seen it coming, he had predicted such an outcome on many occasions and anyone could have found this out if they had bothered to read the papers. Jack Jones from MRBI had written about it all on at least two occasions in May. A Parliamentary Party needed collegiality and consultation and people should remember that the TDs are elected by the public. He felt that he had been treated with exceptional nastiness and that he had been the subject of rumours by staff members. These people carried on in a fashion reminiscent of the regimes of Eastern Europe and given their carry-on he understood why the leadership wouldn't be aware of what was going on in the country. If anyone doubted the distance of Government members from reality then they should spend a night or two at a drugs meeting with him in Dublin. Given the failure of the leadership to accept what had happened then we must surely be on a slippery slope. But it didn't have to be this way; the party could recover. He didn't overtly specify what was needed to make this happen.

Tommy Broughan said that at the root of the problem was the lack of respect shown to backbenchers. The rot set in after the decision to go in with Fianna Fáil; it was all downhill after that. Bernie Malone asked why the myriad of 'handlers' didn't 'see it coming'. She said that she felt hostility towards herself in the room even at that moment. Séamus Pattison suggested that the views of the members who lost their seats should be taken into account – that really would have ignited the tinderbox.

Dick Spring said that he was tired but wanted to answer the charges. I was asked to prepare a report on the elections and the meeting rose for two weeks. By the time it met again, things had changed considerably.

The revelations from this meeting gave rise to considerable talk and comment within the party. Was it possible that Dick Spring hadn't had any idea what way the election was going? I found it hard to believe that I would have been the only one to point this out to him. And yet, some time later Pat Magner was to jokingly say that if Ireland had been hit by a nuclear strike during this time then Dick might be blissfully unaware of it. He would be in his office practising his golf swing, as no one would be allowed to get in to give him the news. His level of self-imposed isolation was immense, added to this was his protective secretary Sally Clarke, who absolutely controlled access to him, and the fact that he didn't like bad news anyway (as I knew all too well myself).

The PLP met again on 26 June and for once this was a meeting with only a little rancour involved. This was because it now appeared that Séamus Pattison would be accepted as a nominee for Ceann Comhairle by the minority Government-in-waiting of Fianna Fáil and the PDs. All members of the PLP expressed their delight. Seamus was another person who had been bitterly disappointed when left out of the ministerial list in 1993. A junior minister in the Fine Gael–Labour Coalition of the eighties, he was universally liked and respected. He was a key figure in Dick Spring's survival at the 1989 Conference. To make matters worse, Labour's leading figure in Carlow, Jim Townsend, was appointed to the Senate, meaning that Seamus had to take him on as a running mate in 1997 – this had almost cost him his seat.

But now all his Christmases had come at once: as the longest-serving TD in Leinster House he'd had the title 'Father of the House', and now he was to be elected Ceann Comhairle, an office enjoying ministerial rank. I went to his luxurious office suite shortly after his election. 'Noeline is looking after me from heaven', he beamed from his high-backed leather chair, referring to our departed friend Noeline Dunphy. The meeting accepted my report into the election; it was merely a constituency analysis of the results rather than a full account. As such, it naturally praised those who had won and the victors were now studying it. A major problem in election analysis is that those who win are somewhat elated no matter what happened to the others. This meeting also decided on the proposal for Róisín Shortall to have a full day meeting early in September to discuss the future of the party. I had been canvassed many times by Willie Penrose about the superior conference facilities of Bloomfield House Hotel outside Mullingar. He had done exceptionally well in the general election, heading the poll, and it was no harm to show him some favour. It was here that I booked a meeting with an overnight stay for the PLP for Tuesday 9 September 1997.

The senate elections

The nightmare of picking five good senate candidates out of the 19 offering now took precedence. Any recovery would be crucially influenced by the performance of our Dáil candidates in waiting and Labour always used the senate as a waiting room to the Dáil. We couldn't squander this opportunity; of the five panels in the Senate, Labour could reasonably expect to elect a member onto four. I was faced with an enormous difficulty: under the new constitution, the Executive Committee had been given almost absolute power in areas such as this. If the Executive Committee alone picked our Senate candidates then only the nominees of the Sally Empire would emerge and an important base for future recovery would be lost. So now I had to establish and have agreed that the much larger and more representative meeting of General Council and the Parliamentary Party was the body constitutionally entitled to make such decisions. Four would be successful in the Senate race: Sean Ryan, Pat Gallagher, Kathleen O'Meara, and Joe Costello.

The election itself became high drama when some of our votes in Dublin North were disallowed because they had not rigidly adhered to the strict rules for Senate Elections. I spent some sweaty days in August with Sean Ryan and Richard Humphries (former Adviser to Mervyn Taylor) who kindly placed himself at our disposal as our legal adviser during the Senate count. This takes place in the Restaurant in Leinster House, which lends a rather surreal atmosphere to the proceedings. But all's well that ends well and we won our four seats in a good humoured and friendly atmosphere.

The Mullingar meeting

By now the members had the benefit of a summer break to clear their heads and with the Senate elections out of the way they could focus on the future. We were at our full day meeting in the beautiful surroundings of Bloomfield House Hotel not far from Mullingar and it was Tuesday 9 September 1997. The meeting started off as it continued, with a row. Pat Upton had agenda items that he wanted discussed. These agenda items were contained in a letter signed by himself, Tommy Broughan, Róisín Shortall, Sean Ryan, and Joe Costello. It was this small group of Dublin parliamentarians who were the dynamic of the meeting.

First of all, Michael D Higgins let it be known that he was available as a candidate for the Presidency; an offer that did not receive much support. He did strike a chord, however, when he said that the idea of the Labour Party supporting Bob Geldof scratching himself for seven years in the Park was offensive. Pat Upton suspected that Fergus Finlay was flying a kite for Geldof as there had been reports of his candidacy on *Sky News* and on the *Vincent Browne Show* on radio. Fergus denied this rumour but said that Geldof had telephoned him.

In response to Dick Spring's initial comments, the Dublin members, excepting Ruairi Quinn, outlined his unpopularity in the opinion polls and their opposition to the appointment of former advisers to positions in head office. The role of the advisers in the previous government was subject to intense criticism. The party was being run by the same people, it was alleged by Bernie Malone, the Dublin MEP. The meeting had become quite heated. It was now that Tommy Broughan spoke. 'It's all down to leadership,' he said, 'the bottom line is that I expect a vigorous role from Dick in the Dáil and if not he should consider his position.' It was as if a bombshell had been dropped. There was a momentary silence, complete and deep. This was the first time that Dick Spring's leadership had been called into question. Michael Bell, who was chairing the meeting, said, 'He's not here at the moment', and Pat Upton retorted, 'I'm sure he'll hear about it'.

The meeting continued on in this vein from midday until 7.53 p.m., breaking for lunch and tea. It was bitter at times, but the members got what they wanted to say off their chests and I thought that was good. Members said things out in the open that they had been saying privately for years and Dick Spring was deeply offended and hurt. The meeting decided to give him leave to present a candidate for the Presidency to the party and to proceed with the appointment of his advisers to head office. The 1983–87 Coalition had needed a much bloodier expurgation; this was mild by comparison and its honesty held the seeds of renewal. The PLP had taken some control in its own party and that must be good. It wasn't what I'd call 'a bonding experience' however.

Then we had dinner. Seating was a bit of a problem as it was decided by faction. I moved in beside Derek McDowell, who is so inoffensive that both the pro and anti-Spring camp considered him acceptable. It wasn't the first time that I ate my dinner sitting on a fence.

Good night sweet prince!

Being morbidly superstitious I was very unhappy when Jackie Ahern, my secretary, told me that a bird was trapped in the basement and asked if I could let it out. It was a little thrush; how it got in I couldn't figure out but I knew for sure what it portended. That was on Tuesday 24 June. The next day Jim Kemmy's Secretary Margaret telephoned and in an unusually subdued tone she said that Jim wanted to talk to me. 'I wanted to tell you something, Ray, I wasn't feeling too well during the campaign and I thought I'd broken a rib. It has now been confirmed that I have multiple myloma, which is bone marrow cancer, and it is irreversible.' I panicked, 'What does this mean Jim?' Almost as if he were describing a new coat he said, 'I'll be happy if I get two years out of it.' I told him that I couldn't believe what he was saying. 'Its true enough', he said almost detachedly. 'I want you to keep it quiet for a while.' He attended his last meeting of the PLP on Thursday 26 June and contributed to the proceedings.

On 11 August I met his train at Heuston Station at 5.30 p.m. and drove him to the Charlemont Clinic from where he was transferred to St James's Hospital. It was heartbreaking to leave him there in hospital, far from home that night, but never once did he complain. Patsy Harrold, his life partner was with him and she too was a rock of strength, they were both far stronger that I thought I could ever be in a similar situation.

Around his bedside now assembled some of the intellectual and political giants of the Ireland of 1997 as well as his family and many of his friends from Limerick. Very much aware of the history of the situation, I took all the staff in head office and many of the Leinster House staff to see him for a last time. I went to see him each weekday and left the weekends to his family and friends from Limerick. His humour never gave up and he was fascinated by his treatment. 'This chemotherapy is very interesting', he told me, 'the only problem is that I'm part of the experiment.' He went through the proofs of his last book, *Limerick Compendium,* from his hospital bed. Mary Robinson, the President of Ireland, was an early visitor as was Bertie Ahern, the Taoiseach and Fianna Fáil leader; John Bruton the Fine Gael leader; and many members of the Oireachtas both past and present. Carolyn Swift the writer and artist, Michael O'Toole the journalist, and Pat Feely the broadcaster, all good friends, were constantly in attendance.

Dick Spring was in America for some of this time but on his return he went to visit Jim with Morgan Stack, the Kerry Executive member. There was to be no deathbed reconciliation. Jim did not share the gentle hypocrisy of the Irish who generally make up with their enemies on their deathbeds. He was too honest in the bluntest sort of way. There was something fierce, something almost Old Testament in his truth that was not softened even by approaching death. Fergus Finlay telephoned him, I was glad of that; a final showdown would have done neither of them any good. Fergus, of course, received the same treatment as Dick.

I had been trying to convince Jim for some time to make a will but he fobbed me off with the excuse that he had so little to leave there was no chance of a row after his death. On the morning of 25 September I was at a meeting of the Presidential Campaign Committee when his brother Joe telephoned. He wanted to know if I could get the party solicitor Niall Connolly to come up to the hospital. Jim had agreed to make his will. Niall came straight away saying this was one aspect of his job that he hated: deathbed wills. Jim was in a bad way, in severe pain. When the will was completed and Niall had left I stayed on with the family. The consultant told us that Jim could not last the day. I walked around the grounds and went for lunch with his partner Patsy and she told me their love story. It was all very poignant. In the afternoon Jim had been given so much sedation and painkillers that we expected him to lose consciousness. I went into his room to shake hands and say goodbye. Unbelievably, he was still conscious and when I rubbed his hand in farewell he looked at me and said, 'Ray, I can't stand the pain'.

He died at 10.45 p.m. that night and the funeral was held in Limerick on the following Monday. Dick Spring gave the funeral oration as per Jim's instructions. Whatever about his personal relations with Dick Spring, Jim took his membership of the Labour Party seriously and nobody was to be left in any doubt; this was to be a Labour funeral.

It was an entirely secular affair in line with Jim's atheism but it was so touching and so moving that many said to me that that was how they wished to be buried. In the funeral home a woman whom he didn't know approached Jim's brother Joe. 'That man,' she said, 'had great respect for women.' Many stories of his humanity and generosity emerged over those few days.

We followed his coffin on foot from the funeral home to the graveyard. At Mulgrave Street the fire brigade took out their tenders and dipped their gantries in respect. At the graveside Professor Gearóid O'Tuathaigh of University College Galway and Dick Spring shared the oration. Mike Finn read the Dylan Thomas poem 'Do not go gently into that good night'. Then, most touchingly of all, a rendition of *Beautiful Dreamer* by the American tenor Thomas Hampson was played. It had all been laid out by Jim and it was his last most beautiful creation.

Adi Roche for president

Mary Robinson was elected for a seven-year term as President of Ireland in 1990. To my real disappointment she was now leaving office slightly early to take up the post of United Nations High Commissioner for Human Rights. I had hoped that she would seek a second term for which she would have been elected by acclaim. All eyes now focused on Dick Spring, could he repeat the 1990 performance, present the electorate with an outstanding candidate and restore his own fortunes and the fortunes of Labour all at one stroke?

My own favourite candidate was John Hume. He was the outstanding politician in Ireland in the second half of the twentieth century and almost single-handedly brought peace to Northern Ireland. He was also winding down a career that involved membership in the legislative assembly in Northern Ireland, membership of the Westminster Parliament, and membership of the European Parliament. He would have easily been elected, as his world stature would have proscribed opposition to him from Fianna Fáil or Fine Gael. Since he was a member of the Socialist Group in the European Parliament and because the SDLP, like Labour, is affiliated to the Socialist International, we would have been able to claim some credit. The party and the country would have benefited. But it was not to be – unless he was given all-party support, John Hume would not run. He wanted to be a President with popular support and he was not approached by

Labour. An IMS/*Sunday Independent* poll published on 16 March verified it all; John Hume was the popular choice for President. A great opportunity and a great President were lost.

It was soon leaked out that Labour's candidate would be Adi Roche, the Cork Director of the Chernobyl Project. This group had raised millions of pounds worth of aid for the children affected by the terrible conditions in Belorussia due to the fallout from the nuclear accident at Chernobyl in the eighties. Many of the Chernobyl children had been taken to Ireland for fosterage or medical treatment. Adi had done more for suffering humanity than anyone in Ireland.

But there was one important qualification that she lacked: she was not a politician and unlike Mary Robinson or Mary McAleese, she had never stood for office. She wasn't even much of a self-publicist; she was in fact a rather shy and private person. It later emerged that Adi was aware of all of this herself but that Fergus Finlay and Pat Magner had spent four hours convincing her to run. Of course she gave in to them; they were the big guns down from Dublin. It was most unfortunate.

Fianna Fáil was on the verge of picking Albert Reynolds as their candidate and I suppose on that basis it wouldn't be too hard to cobble together an anti-Albert coalition. However, the Sunday before Fianna Fáil was to pick their runner, Adi's candidature was leaked. This was a monumental blunder. Fianna Fáil then reassessed the situation, dropped poor Albert yet again and chose Mary McAleese – it was all over for Adi. Mary McAleese was an experienced politician, broadcaster and university don, she was in fact a clone of Mary Robinson on the nationalist, Catholic side. Fine Gael also picked a Mary Robinson clone in Mary Banotti MEP, though not such a good copy as the Fianna Fáil one, but at least she had the pedigree, being the grandniece of Michael Collins. The whole thing reached ludicrous proportions when the fundamentalist far right picked another Mary Robinson clone in Rosemary Scallon, previously known as the Eurovision Song Contest winner Dana. There was even an ex-garda to vote for in Derek Nally, obviously for those who had an aversion to Mary Robinson clones!

The campaign was launched on Tuesday 16 September 1997 in The Gallagher Gallery in Ely Place. Adi was bubbling with enthusiasm and innocence. She announced that one of her reasons for contesting was that she thought 'it was the right time for her'. She looked very well in her campaigning designer gear and she exuded sincerity and altruism but she lacked the vision of Robinson. A Campaign Committee was set up and

Ruairi Quinn chaired it initially. It was a high-powered committee and its membership was very impressive. It included Liz McManus TD and Tony Heffernan of Democratic Left, Trevor Sargent TD of the Green Party and other non-aligned friends such as Don Mullan, the Derry Civil Rights activist, and Billy Fitzpatrick, the former president of the ASTI. A bus was hired and Pat Magner went on tour with the candidate.

From the very start things went badly wrong. From Cork I received the phone calls alleging bad behaviour by Adi towards her employees on the Chernobyl Project. These were later given wide publicity. Reports from around the country were not good. In Kildare the constituency asked if we could get her a scriptwriter, her address to the party there had lasted a mere eight minutes and was mainly on the theme of 'My halo has slipped'. Pat Magner reported that small crowds or no crowds were turning up to meet the bus.

The Campaign Committee met every second day. Neither Fergus Finlay nor Ruairi attended after the first few meetings but I held on with a sinking heart. We tried to re-launch the Campaign in Jury's Hotel in Dublin. It was not a success. At the end of her speech she bowed to the audience like a cabaret singer, losing all eye contact. I was sitting beside Ali Hewson and I got her to stand up and wave at Adi so that she would stand and wave at the audience – she just wasn't a 'natural'. The Committee tried to shift the campaign to Dublin on foot of reports of its break-up and also because the floating vote is largest in Dublin. Meanwhile, Dick Spring joined up with Adi in South Tipperary. This is where the TV cameras filmed some impromptu entertainment given by singer Luka Bloom. Instead of just listening, Adi joined in and started to gyrate. The TV camera then panned to Dick Spring who was treating her to one of his special sour grimaces. These images were dutifully covered on the *Six O'Clock News* giving the nation great entertainment at our expense. It got worse and worse.

On Thursday 24 October, we had her in Dublin to do a walkabout in the city centre and in the evenings to visit the suburban shopping centres. The Green Party supplied the music: it was a 'bongo' band, very alternative in a hallucinogenic sort of way. As she left the new Jervis Street Shopping Centre they lined up on either side and played the *Batman* theme! 'Du ee, du ee Batman, Batman, Batman'. I could imagine what Bride Rosney would have made of them, she would have given them a clip on the ear and sent them home to their mammies. But Adi seemed oblivious to any discrepancy between the Caped Crusader and Uachtaráin na hÉireann. I was exasperated and remarked to Carol Coulter, the *Irish Times* journalist covering the walkabout, that I felt the bongo band might frighten the little old ladies. I was a bit too frank about my opinion and I'm afraid I was rather ungracious to the Greens who had brought the band along. Carol published the story in the following morning's *Irish Times* under the headline 'Greens send skinhead and bongo drum to aid of Adi'.

My comments effectively ended the Labour Campaign. The members had had enough at that stage. Dick Spring had gone to ground after the Tipperary incident and Fergus Finlay had disappeared, maybe to write a book on the campaign as he had done on the Robinson campaign. Ruairi Quinn, Chairperson of the Campaign Committee, I later learned, had gone to America. What a fiasco! Only one or two pockets held out. Gerry Ashe, the Constituency Organiser in Dublin South-East, and her brave troops continued on from their headquarters in Camden Street even though Gerry was the first Dublin member to point out to me the unsuitability of Adi Roche as a Presidential Candidate.

Polling day was on the following Thursday, 30 November, and the count was on Friday. The co-ordination centre was in Dublin Castle and I was the Agent for Adi Roche. After the early indications of a heavy defeat the Labour crowd surrounding Adi disappeared. It was the same old story over again; in victory everyone stays around to claim credit, in defeat everyone runs away in case they are blamed. But one other person stayed – it was Bernie Malone MEP and I really liked her for that. I then sat Bernie down and told her the hot news: on the previous Wednesday an impeccable source told me that Dick Spring would resign the leadership on the weekend of our heavy defeat in the Presidential Election. She wasn't too surprised. It would have been difficult enough for him to regain his authority after such a blunder. He would be the second party leader in seven years to lose out as a result of the previously irrelevant Presidential elections. Bernie and myself then discussed the scenarios for the succession.

But now it was becoming embarrassing up in Dublin Castle with the results to be announced. There was no Adi Roche. This was bad. It would appear that she was unable to take a defeat. It is a gracious custom for all candidates to be present, at least at the final result to thank the electoral officials and their own workers and to congratulate the victor. For Adi to have missed this would have reflected very badly on her and it would have been most unfair to let her end the campaign this way. I knew where they were all holed up; it was in Bono's house in Killiney. His wife, Ali Hewson, was throwing a party for the campaign at the luxurious house, swimming pool included. I became quite frantic, as naturally enough I didn't have access to Bono's home phone number. Fortunately, I did have the number of a Cork friend who would have it and was able to summon Adi to the Castle in the nick of time. The National Returning Officer, Mr Greene, had held back the declaration three times for me and now the Taoiseach was getting impatient. Adi arrived with two carloads of hangers-on. Bernie Malone took one look at them and paraphrasing Churchill's words turned to me and said: 'Never in the field of human endeavour has so little been owed to so many.' Good on you Bernie! But at least Adi got to speak at the declaration of the result and she graciously congratulated the winner, Mary McAleese.

Mary Banotti, the Fine Gael candidate had come in second and Rosemary Scallon (Dana) was third. Adi came fourth, ahead of Derek Nally. Dana had been nominated by the County Councils and not by the members of the Oireachtas, which is the more usual method of nomination. She said to the journalist Carol Coulter that night, 'I may not be President but I am a precedent'. She had turned out to be quite a substantial candidate.

The death of Anne Spring

My old friend Anne Spring had been sick for over a year and for such an active woman both physically and mentally it was torture for her. The phone calls had ceased, as had the advice and the decisive and fine character assessments of party figures. She was mainly interested in the progress of her son Dick and in that regard I'm glad that she wasn't around when he left the leadership. She wouldn't have understood or accepted in spite of her frequent assertions that it was all doing him no good personally.

She died in September 1997 just before the Presidential Campaign started. She was buried on Sunday 14 September after an enormous funeral mass attended by many of her Labour friends and admirers from far and wide. John Hume MP MEP, the leader of the SDLP, was there. I believe that this woman and many of the great women of her generation would have been TDs in a more equal society. Nevertheless, their pivotal role in Irish politics has never been appreciated. Their managerial, financial, and organisational skills enabled the election of their husbands and in some cases their sons. There are very few examples of this type of relationship in current Irish politics.

By the end of 1997 I had lost three of my greatest friends and allies in the party. On February 17 Noeline Dunphy, constituency Secretary and Executive member from Carlow-Kilkenny had succumbed at a tragically early age to cancer, and by September, both Jim Kemmy and Anne Spring had passed away. I was a much lonelier and isolated person without them.

Leaving five minutes too soon

The phone call came on Saturday evening; the story of Dick Spring's resignation as leader of the Labour Party was to be carried by Stephen Collins in the next morning's *Sunday Tribune*. It was a strange feeling of ending, closing, and passing. Dick was just 47 years old, far too young to retire from anything, yet he had been party leader for 15 years. He had been Tánaiste three times and of his 15 years of leadership, eight and a half had been spent in Government.

He had become very unpopular in recent years but had been the leading figure of the new Ireland in the early nineties. I remembered the ladies bursting into spontaneous applause when I crossed Kildare Street with him in 1992. Political popularity is fickle and transient. If he wanted to brave it out I have no doubt that the members of the party would have stood by him in large numbers. But we must also remember John Biffen's words. He had been a Cabinet Minister under Margaret Thatcher and in his resignation letter, he had written: 'In politics it is better to leave five minutes too soon than to continue for five years too long.' He was now about to part with grace, dignity, and even some good humour.

The king is dead, long live the king!

Canvassing started even before the ink was dry on the *Tribune* article. There was always the possibility that Dick Spring might change his mind. Resignations are like that; they are never final until committed to paper. And so that Sunday morning 1 November 1997 the succession race began.

Under Labour rules, the leader and deputy leader are elected every six years. In 1996 there had been no contest and Dick Spring had been elected leader and Ruairi Quinn deputy leader unopposed. The next election would take place in 2002. In the meantime, the General Council and the PLP would elect the replacement. There were to be 74 electors. At the outset Ruairi seemed ahead, in fact his constituency members were rather surprised that he would be challenged at all, but it was hardly going to be as simple as that. Worryingly, from early on it looked as if Ruairi was having difficulty getting support from rural Ireland even though Dublin was solidly behind him.

My position was plain from the outset. As General Secretary I was a voting member of the General Council as was my Deputy, Marion Boushell. It was a position I jealously guarded as I considered the position of General Secretary to be a representative as well as an executive one. As a constituency member of Dublin South-East and as a long-standing acquaintance if not friend of Ruairi Quinn's, I was voting for him. There were other factors, mainly associated with a change in the style in leadership, determining my choice. I believed that the removal of the influence of the unelected advisers would mark a leadership of Ruairi Quinn's rather than of Brendan Howlin's. This was an important issue, perhaps the major one in the election. There was also the case of the women infected with Hepatitis C, which had not been dealt with adequately during Brendan Howlin's term as Health Minister. This would be a serious handicap to his ever becoming party leader. I explained all this to Brendan when he canvassed my vote so that there would be no doubt as to my position. I did not, however, take a public stand in the party, keeping very much in the background.

As it happened I was out of Dublin during much of that week, which suited me well. It also coincided with the plans I had for the next few years: I intended to concentrate on organising and campaigning in the constituencies and this would necessitate my frequent absence from my Dublin office. On Friday I went to Kenmare in Co. Kerry to the funeral of Toni O'Connor, wife of an important party member. I had lunch afterwards with Breeda Moynihan-Cronin, the local TD, and her husband DC. Breeda was supporting Brendan Howlin and was very firm in her views. Ruairi had not responded to the needs of part-time workers in her constituency during his term as Minister for Finance. The chickens were really coming home to roost. On Tuesday (11 November) I travelled to Stradbally in Co. Laois where our old comrade and former Laois County Councillor Paddy Bray was to be buried. Pat Gallagher, now the local senator and former Laois-Offaly TD, was also strongly supporting Brendan Howlin, as were all of his non-Dublin-Leinster comrades. At this stage the whole thing was becoming a real Dublin versus rural split.

Nor was I reassured that evening at Dublin Castle, where the reception in honour of the new President, Mary McAleese, took place. It was the usual glittering affair but sad for me as my Mary had moved out. Nevertheless, when I got there it was a major culture shock – where were the women with histories, the trendy barristers, the separated spouses and the earnest lefties all eating dainty pieces of salmon or cream cheese from savoury crackers? All banished, banished completely, the place had been taken over by ham sandwich eaters and 'Fields of Athenry' singers of the Fianna Fáil persuasion. It was as if Robinson had been a figment of our imagination. They munched and drank and roared with laughter as they repossessed

Dublin Castle. It was enough to bring back memories of the eighties! Thank God the clock just can't be turned back in politics.

At the reception I spoke to Brian O'Shea, the Waterford TD and a very steady political judge. I tried to explain to him how alienated the Dublin party had felt over the previous four years. 'But don't you see,' he said, 'if Quinn is elected then the rural party will feel alienated.' Michael Ferris, the South Tipperary TD who was also in our company, agreed, but was more up front about it. He had gone public in his support for Brendan Howlin. John Mulvihill the former TD from Cork East was also there and he supported Ruairi Quinn, but was not a member of the electoral body. The urban/rural split was a worry even at this stage.

On the Monday of that week the *Irish Independent* had published a poll indicating that the general public favoured a Quinn victory. I wasn't at all surprised at this; Ruairi Quinn had been a popular Minister for a total of eight and a half years at this stage and had an enormous public profile. During the general election, he told me, research had indicated that he was the most popular Minister in the Government, yet he had been given no public profile during that campaign. He was very bitter about that as well he should have been. His presence on the airwaves might have saved a Labour seat or two.

The joint meeting of the General Council and PLP took place on Thursday 13 November 1997. It was a short enough meeting lasting a little over an hour. As expected, Ruairi Quinn won by a handsome margin of ten votes. Thirty-seven had voted for Quinn and twenty-seven for Howlin, who was then proposed as deputy leader by the victor. The ordinary party members representing the constituencies and the organisation had voted massively for Ruairi Quinn, though he failed to win a majority in the PLP. This was interesting, as it was the PLP that was the electoral body under the old rules; it would not have elected Ruairi Quinn as leader.

After the election and the press conference, the electors, who were now swollen with Quinn family members and well-wishers, headed for the Dáil Bar where there was already a large group of Howlin supporters in occupation. It didn't make for a comfortable mix.

Fergus departs

In the afternoon a small group gathered to make a presentation to Fergus Finlay whose resignation letter I had presented to the PLP on 5 November. He had worked for the party for almost 15 years and had every intention of leaving earlier. He stayed on, I believe, to facilitate Dick Spring.

Nevertheless, his star had sunk within the party, and the success of his term as Political Director was open to question as the party had gone from 32 seats to 17 in that period. Furthermore, as inventor of, and chief apologist for, the system of advisers which ran the Labour side of the governments from 1993–97, he was held responsible by some in the PLP for the subsequent halving of its numbers. Ironically, he was blamed by a totally different group within the PLP and the party for bringing Labour out of government with Fianna Fáil.

Now at his departure, I stood with Pat Upton TD at the back of the small crowd that gathered in the Dáil Bar to wish him well. It was the first function of the new party leader. 'Fergus Finlay's contribution to the Labour Party was unique,' began Ruairi Quinn, 'there was never anyone quite like him in the Labour Party before and there will never be anyone quite like him again. His contribution was enormous and will never be forgotten.' When the short speech ended, Pat Upton turned to me. 'That,' he said approvingly, 'was adequately ambiguous.'

CHAPTER 17

THE QUINN AND I

DURING DICK Spring's decline in popularity in 1996, Pat Upton had said, 'Yes, Boss Quinn will have to take over. He'll probably surround himself with advisers from the Irish Management Institute (IMI), but anyone would be better than the present lot.' It was now widely felt within the party that new blood would arrive and reinvigorate the party but Ruairi chose the cautious approach. He just promoted existing people into vacated positions. Ronan O'Brien, the Research Officer, became his adviser; Tom Butler, the Press Officer, became Press Director, a kind of derivative of Fergus's job; and Pat Magner and Anne Byrne remained on, though they had both supported Brendan Howlin. There were no radical changes and no new personnel.

In the policy area he was bound to be more liberal than his predecessor, coming from and representing one of the most liberal constituencies in Ireland. On the economic front, however, he was very cautious. He expressed, even as far back as the seventies, a belief in the excuse theory of 'the rising tide lifts all boats' and his attempt to sell off the TSB Bank during the dying days of the Government of Renewal was still remembered. It remained to be seen how he would handle Labour's traditional support for and protection of state services and sectors.

On the positive side he was very popular with a very good image as a successful minister and as an articulate and sensitive performer in the media. He was very well liked by the people who worked in RTE. His enormous experience in the party now made him one of its longest-serving TDs and he enjoyed an excellent relationship with the leaders of the trade union movement.

A strong, vigorous opposition in the Dáil matched by an organisational drive in the constituencies, sustained over a two or three-year period could lift the party's fortunes as it had in the late eighties and early nineties. The urban/rural divide could be healed; after all, it was the rural members of the General Council who had tipped the balance in favour of Ruairi Quinn so decisively. A more serious problem was the pro-Fianna Fáil image which haunted him; this too could be lifted after a year or two of stern, unrelenting opposition. These were my thoughts in the first few months of Ruairi Quinn's leadership.

Carry on Mandy!

In the last weekend of November I travelled to London for the first meeting of a group established to prepare the Socialists for the European Parliament elections of 1999. The British Labour Party put all their facilities at our disposal. In a way it was to be a showcase for them to demonstrate how they had ended 18 years of Conservative rule. We were a small group representing the Labour and Social Democratic Parties across the European Union and we met at their headquarters in the Millbank Tower on the Thames. On Sunday, Peter Mandelson, who was Cabinet Minister without a portfolio at the time, flew over from Paris to address us. It was most impressive. I had been anxious to meet Mandelson to see if he could throw any hints on the Irish situation our way. 'The Labour Party had been simply dreadful,' he droned, 'there were people in it who simply didn't want to win elections, could you imagine that?' The voice was at falsetto level with mock indignation and the hands were flying helicopter-like across the small stage to express his horror at these 'awful people'. I stared at him trying to keep my jaw from dropping. Was he for real? And yet he seemed so familiar to me – had I met him before, at a British Labour Party Conference perhaps, or maybe on holidays? I couldn't place him and yet I had this strong feeling of familiarity. Then it dawned on me, he was an almost exact replica of Kenneth Williams in the *Carry on* movies with his oohs and aahs, his waving hands, and his facial gestures. I decided that he wouldn't go down too well with our crowd and in any case, the clean up and modernisation of our party, accomplished ten years previously, had been superior to what had been accomplished in England. We were better off with our own counsels. When Mr Mandelson had left we all trooped out to a rather posh gourmet restaurant in Islington, *Frederick's*, where Frank Dobson, the Health Secretary, was our host. Nobody at the dinner mentioned Peter Mandelson.

Three by-elections and a conference

Two by-elections were scheduled for 1998 and both were in strong Labour constituencies. They would therefore be great indicators of the state of the party, the public attitude towards it, and of course the popularity of the new leader as well as the perception of the Fianna Fáil/PD Coalition Government. There was to be an election in Limerick East to fill the vacancy caused by Jim Kemmy's death. There was no doubt as to his replacement, it was to be his running mate, former senator Jan O'Sullivan, and she was duly selected in December 1997.

Jim's old friends, tough men who had come through his many campaigns with him formed an essential part of the campaign. This was the famous 'Dad's Army' with an average age of 70 years. Many had not made the transition from DSP to Labour but they were always ready for an election and were they full of spleen! Their knowledge of the city and its people was encyclopaedic and invaluable and their memory was as long as their insults were vitriolic. Mick Mulcahy had it in for Willie O'Dea, the sitting Fianna Fáil TD and Junior Minister. Seemingly O'Dea's aunt had fired Mick's sister from Shaw's Bacon Factory in 1940 for 'borrowing' some bacon scraps. Liam O'Connor, the philosopher of the group said, 'It's all a game. Your boss wants you to do as much work for as little money as possible and you want to do as little work for as much money as possible!'

There were two enormous assets to the campaign. One was the candidate herself: Jan was positive, confident, tireless, and thoroughly organised. She reminded me of Mary Robinson who had displayed similar qualities during the 1990 Presidential campaign. The other major asset of the campaign was the memory of Jim Kemmy. Just mentioning his name on the doorsteps evoked almost a reverent response. Dad's Army referred to it as Jim Kemmy's last campaign.

During the day I worked in the office in Hartstrong Street doing clinic cases with Jim's secretary, Margaret O'Donoghue, and in the evening I was out canvassing with Dad's Army. The out-of-Dublin PLP came in great numbers, Michael D Higgins being a particular hit as he was born in Limerick, quite near our headquarters.

The result was very gratifying with Jan O'Sullivan heading the poll and being elected quite easily.

Dublin North

Meanwhile in Dublin North a similar story unfolded. The by-election had been caused by the resignation of Ray Burke of Fianna Fáil from the Dáil. Sean Ryan who had been defeated here in the general election of the previous year was the Labour candidate. He had since gone on to win a senate seat. The campaign was very different to the Limerick one, being thoroughly modern; it was high tech and paper driven with responses reflected upon and everything assessed. It too was a great victory with Henry Haughton as the successful Director of Elections.

The winning of two by-elections was a great victory for the Labour Party coming as it did just nine months after the crushing defeat of the general election. For Ruairi Quinn it was both a great personal success and a great danger. It was a success in that it was a brilliant start to his leadership of the party and its danger lay in the fact that he might think that it was all going to be this easy. It was like a person becoming a minister on his or her first day in the Dáil – it can be a poisoned chalice.

Policy Conference 1998

If anything demonstrated the transience of the by-election victory it was the Special Consultative Conference that was held on 28 March in Jury's Hotel in Dublin. It was just after the double by-election victories of Dublin North and Limerick East and was the first Conference of the party with Ruairi Quinn as the new leader. As such, it was supposed to point to a new policy direction and relevance for Labour.

Central to the Conference was an economic proposal to be made by Emmet Stagg as Public Service spokesperson on the sale of public utilities, in particular the ESB. Granted, Emmet was not too convincing in his proposition and the naked copying of this from the British Labour Party's policy platform was a bit too obvious. Anyway, it was not acceptable to the Conference. James Wrynn, the Deputy Chairman of the ESB, who was International Secretary of the party, rounded on it with particular vehemence. It was also strongly opposed by Cllr John McGinley of Kildare, Emmet's right-hand man. This policy was to have been the centrepiece of the Conference and it had to be dropped. Ruairi Quinn, the eternal optimist, had said to me that he expected the party to rise in the opinion polls after the Conference. I didn't think it was going to be as easy as that, instead it registered its first drop since he had become leader.

The Cork South-Central by-election of 1998

As soon as I got back from Limerick the news broke of the tragic death of Hugh Coveney, the Cork South-Central Fine Gael TD. He had fallen from a cliff face while out walking. In this constituency Labour's Toddy O'Sullivan had lost his seat in the general election and was full of fight and ready to win it back though he was now almost 64. He was a highly-strung and excitable candidate.

The situation was much more complex here than in Limerick. Toddy had had a very public falling out on the night of the count with Ruairi Quinn, then the deputy leader. Speaking just after he had lost his seat an angry Toddy had called on Dick Spring to put information into the public domain relating to Independent Newspapers, who were believed to be hostile to the Rainbow's return to power. In studio, Ruairi Quinn was asked about this immediately after Toddy went off air. Ruairi indicated that he knew nothing of what Toddy was talking about. This went down very badly in Cork and was seen as Ruairi undermining a defeated TD at his weakest moment. The constituency secretary sent a letter to Ruairi Quinn telling him that they felt he was unworthy of being deputy leader of the party. Matters got a little more complicated when a few months later Ruairi became leader. Now that there was to be a by-election, who was to be Director of Elections? Well who else except the very man who had penned the letter, Cllr Mick Ahern? This was going to be fun.

The campaign picked up well and for a while in that optimistic lacuna between opinion polls we thought that we could win. Fine Gael, however, had produced their ideal candidate in the deceased TD's young good-looking son Simon. Two weeks into the campaign I was told of two women seen removing one of his posters in Turners Cross. They were removing the poster to put it up in their bedroom. Not many Irish politicians either male or female would pass that test, but Simon Coveney could. After that I dropped whatever lingering doubt I had about his winning the campaign.

Polling day was 23 October 1998 and Toddy got 19 per cent of the vote. This was a very good showing indeed and well within the range for his winning back a Dáil seat. As expected, Simon Coveney easily won the seat previously held by his father.

Mo under threat!

My old acquaintance from the British Labour Party, Dr Mo Mowlam, had been appointed Northern Ireland Secretary by the incoming Labour Government in 1997. Now in Dublin for a meeting with the Irish Government she surprisingly indicated a wish to meet Labour representatives. This is most unusual for office holders who must strive to be separate from their own party affiliations. The meeting took place at head office on 29 October 1998. Mo was accompanied by her handsome young adviser Nigel Warner. Ruairi Quinn was there with his adviser Ronan O'Brien.

My secretary, Jackie Byrne, served tea and biscuits. 'Look Nigel,' the Secretary of State exclaimed, 'they have Jaffa Cakes.' Poor Nigel looked very embarrassed, as he was force fed Jaffa Cakes by his boss. 'Oh do have another Nigel', she would say.

She wasn't long though about getting down to business. 'Tony' as she called the British Prime Minister Tony Blair, was very taken by David Ervine, the leader of the Progressive Unionist Party in Northern Ireland. Could we assist in having that party recognised by the Socialist International? I couldn't believe what I was hearing. This is the parent body of all Labour and Social Democratic Parties in the world, its recognition of the PUP would seriously undermine the position of the SDLP, its only member in Northern Ireland. I explained to her in as indirect a fashion as possible of the solidarity between our two parties and how John Hume in particular had stood by us on the European stage when we had lost all our seats in the European Parliament elections in 1984.

The meeting ended and I was able to give Mo a scarf from the Kilkenny Design Centre in memory of the whisky she had sent me in 1989. But the meeting had very serious implications. The PUP was a party that got 2.5 per cent of the vote in the 1998 Northern Ireland Assembly elections, while the SDLP got 22 per cent. To try to promote a Party of 2.5 per cent as against one of 22 per cent indicated a lack of knowledge by Downing Street that was alarming. Furthermore, such a level of interference in the work of the Secretary of State boded ill for Mo herself. Sadly my worries proved well founded and Mo was removed from her position in October 1999. She had been the most popular Northern Ireland Secretary ever.

Labour and Democratic Left merge

The unity of the left, which is a very varied and multi-coloured animal, had always been an aspiration in Ireland. Labour had always dominated but never monopolised it. In the first 80 years of the Irish State, only the Communist-aligned Workers' Party came anywhere near Labour. The greatest challenge ever to Labour's position was in the 1987 and 1989 general elections when the Workers' Party had increased its number of TDs to seven. But this was still a long way from overtaking Labour. On the trade union front, the Workers' Party had also posed a similar threat to Labour influence, particularly in the ITGWU. Its merger with the FWUI in January 1990 put paid to that one. The new union would have a strong officer corps, which would be able to repel all boarders.

Things changed very dramatically in 1992 when the Workers' Party split. The Parliamentary group had become increasingly unhappy with the centralised control of the party and six of its seven TDs, including the party leader Proinsias De Rossa, left to form a new party. After some false starts this group emerged as Democratic Left, winning four seats in the 1992 general election. Besides the party leader, this group included Pat Rabbitte in Dublin South-West, Eamon Gilmore in Dun Laoghaire, and Liz McManus in Wicklow. In 1993 it won the by-elections in Dublin South-Central and Cork North-Central with Eric Byrne and Kathleen Lynch respectively.

When Labour split with Fianna Fáil in 1994, Democratic Left, along with Fine Gael, comprised the new Government. It worked with surprisingly few hiccups. After the general election in which Democratic Left dropped the two seats they had won in the 1994 by-elections, they began a fundamental internal assessment and they didn't like what they saw. During their term in Government, the four TDs had each been ministers. Now, having tasted the nectar of power they wanted more. Being a small marginal party of the left was hardly the way to achieve it, after all, it had entered Government in 1994 almost by accident. Labour on the other hand, found Democratic Left a most desirable match, at least as far as their personnel was concerned. In April of 1997 Jim Kemmy and myself had discussed Pat Rabbitte's situation: he was a very successful and popular minister and Jim offered to approach him with a view to joining the Labour Party. We agreed to put it off until after the general election. Another likely recruit would be Eamon Gilmore, the TD for Dun Laoghaire.

What was offered though was much more extensive. When Proinsias De Rossa approached Ruairi Quinn he offered a merger of the two parties to make a new political entity. That one was soon dropped in the face of fierce Labour opposition though Ruairi Quinn had considered it. There was a history of intense rivalry verging almost on hatred on the ground. Overcoming this would be a difficult though not impossible task – there had been similar hatreds in Limerick. The practical problems of a merger were centred on candidate strategy. Who, for example would contest in Dublin North-West, where Róisín Shortall and Proinsias De Rossa both held seats in what was soon to become a three-seater constituency? This situation was to be mirrored all around the country, not only at Dáil level, but also at the level of local government and the European Parliament. The subject was first broached at the Parliamentary meeting of 27 May 1998. Those deputies most affected by it, namely the Dublin ones, were the most wary. They were strongly supported by Brian O'Shea of Waterford, where the left seat had once been held by Paddy Gallagher of the Workers' Party from 1981–82. He predicted that a merger would give only a short-term boost. It was the Dublin TDs, however, who outlined the most serious problems of a merger.

Proinsias De Rossa eyes Brendan Howlin suspiciously as Labour and Democratic Left merge in 1999.

As was to be expected, Pat Upton took a leadership role in this. Rivalry had been bitter in his constituency between Labour and Democratic Left and indeed with its predecessor, the Workers' Party, right back to Frank Cluskey's time. Labour has come out on top on all occasions bar one. That was in the election of 1989 shortly after Frank Cluskey's death. The vehemence of his opposition should have rung alarm bells with Ruairi Quinn and his advisers but it seemed to have no affect at all. He spoke of his deep suspicions of the baggage of the Workers' Party and the possibility of its re-surfacing and of the detrimental effect a merger would have on existing Labour candidates who would be moved aside to facilitate the newcomers. Róisín Shortall spoke of the way herself and Proinsias De Rossa had kept down the Provo vote in her constituency. She felt that it was very important to have someone on the left to do this. There is a small hard left vote that Labour finds it hard to hold, but Democratic Left could. Without that party it would go to Sinn Féin, who were on the rise. This point was never adequately answered. The concerns of the TDs weren't answered either and Ruairi Quinn talked about the process ending by

Christmas. The problem here was that he was reacting to someone else's initiative, lured by the bait of four seats.

Róisín Shortall soon made it clear that she would not commit electoral suicide and take Proinsias De Rossa as a running mate. Then the question arose as to where he would run. He quite understandably refused to move to the new constituency of Dublin Mid-West, a three-seater centred on the dormitory town of Rathcoole. He had been an MEP, elected in 1989 but he had handed over to Des Geraghty during his term. Bernie Malone was the sitting MEP and had been one of Ruairi Quinn's strongest supporters. I met her at Vicky Somers' annual party on 20 June 1998 and she knew the score. 'I'm to be sacrificed for the merger because I can provide least opposition to it', she predicted accurately.

The General Council was presented with the idea and as expected was very supportive. Many had been around for the positive benefits of the mergers with the Democratic Socialist Party and the Independent Socialist Party of Sligo/Leitrim. Very few understood how much work and time had gone into these to remove all obstacles before merger. This was different, the timescale had been set even before the viability of the project had been tested. It was bound to get very messy. Meanwhile, the people who would be affected were at their wits' end. There was no attempt to analyse the effects of the merger from an intellectual or political viewpoint. Newspaper articles against the merger, particularly in the *Sunday Business Post,* were rubbished. Róisín Shortall's concern that narrowing the left's diversity left space for Sinn Féin was never answered, but eminent independent political scientists supported her argument. Only the cliché used extensively by Brendan Howlin that 'the sum of the two parts would be greater than the whole' and the sentiment that the merger would create 'a synergy' were held out in reply.

For the first time since his departure, members began to compare how Dick Spring would have handled Proinsias De Rossa's overtures as opposed to Ruairi Quinn. The pressures centred on Pat Upton and he bore them personally and for the others. After his death, one TD told me that if Pat Upton had led a breakaway party he would have joined him. But Pat would not do that; even at the Merger Conference he called for party unity and for people to stay in the party. In this way he saved much for Labour.

There were many others however who could not accept what had happened or the way in which it had happened. The most notable of these was Brian Fitzgerald, the Meath Dáil candidate and former TD who left the party along with fellow Councillors Jimmy Cudden and Robbie Griffiths. In

Carlow, Cllr John McNally left. These were more nails in the coffin of Labour in rural Ireland. The Dublin Labour Party mainly stayed intact due in large part to Pat Upton's influence, but we lost Charlie Callan, the Secretary of the Labour History Society. He was particularly concerned about connections between persons in Democratic Left and the former regimes of Eastern Europe. In many places it was a merger in name only, the two groups remained separate and led separate existences. As Mervyn Taylor said to me at lunch one day: 'The problem about the merger is that it didn't take place.'

It was very sad and frustrating because it was so unnecessary. The merger could have happened without losing a single public representative. A bit of consultation and consideration of the problems on the ground and everyone could have been brought around. It would have taken time, patience and the long view of Labour and politics; attributes now sorely lacking.

The positive spin-offs were immediately obvious. Proinsias De Rossa, Pat Rabbitte, Eamon Gilmore and Liz McManus joined the PLP and were soon senior and respected spokespersons for Labour. Their councillors too fitted in well with their former rivals, but this was more in the nature of a lull before the local elections, which were scheduled for June 1999. These would be the first electoral test of the merger.

For whom the bell tolls

For almost 20 years now Labour had performed very badly at European Parliament elections. In 1979 the party had won four of the 15 seats, in 1984 it won no seats at all, in 1989 it won just one and in 1994 it also returned one seat. It was clearly under-performing and a drastic re-vamp of its candidate strategy was required. What was going to happen in Dublin was a bloody battle for survival between outgoing MEP Bernie Malone and former Democratic Left leader Proinsias De Rossa, but there was at least an outside chance of two seats. Barry Desmond and Proinsias De Rossa had won a seat each in 1989, but at that time Mr De Rossa had been a Workers' Party candidate, now the entire premise on which the merger had been rushed through would be tested, would Bernie Malone and Proinsias De Rossa win two seats contesting for the same party? If they did, then the haste of the merger would be justified.

In the Leinster constituency the situation was more clear-cut. Michael Bell, the rotund sixty-two-year-old Louth TD had contested twice and intended to have one last winning shot. He was a man of enormous appetites and generosity. He had been returned to the Dáil at each election since 1982 though he had a very close shave in 1997. Though he almost won the European Parliament seat in 1989, he had since been in very serious trouble with the party. In 1991 he had declared of Rhonda Paisley (daughter of Dr Ian) that 'The only way this country will ever be united and at peace is when people like her return to Britain'.

He had received further bad publicity when while serving as Labour's Defence spokesperson he announced that he had applied for compensation for deafness inflicted while serving in the FCA. Anyway, his profile was all wrong. Even a casual perusal of the European Parliament campaigns would show that the electorate did not want retiring older TDs as candidates, they wanted young articulate representatives for the European Parliament. Sean Butler, a sales executive from Kilkenny and a member of Labour Youth fitted the bill. He swept the Selection Convention and became Labour's Leinster Euro candidate. The Labour members demonstrated yet again that they have minds of their own. Michael Bell thought it had all been a big plot against him and resigned on the following day, but he was to return before year's end though he did not contest the local elections.

The Munster European Parliament constituency did not hold out the same prospects as the Leinster one. It was also a four-seater but its four MEPs were contesting again and each had strong electoral bases and high profiles. They were Brian Crowley and Gerry Collins, both of Fianna Fáil, John Cushnahan, the former Alliance Party leader, now a Fine Gael MEP, and Pat Cox, formerly of the PDs, now an independent MEP. Nevertheless, this is exactly the type of challenge that is made for a young enthusiastic candidate who is prepared to fight more than one campaign for the seat. As ever in politics, those who persist win.

The obvious choice was Cllr Paula Desmond of Carrigaline in County Cork. She was popular and well known in the party having served her stint as Chairperson of the Labour Women's National Council and the AC. She was the daughter of Eileen, former TD, Minister, and MEP and her father Dan Desmond had also been a TD. The last time we had won the seat was with Eileen back in 1989. When Ruairi Quinn asked Paula to stand I thought that at least he had done the right thing for Munster, but sadly it was too good to be true; in January 1999 a source told me that Brendan Ryan, the independent senator, had been asked to contest for Labour. I went straight to Ruairi Quinn who confirmed this. It was madness in my view, bound only to antagonise the Munster membership and for no gain whatsoever. Seemingly the decision had been reached at a meeting in the

Ferrycarrig Hotel in Wexford. I remembered the words of Anne Spring: 'Never trust anyone who makes up Labour policy in a pub.' I was beginning to despair of the current style of leadership.

Senator Brendan Ryan was a highly respected and radical character with connections to the Simon Community and the Irish Campaign for Nuclear Disarmament. We had hoped to get him to join Labour back in the late eighties. He said himself that a local approach he made was rebuffed in those days, but it had never come to my desk, I would have been delighted to have him in the party. But now it was different, we already had a candidate who had been invited by the party leader to run, and to expect the Munster membership to drop her just was not on. I explained to Ruairi Quinn that the Labour Party just doesn't act that way, nevertheless, the project was proceeded with and the inevitable happened: Brendan Ryan was humiliatingly defeated at the Munster Euro Selection Convention. It had been postponed twice, much to Paula Desmond's chagrin, but she came through convincingly in the end.

For Connacht-Ulster I had been approached by Ger Gibbons, who worked for Bernie Malone MEP in Brussels, as a prospective candidate. As a young candidate with experience in Brussels and Strasbourg he would have made an ideal MEP. His constituency, however, became a battleground of high profile independents that gobbled up his potential vote. He was selected on 21 February at a convention in the Sligo Park Hotel. I drove up and down that day, giving Bernie Malone and her secretary Margaret Dowling a lift in my car. She was travelling west to support Ger who was her employee and protégé, though she giggled when she said that she didn't think that Ger had her 'killer instinct'. It was a hilarious trip as Bernie berated her enemies, praised her friends, and poured scorn on her detractors. Yet again she was ready to carry her fight onto the streets of Dublin – but alas, she had met her match. At a European Parliament-funded Conference on the Elderly, which was attended by her running mate Proinsias De Rossa, Bernie, in full flight, announced that she was descended from the famous street trader Molly Malone at which remark De Rossa was heard say, 'Wasn't she a whore?'

The death of Pat Upton

The stress of politics was having a serious effect on Pat Upton. He seemed to be taking everything to heart and carrying an increasing burden on his own shoulders as he internalised each problem that affected the constituency and the party. He was never a complainer and looking back I can see quite easily that he had little or no means of relieving his stress. He was the only person I have no hesitation in saying would not have died at the early age of 55 years if he had not been in politics. He was a tremendous loss to his young family of three sons and one daughter and the dignity of his wife Anne all during the funeral ceremonies added immeasurably to the poignancy of the event.

I was at a lunch for the European Person of the Year in the Berkley Court Hotel on 22 February 1999 when I heard the news. The Taoiseach Bertie Ahern was there and when I told Joe Lennon, his Press Secretary, he said that there was a curse on the present Dáil; already after just 20 months three of its members were prematurely dead.

Pat was a straight talker to two Labour leaders and a devastating critic of humbug and cant. He was even listened to by Bernie Malone, which was an almost unique attribute. At his funeral I too felt a devastating personal loss. This was the type of public representative I had always admired: fearless and incorruptible. It was very hard to move on from here.

National Conference 1999 and the local election preparations

In 1999 the sequence of events were to include a National Conference of the party to be held in Tralee in deference to the former leader Dick Spring. After Paula Desmond's selection against Brendan Ryan's for the Munster Constituency, Ruairi Quinn asked me to go to Munster to run Paula's campaign. I laughed when he said it asking, 'Is this punishment for supporting Paula?' It was a bit too obvious, yet I thought maybe I'd do it as it might be a bit more productive that staying in Dublin adjudicating in the rows between Bernie Malone and Proinsias De Rossa. Besides, there was unlikely to be much of a campaign without me in Munster; Paula, by her own admission is not an organiser.

It was towards the local elections that I now set my plans. They had been the launching pad from which we gained our massive victory in 1992. The complicating factor was that we had now to take into account the Democratic Left vote, the number of candidates, the narrowing of the range on the left, and the rise of Sinn Féin. I set off on another marathon tour of the country. I met with great success in many places. In Cork County I was able to get candidates to contest all council areas; something I was unable to do in 1991. At a convention in the Celtic Ross Hotel in Rosscarbery on a freezing Friday night 22 February, candidates and supporters came to a monster Selection Convention that covered most of the county. Some would make a round trip of over a hundred miles that night. It was clear yet again what commitment there was for Labour if only it could be harnessed. There were problems too: in Limerick City and in Cork City the candidate list was comprised of the former Democratic Left plus the existing Labour representatives, the ticket was built around the merger, not around a strategy to win seats. It reached ludicrous proportions in Limerick City Area No.3. Here was a four-seater electoral area in Limerick City Council and two candidates were proposed by the former Democratic Left in Limerick and three had been put forward by Labour before the merger. That meant there were five Labour candidates in a four-seater ward. Pat Magner was put in charge of these aspects of the merger and yet this was allowed to stand. In 1991 we had won two seats here. In these elections, not surprisingly, we won none. The party was becoming a laughing stock with carry-on like this.

Back in Dublin I was informed by means of a letter from Ruairi Quinn that Brendan Howlin was to become Chairperson of the Election Campaign Committee and that I was not to be even a member of that committee. Well, I wasn't having that and after a row, Ruairi reversed his decision. I was too busy anyway to sit around in committee, there was too much work to be done on the ground but this was a point of importance. The idea of having an election committee without the General Secretary was surreal but demonstrated again the fantasy nature of the strategy being pursued. Meanwhile the Euro Directors of Elections in Dublin, Leinster, and Connacht/Ulster resigned for different reasons. In fact, as Euro Director of Elections in Munster I was the only one to hang on until the end of the campaign. Most astonishingly of all, there was to be no dedicated Director of Elections for the local elections. Brendan Howlin's Campaign Committee met on several occasions and I attended the first few meetings but it had no grasp and little knowledge of the situation. After I left for Cork I didn't hear of it again.

What happened next was far more serious for my work: Marion Boushell, the Deputy General Secretary, was diagnosed as having breast cancer. Her treatment meant extensive surgery and chemotherapy and her extensive workload was devolved onto my desk, as she would be sick for some time. It was a small price to pay for her recovery.

Marion hailed from Manchester originally and had come to Dublin in the sixties. Her personality fitted in so well with the Irish temperament that it is hard to imagine her not being Irish. In 1990 at an AC Meeting, a member who usually had a good few pints of Guinness on the train coming up to the meetings was in vocal but not very sensible form. The party was always totally broke in those days and so depended very much on the small membership fee. The person involved suggested that part of this fee be returned to the constituencies to which Marion retorted 'For fuck's sake'. It was said with such meaning and derision that it showed that she had totally captured the idiom – she had absolutely gone native. The extra workload necessitated by Marion's absence did not interfere with the preparations for the National Conference in which she usually played such a key role. There were some areas though, such as the preparation of the Report to Conference Document, to which I would normally have given more time. She was also the bookkeeper to the party and its high reputation for honesty in those years owed much to her meticulous keeping of the accounts. Ita McAuliffe did what she could to help, particularly in relation to National Conference but she had her own busy job. To be fair, Denise Rogers, Ruairi Quinn's secretary, did offer to help to fill in for Marion but I felt that this would not be appreciated by my missing colleague.

The Conference was held on 31 April through to 2 May in the Brandon Hotel in Tralee. Dick Spring arrived in to meet us on the previous Thursday and he was transformed. Jovial and dressed in tweeds, very much the country gent, he now travelled in a four-wheel drive jeep and he seemed much happier in his new role. He was certainly less of a grouch. During the Conference he was given a rousing reception by the delegates.

The centrepiece of Ruairi Quinn's speech was a section on refugees which Ronan O'Brien, his adviser, assured me would be 'very powerful'. I would have preferred a conference around the local and European elections. The Conference was technically successful, everything worked well and there was no negative undercurrent. It did, however, lack excitement and relevance. I suppose this was part of the *malaise* of not only the Conference but also the party at this time. We can forgive anything in politics except boredom. Even during the Labour civil wars in the eighties when the Springites were beating the Staggites over the head, at least neither side was dull. Now the whole party mass had become a grey blob. Only some few bright sparks like Pat Rabbitte or Jan O'Sullivan stood out.

Back in Dublin in the first week in May after the Conference, I was preparing to move myself to Cork for the eight weeks or so that would take us up to polling day. I took a short-term lease on an apartment in the city centre, bought a second-hand jeep in which to transport the candidate, and prepared to take on the Munster Euro campaign. Already at John Mulvihill's suggestion I had hired AJ Cotter, a former County Council PR person, to be the campaign's Press Officer and with an office contributed by SIPTU was ready to head for Ireland's southern capital. I didn't get out of

Dublin a second too early. At a meeting in Ruairi Quinn's office before I left, it was decided that as regards the local and European elections, the Press Office 'Would not be taking its eye off the Dáil'. This was strongly supported by Brendan Howlin, who was Chairperson of the Election Committee. Such a downgrading, especially of the local elections, betokened a lack of understanding of their importance and of the role of local councillors in the ebb and flow of the party.

I loaded my gear and the party accounts into my jeep and headed down the road to Cork. It was 5 May 1999 and I would not return to Dublin full-time until 15 June.

CHAPTER 18

EURO ELECTIONS, LOCAL ELECTIONS AND EXIT

IT WAS a wet and depressing Wednesday afternoon when I unloaded my bags in Washington Street in Cork. I moved into the Campaign Office that night and by the weekend the campaign was up and running. The strategy was to get Paula Desmond's vote in between that of the two Fine Gael candidates. The weaker of the two was Jim Corr and as he was from Cork. Paula would benefit disproportionately from his transfers and after that things would be in the hands of providence. So we hit the road, Paula and I, in our Mitsubishi Pajero, soon re-christened the 'Paulamobile', while AJ Cotter held fort at the office pumping out the press releases and briefings. We returned to Cork almost every night, though we did overnight in Ennis, Limerick, Tralee, and Dingle. Cork is a very central location for the Munster constituency and it has excellent access roads. It was a great pleasure canvassing with a candidate in such command of her brief and meeting all my friends in the Munster Labour organisation.

Paula's main campaign plank was protection of the consumer from genetically modified foods and she had produced a paper for the party on the subject. The Munster constituency, even though it boasts the cities of Cork, Waterford, and Limerick as well as large towns such as Tralee, Killarney, Ennis, Clonmel, and Thurles is dominated by the agricultural lobby to the detriment of the consumer. Everybody was busy with the local elections in their own areas but gave us a genuinely warm welcome when we headed in the road. I think they probably looked on our arrival as a pleasant break from real campaigning. There was more than a touch of the Don Quixote and Sancho Panza travelling about the country in our campaign!

While all this was going on I kept in touch with the local election situation as best as I could by phone. In Waterford's Dooley's Hotel on

17 May I received a call from Mary O'Reilly from Granard in Longford. She had telephoned me in 1994 and asked if she could contest the local elections for the Granard Town Commission. I had never met her but could tell that she was a decent kind person. She wasn't elected but I was always happy to present the electorate with decent candidates. After the election we lost contact and she didn't get round to joining the party. 'You probably don't remember me', she started. 'Of course I do', I replied. 'Can I run again for Labour?' she asked. I was delighted but told her that it was now very late for me to get her canvassing cards. That didn't put her off though: 'I've still some left from the last election', she assured me. No, she didn't think they were a bit out of date but were Mr Pattison and Mr Bell running again for the European Parliament as they were mentioned on her literature left over from 1994? When I told her that we had new candidate called Sean Butler she was not put out at all. The European Parliament elections were mentioned at the bottom of the canvassing cards, she would just trim off that bit with a pair of scissors! This is the story of how Labour won its first seat ever on Granard Town Commission. Of all our results I was thrilled to read of Mary O'Reilly's election. I was delighted to meet this charming lady shortly afterwards.

In other places things weren't going quite so swimmingly. In Limerick the party was fielding far too many candidates and was headed down the road to losing three city seats and our one seat in the county. It was heartbreaking to see all that Jim Kemmy and the Labour/DSP merger had built up going down the Swanee River, but we had great people in Limerick and I was confident that they would rise again. In Dublin things went very well from the start. I was hardly bothered by news from the capital; a sure sign of campaign success. Cork City was perhaps the worst example of the failure of the merger. All candidates seemed to be campaigning separately and in competition with one another. I tried fairly successfully, I think, to steer Paula clear of any partisanship and as a consequence all candidates treated us very well. In fact the Euro campaign seemed to be the only unifying factor in the southern capital.

I campaigned during the six weekdays and on Sundays I headed down to the office to do the party accounts. I was able to pay the party's bills and keep an account of our affairs by dedicating this one day a week to our finances. In reality, I was only keeping our head above water until Marion returned from her treatment. Thankfully, from July onwards she was to make a remarkable recovery and by the end of the summer she resumed her job full-time. In the meantime, on dreary and wet Sundays I struggled with the accounts in a back-street office in Cork City. There was a sex shop across the road and AJ Cotter promised a guided tour, but we never got round to it. It was a real case of 'the nearer the church the farther from God!'

Travels in Munster

Travelling around Munster in May time has its advantages, I certainly got an insight into life in the province that few have shared. In Portlaw in Waterford at lunchtimes on Mondays the pubs are full. 'It's an old custom', Brian O'Shea the local TD told me unconvincingly. An advertisement in an auctioneer's window in Carrick on Suir told me that one could still buy a house in the Comeragh Mountains for about £20,000 or so. Dick Spring took us for a drink in Tralee and related how he had baffled them at a lunch in the House of Commons by referring to a portrait of his fellow Kerryman in a Committee Room. It was of Lord Kitchener, who was born in Ballylongford. We stayed in the Old Ground Hotel in Ennis, that last survivor of gentry life and the landed ascendancy in Munster. While the staff turned a blind eye we smuggled in Chinese takeaways and ordered wine from room service. We hadn't eaten all day so we turned necessity into an opportunity and entertained our Shannonside candidate Betty Walsh and her son Ciaran with an impromptu pyjama party.

Ruairi Quinn travelled down to canvass with us on a number of occasions. On 4 June we finished in Mitchelstown having done a circuit that included Macroom, Kanturk, and Charleville. Here we were met by local candidate Tadhg O'Donovan dressed in an off-white sleeveless shirt that had obviously seen many campaigns with him; there were distinct traces of brown sauce on the front. Beside him stood Ruairi Quinn in his immaculate £400 plus Hugo Boss olive green suit and flamboyant tie. Never before was the contrast between Dublin 4 Labour and rural Labour so starkly posed. They were the odd couple if there ever was an odd couple. The scene was enhanced by the look of total discomfiture on Ruairi's face. 'Tell him to wear a clean shirt in future', he growled at me before he sat into his car and headed off the Dublin Road. Paula and myself laughed all the way back to Cork.

The Cork count

But even a campaign as long as this must come to an end. The count was in the now familiar Neptune Centre in Cork City. As expected, Brian Crowley, the sitting Fianna Fáil MEP, headed the poll. His astonishing vote of 154,195 was almost twice the quota. At just 35 years of age he was heading into his second term as an MEP. I had met him at the start of the campaign when RTE were recording an item for the *Six O'Clock News* in University

College Cork. Our paths didn't cross again until the day of the count. Without the slightest hesitation or obvious sign of trying to remember he said 'Hello Ray' – no wonder he was a poll topper. Paula Desmond came fifth in this four-seater: a remarkable achievement and right as near to target without winning the seat as we wished.

It was Sunday 13 June 1999 and the dreadful news from the local elections had been pouring in since Saturday. I had been in Dublin on Friday to cast my own vote but had returned to be present for the Munster Euro count. Paula had also been a local election candidate and had been returned. Sadly, many of her colleagues bit the dust, including two former Labour Lord Mayors of Cork Frank Nash and Joe O'Callaghan. Her hard-working County Council colleague and Dáil candidate Sheila O'Sullivan had also lost out. It was a sad day for many but others were just starting their political careers; in Skibbereen, Michael McCarty at 21 and as Labour's youngest candidate in the state came through to hold the West Cork seat.

The Euro Count dragged on until Monday. At lunchtime so many transfers were heading towards Paula that Toddy O'Sullivan the former TD went on RTE's lunchtime radio show to say that Paula had a chance of winning. It was a lovely moment and must have given just a little lift to many flagging Labour hearts around the country. But it was just Toddy's natural excitement and exuberance coming to a head. Shortly afterwards my mobile phone rang. It was my sister Mary calling from Tullamore Hospital. She was with my brother Vincent and had the results of his catscan. It had revealed that he had multiple brain tumours. 'Could you come immediately?' she asked. I froze just thinking of my brother, my sister and that now frequent visitor of cancer. 'What's the matter?' Toddy asked gently as he saw the change in my demeanour. I told him and left the count centre. I drove to my apartment, emptied it as best as I could and drove to Tullamore. During the trip my phone rang several times but I was unable now to share my personal news with my colleagues.

Dublin again

It was a more depressed and chastened party that I had to overview from my office in Dublin. On the positive side, Marion was now recovering from her treatment and was able to come in to work more often. On the following day (15 June) I travelled again to Tullamore. Ruairi Quinn telephoned me on the way. 'Could you prepare a report on the local and European elections for the Parliamentary Party?' I was a bit taken aback. After all he had appointed

Brendan Howlin to chair the Election Committee and had initially tried to keep me off the Committee completely. When I put that to him and asked why he didn't ask Brendan Howlin to do such a report he told me that Brendan had refused. I felt sorry for him then as this would make him look totally ineffective. He never had majority support in the PLP and for the past year many members didn't bother even turning up. I agreed to do the report but it couldn't be for the following day, it would have to be for Wednesday 22 June.

The party had done fairly well in Dublin in the local elections. It was provincial Ireland though that caused me most concern. Whole areas were now without Labour representation. There were now no Labour members, in some cases for the first time since the foundation of the state, in Meath, Clare, Laois, or Limerick County Councils and we had just one member on Tipperary North Riding, Tipperary South Riding, Wexford, Offaly, Kilkenny, Donegal and Sligo County Councils. Clawing our way back would be harder than I anticipated. Overall the party had lost 17 county and county borough council seats over its numbers at close of nominations. The party would have to be rebuilt from the very foundations in some areas. I was not looking forward to the prospect but I wouldn't let the party down. If it had to be done then it had to be done. I would give it another five years at most.

When I presented my report to the PLP there was shock at the level of our losses – 17 seats are the makings of a small political party. I think the former Democratic Left people were a bit embarrassed as theirs had held on well, and they deserved congratulations for this in my opinion. Brendan Howlin did not show up. Jack Wall, the TD from Kildare South, said that one of the reasons the party did badly was that the General Secretary was not in head office during the campaign. I took his words to heart. There were many things I could have done in the local election campaign regardless of whether I had the title of Director or not. There was a large section of the Labour organisation that always responded to me and I could have done something for it as I had done so often in the past. It would have meant that I would have had to abandon Paula Desmond and the Munster campaign though and I hadn't wanted to do that either.

Implications of the local elections

Leadership of a political party is akin to tribal leadership from which it is descended. One of the primary duties of leadership is to protect one's own. In this, Proinsias De Rossa succeeded brilliantly. Of the 17 Labour seats lost only one was from former Democratic Left and that was a fluke.

Seamus Rogers in Glenties was a long-serving and well-respected member of Donegal County Council and was squeezed out in an unusually vigorous Fine Gael campaign. Of the 16 other seats lost all belonged to long-standing Labour members most of whom had been elected in 1991. The implications for local government were very serious where Labour lost so much influence in Council chambers. For the general election there were also the most serious of consequences as councillors are usually the basis from which Dáil seats are won and now these bases had disappeared. As regards the Senate, there were similar implications as councillors form the Senate electorate for 43 of the 60 senators. One of Labour's four Senate seats must now be under pressure. I'm sure this was taken into account when, shortly after the local elections, Senator Pat Gallagher resigned his seat to take up a job with Westmeath County Council.

Bernie Malone was putting a brave face on it. She had lost the seat to Proinsias De Rossa as she had so accurately predicted herself just a year earlier. De Rossa had won fair and square but there was a general feeling abroad that Bernie Malone had been mistreated by the party. In Connacht-Ulster Ger Gibbons was to suffer from the popularity of independent candidates Rosemary Scallon (Dana), and Marian Harkin from Sligo. Dana went on to win the seat in a surprise result and Ger got over 10,000 first preference votes. Sean Butler had done remarkably in the Leinster Euro constituency garnering over 38,000 first preferences on his first outing. Sadly he was to leave politics before the year was over; he had been refused permission by the party to contest in the local elections and now he had no political role. The same rule had been imposed on Paula Desmond but she had just refused to accept it.

Exit stage left

For me too it was time to make an exit. I was greatly relieved when Ciaran O'Mara, Ruairi Quinn's adviser, approached me to see if I would be interested in a deal. Was I ever! I was exhausted after the campaign in Munster and now needed time for my brother who was very much on my mind. I was very conscious of my friends in the party and any feeling they might have that I was deserting them. Nevertheless, I was very flattered when a TD suggested that I fight on and another friend sketched a campaign. It was a lovely suggestion but General Secretaries must never fight party leaders; that is a recipe for chaos. Anyway, a change might do the party good.

I resigned formally at the General Council Meeting held in the Mansion House on Thursday 22 July 1999 and the members were kind enough to give me a standing ovation. On the way out Róisín Shortall TD winked at me and whispered 'Congratulations'. I finished in the office the next day and went with the staff – Marion, Angie, Dermot, Jackie, Marie, Pat, Anne, Marian Gaffney, Angus and Cathy – for our last boozy lunch together. Afterwards I was joined by my personal friends, I looked around the room and saw exactly the same people as had come to my flat to congratulate me on my appointment in 1986. That felt very good indeed.

I had been General Secretary of the Labour Party for thirteen and a half years almost to the very day and I had enjoyed every minute of it. The party held a farewell function for me in the Oak Room of the Mansion House on 25 November. They were all there: the good, the bad and the ugly, plus most of my friends who had worked with me for the past thirteen and a half years and enjoyed them with me. I was able to say quite truthfully that to me being General Secretary was the best job in the world. I had worked with some of the greatest people of my generation and had helped to shape a new Ireland, unrecognisable to those who had lived only a few decades earlier.

Now I often think of the words of Cllr Tom Brennan of Ennis when I approached him in 1989 with a view to his running for Labour. When I said to him 'I'm Ray Kavanagh, the General Secretary of the Labour Party', he turned to me and said with a smile, 'That must be a cushy number'. Now it's my turn to smile.

INDEX